The Storytelling Classroom

THE STORYTELLING CLASSROOM

Applications Across the Curriculum

Sherry Norfolk,
Jane Stenson, and
Diane Williams

LIBRARIES
U N L I M I T E D
A Member of the Greenwood Publishing Group

Westport, Connecticut • London

Library of Congress Cataloging-in-Publication Data
Norfolk, Sherry.
    The storytelling classroom: applications across the curriculum /
by Sherry Norfolk, Jane Stenson, and Diane Williams; foreword by
Syd Lieberman.
        p. cm.
    Includes bibliographical references and index.
    ISBN 1-59158-305-5 (pbk. : alk. paper)
    1. Storytelling—United States. 2. Teaching—Aids and devices.
3. Education—Standards—United States. I. Stenson, Jane, 1941-
II. Williams, Diane, 1953- III. Title.
    LB1042.S82   2006
    372.6'77—dc22   2006026486

British Library Cataloguing in Publication Data is available.

Library of Congress Catalog Card Number: 2006026486
ISBN: 1-59158-305-5

First published in 2006

Libraries Unlimited, 88 Post Road West, Westport, CT 06881
A Member of the Greenwood Publishing Group, Inc.
www.lu.com

Printed in the United States of America

⊗™

The paper used in this book complies with the
Permanent Paper Standard issued by the National
Information Standards Organization (Z39.48–1984).

10 9 8 7 6 5 4 3 2 1

To Bobby, for his continued inspiration, support, patience,
and understanding (above and beyond the call of duty!) — sn

To John, who smiles every day, and to my colleagues at the
Baker Demonstration School, Evanston, Illinois, because we make the
daily journey together. — js

To my sons, Perry and James, and my husband, Ray. — dw

CONTENTS

Contents

Contents

FOREWORD

Syd Lieberman

In this computerized world where speed and instant communication rule, storytelling might seem like a quaint or exotic school activity. But storytelling is a teaching tool that can transform a classroom.

Children are in the identity business. To discover who they are, they need to know where they came from, what the world is like, and where they might be going. Storytelling can teach these things. Stories have always been the repository for a culture's values and ideas. They present life in an interesting and understandable form. They parade the whole panoply of saints and sinners, the wise and the foolish, before our eyes. And, if you add the telling of personal stories to the mix, the students themselves can join the parade, finding answers to essential questions: Do people care? Do they understand? Can I make people laugh? Can I make them cry?

A quiet student once came to life when our class was reading *The Call of the Wild*. It turned out that he volunteered for both the city's dog-catcher team and a pet shelter. He wanted to become a veterinarian. His fellow students peppered him with questions. Suddenly, this shy student was telling story after story about his experiences. One of his stories won the school-wide contest for his grade and level.

I would take paragraphs from all the winning entries, enlarge them, and hang them in the hallways, so the whole school could celebrate good writing. The first day they went up, the shy would-be veterinarian caught me and asked excitedly where his paragraph was. After I led him and a friend to it, I watched him read it with a smile on his face. Then he pointed out his name and announced, "That's me."

Once students see that their stories are valued and recognize how their own tales connect to the stories of others, a metamorphosis takes place. When that happens, the classroom no longer contains a teacher merely feeding students facts. It becomes a group of people communicating on a real level. You can be yourself; they can be themselves; and together you can take an amazing journey of self-discovery.

Syd is an internationally acclaimed storyteller, an author, and an award-winning teacher. Many of his best-loved stories deal with growing up and raising a family in Chicago. He is also known for his original historical pieces and his signature versions of Jewish and literary tales. His work has garnered awards from ALA, Parent's Choice, and Storytelling World. He has taught storytelling at the Kennedy Center and Disney World, and has received commissions from NASA, the Smithsonian Institution; Johnstown, Pennsylvania; Historic Philadelphia; and the Van Andel Museum Center.

ACKNOWLEDGMENTS

We would like to acknowledge ...

Judy Sima for her encouragement and help from concept to finished product. In addition to her efforts in that regard, she generously offered to prepare our bibliography—a usually thankless task for which we truly thank her!

Our acquisitions editor, **Sharon Coatney**, for her patience, guidance, and support in helping us make this book a reality;

The **Mississippi Arts Commission** for sharing information from their research for the Whole Schools Initiative. Special thanks to **Larry Morrisey** and **Bill Edwards**;

Veronica Gates and **Linda Calvin Johnson** for their assistance;

The **Jefferson National Expansion Memorial** for the use of their photographs of "Through the Eyes of York," photographed at the Museum of Westward Expansion in St. Louis, Missouri;

Milbre Burch, Betsy Doty, Jeanne Haynes, Angela Lloyd, Greg Weiss, and **DWe Williams** for going the extra mile to provide their wonderful photographs;

Jamestown Elementary, in Florissant, Missouri, for the photographs of Ms. La Rue's third-grade class;

Photographer **Philip Kaake** of Oakland, California, for his excellent photographs and endless patience;

The **Baker Demonstration School**, Evanston, Illinois, for its continued embrace of storytelling from pre-kindergarten through eighth grade;

Cary Cleaver for assisting us in surmounting the technical challenges inherent in the manuscript preparation process;

And all of the **storytellers** and **storytelling teachers** whose dedication and creativity inspired this book.

INTRODUCTION

Sherry Norfolk, Jane Stenson, and Diane Williams

This book is a collaboration. It brings together story artists and teaching artists who live and work and tell stories among children. Both professional communities have much to share with each other and much to learn from each other ... to benefit children. So, this book is not for teachers from storytellers, and it is not for storytellers from teachers. It is authored by artists to share and use and encourage storytelling in classrooms, all kinds of classrooms.

By displaying the national curricular standards at the beginning of each contribution, the editors show that storytelling belongs in education in an ongoing and fundamental way. The standards give credence to tellers wanting to work well in schools, but tellers must understand the curriculum schools need and want. The standards demonstrate to teachers that it is time to tell stories with and for children. Storytelling teachers change the way teachers manage children and the way everyone speaks to each other; it's democratic; it's fun; it's whole; and it's very, very humane.

Storytelling is a power tool for education. When storytelling comes to school, everybody wins! Everything we do in the modern world is connected to story, and the more adept we are at telling stories, the more connected our society will be as it relates to all forms of communication.

From the beginning of time, storytelling has been the means by which cultures and societies have preserved and celebrated their memories, passed on their values and belief systems, entertained, instructed, and reported. Long before there were written records, storytellers taught through the oral tradition.

Today, teachers can employ this age-old educational tool with the assurance that *it still works*! In fact, recent brain-based research supports intuitive belief in storytelling with empirical evidence. In *Making Connections: Teaching and the Human Brain* (Addison-Wesley, 1994), Renate and Geoffery Caine state, "There is strong reason to believe that organization of information in story form is a natural brain process.... We suggest that the brain research confirms that evidence and begins to explain why stories are important."

Dr. Hank M. Bounds, Superintendent of Education in Mississippi, shares an example of how a child's brain function changes once he or she matures into adulthood. In children, brain cells constantly replace dying cells, allowing the child to learn and absorb volumes of information. He notes that the replacement of cells slows once that child becomes an adult. Dr. Bounds holds up a white Styrofoam cup and asks the audience to think about the color of the cup. The audience looks at the cup, and everyone makes a mental note that the cup is indeed white. He then asks the audience to respond aloud to his question, "What do cows drink?" Two-thirds of the audience respond, "Milk!" Then everyone has a good laugh. This is an adult audience; it is a quick response. If one were to ask the same question in the classroom, there would probably be a different answer. Providing students with stimulating avenues for learning is imperative now, while they are young.

Neuroscience is discovering that the brain is wired to organize, retain, and access information *through story*. If that is true—and it *is* true!—then teaching through story means that students will be able to remember what is taught, access that information, and apply it more readily. Story aids memory because it puts information into a meaningful context, to which other information can be "attached." Storytelling lays down the narrative or contextual track where knowledge can reside. It's storytelling that creates and maintains connections between isolated pieces of information. Storytelling is the opposite of the sound byte that blares and jumps erratically here to here to there.

Story also puts information into an emotional context, and research indicates that emotions play an essential role in both memory and motivation. When emotions are present, hormones released to the brain act as a memory fixative. Story is engaging—it evokes emotion, which provokes learning!

Storytelling and literacy comprehension go hand in hand. Students learn to construct meaning from an increased engagement in storytelling, and language skills improve. The principal evaluators for the Mississippi Arts Commission's Whole Schools Initiative conducted educational research on integrating the arts into the curriculum. In the book *The Arts Are an "R" Too*, they tracked student and teacher performance and improvement as teachers used the arts to teach. Teachers create situations in which academic content is taught and/or reinforced in and through the arts, thus "inspiring" student learning. What the art lessons add to the classroom is the opportunity for students to understand, remember, think, work together, become confident, and be motivated.

Arts integration enables students to be active, to experience things directly, and to express themselves in ways that best suit the students. In the process, of course, students have fun and enjoy themselves and are enthusiastic, which, in turn, makes them eager for the next time they can engage in active, hands-on, and varied lessons. Ultimately, students will acquire knowledge about, appreciation of, and a talent for the cultural aspects of being a citizen in their community, state, and country. The Whole Schools Initiative addresses the infusion of all art forms, but the conclusions of their research can be interpolated for storytelling. The evaluators (Dick Corbett, Bruce Wilson, and David Morse) conclude that the teacher's (artistic) instructional repertoire enables him or her to tap students' varied strengths and provide multiple ways to acquire, process, and demonstrate what they learn.

We want to make it easy for teachers and storytellers to explore the power of story in the classroom, which is the whole purpose of this book! In *The Storytelling Classroom: Applications Across the Curriculum*, we have collected an astonishing variety of lesson plans from classroom teachers who use storytelling as a successful teaching tool, and from storytellers who work in the classroom, teaching curriculum material through story. These lesson plans exemplify the creative, innovative, and highly effective ways in which story can transform standard teaching methods.

Our organizational plan is simple: in each chapter you'll find language arts, science, math, and social studies lesson plans appropriate for specific age groups. Each is linked to national education standards in its field, and has been field-tested by its author(s) to ensure that you can pick it up and DO IT!

So have fun, experiment . . . and discover the joy of a Storytelling Classroom!

THE NATIONAL STANDARDS

Throughout the book, the same highly respected sources have been cited for the National Standards in each subject area. The following abbreviations have been used when referencing the sources for these standards:

NCTE = National Council of Teachers of English
NCSS = National Council for the Social Studies
NCTM = National Council of Teachers of Mathematics
NAS = National Academies of Science
HCOF = Head Start Child Outcomes Framework
CNAEA = Consortium of National Arts Education Associations
NETS = National Education Technology Standards
NASPE = National Association for Sport and Physical Education

CHAPTER ONE

The Story Behind the Stories

How do you start the journey toward creating a storytelling classroom? In these insightful articles, our contributors offer glimpses of their individual paths, their experiences, and their joys. So, as you begin (or continue) your own voyage of discovery, here's The Story Behind the Stories!

FROM THE LIBRARY MEDIA CENTER: STORYTELLING THROUGH THE GRADES
By Anne Shimojima

One day several years ago, I had just finished telling a story to a second-grade class. As the children were coming back from the images in their minds, one little boy several rows back from the front raised his hand. "Ms. Shimojima," he said, "when you tell us a story and I look at you, it feels like you are right here next to me."

I knew what he meant. In over twenty years of telling stories to my students in the library media center, I've realized that storytelling, more than any other activity, has deepened the relationship between my students and me. We travel down an intimate road together, journeying to faraway places and learning about life and love and truth. I believe I've nurtured their spirits as well as expanded their minds.

Storytelling is more than just fun in the library. It enhances visualization, imagination, and creativity. Storytelling introduces children to literature and the beauty of language. It develops a student's sense of story and the knowledge that stories have a beginning, a middle, an end, characters, a setting, a problem, and a resolution. And what better way to develop listening skills? Best of all, this is active listening, where children must provide the images in order to fully experience the story. In addition, I tell world folktales, and so I introduce students to other cultures. They learn that all people share the same hopes, fears, and dreams; that love and betrayal are universal; and that tricksters, heroes and heroines, silly folk, wise elders, and evil villains exist everywhere.

It starts in kindergarten, the very first week of school. My goal is to teach the children what to expect in the storytelling experience and to provide them with food for fantasy and imagination. Weekly storytelling teaches them to get ready, listen, and not raise their hands until the story is over. Sometimes a participation story invites them to become part of the action. I pick stories to complement their letter of the week, and as the year progresses their ability to sit still and listen increases noticeably. Occasionally they vote on a story to be repeated, so that they can delight in it again.

Kindergarten students also love to act out stories. The ideal story is one with many characters and a very simple plot that can be grasped immediately. I begin with *The Great, Big, Enormous Turnip* (Alexi Tolstoy, Franklin Watts, 1968). I tell the story and invite children to choose a part to play. We repeat the story three times so that all students have a chance to act. Another option would be to have only some students act while the others know their chance will come on another day. When the parts are assigned, I tell the story again, and when it is time for a character to speak, that child supplies the dialogue. Repetitious stories are the best, because children learn the plot easily and quickly.

The first-grade experience provides an opportunity for librarian-teacher collaboration. The classroom teacher is an important part of reinforcing the idea of story elements. I choose fairy tales and simple folktales that engage students with an obvious problem and resolution. After I tell a story, the teacher leads a discussion on the characters, setting, problem, and resolution. We always leave time for the students to voice the questions that the story has raised in their minds. (Why didn't the mother go to watch 1-Eye in the pasture instead of just sending 2-Eyes or 3-Eyes? How did the sixth brother go through life with a wing for an arm?)

In second grade, the students love the yearlong folktale unit. All of the stories are put into themes: Cinderella stories, tricksters, creation stories, strong women, little folk, magical creatures, noodleheads, the third child, the good/bad character story, funny stories, and stories with a surprise ending. Classes come to the media center twice a week for a story, and teachers receive a stack of folktale picture books to read in the classroom as well.

Sometimes the story is enjoyed on its own without activities, but often there is an application that follows. Perhaps a story map is filled out with protagonist, antagonist, setting, initial action, problem, and resolution. I may ask the students to retell the story in their own words while I type it on a computer and project the words on a screen. Sometimes I rewrite a story simply and cut the sentences into strips. Pairs of students then work together to put the sentence strips into the proper sequence. The good/bad character stories include a lesson on the Venn diagram—two intersecting circles that the children fill in with the good character's traits on the left, the bad character's traits on the right, and traits in common in the overlapping space in the middle.

We use the story *Wiley and the Hairy Man* (Molly Garret Bang, Macmillan, 1976) to create a class picture book. After hearing the story, the children recall each scene. I write the key words for each scene on a different sheet of paper and then each student chooses a scene to work on. In the classroom they will each write the narration for their scene. When the scenes are rewritten, we gather together again for an oral reading to make sure nothing important is omitted. I remind them to be descriptive and to include what characters say and feel. After the pages are typed, each child illustrates his or her page. The entire book is duplicated so that each child has a copy to take home.

The Battle of the Folktales provides an exciting culmination. I've prepared recall questions for each story they've heard in the library media center. (In what story does the youngest son inherit the family pet when his father dies? What was it that Molly Whuppie could get across but the giant could not?) The entire second grade comes to the library media center. Each child has been put onto a team, for a total of ten teams. We have five battles, two teams in each battle, ten questions per team. Each team has students from all the classrooms, to minimize the competition between classrooms. It's a satisfying finish to a yearlong celebration of story.

Third grade participates in a unit on Jack Tales, folktales of the Appalachian Mountains with roots in the British Isles. Each story has an activity to follow. Students have their first chance to try storytelling when I put them into a circle and start the story a second time. Each child continues the story until I say stop. The story continues around the circle, and the students are at ease because they don't have the pressure of remembering an entire story.

I also fold a paper into three parts and students draw pictures and write sentences from the beginning, the middle, and the end of the story. Perhaps they may write a poem about the story, write an epilogue, or create a comic strip. A story with many locations in the plot provides an opportunity for students to create a map of the setting with all of the locations pictured and labeled. The word list is one of their favorite activities. I give the students five minutes to write a list of all the words they can remember from the story (Jack, mama, fortune, basket, farmer, seven, cow, hen ...). The room is dead silent as the pencils are moving across paper. After giving an extra minute to write, I have all students stand. They sit down if they have fewer than ten words, twenty words, thirty words, and so on until the student with the most words is the only one left standing. Then we go around the room and each student says a word from his list that he thinks no one else has. How many other students have thought of that word?

The culminating activity for the Jack Tales unit is similar to the class picture book. We divide a story into scenes in the same way, but here the students each draw a picture of the scene on $18'' \times 24''$ paper. Each child writes the narration for his or her scene and the pictures are videotaped with the child off-camera reading the narration. The resulting video is circulated among the students so that they can show their parents the final class creation.

Fourth graders develop their writing skills with the rewriting of folk-tales. This requires them to listen carefully and recall the sequence of the plot. Very short stories with no repetition are ideal. The first session has a demonstration with word processing projected onto a large screen as students help retell the story. Subsequent stories have students writing individually. We discuss what details can be changed as the children put the story into their own words and what important themes or ideas must remain the same.

When I was asked by fourth-grade teachers to provide an activity to develop listening skills, I immediately chose to tell fairy tales, because of their rich detail and universal themes. After each story, students are asked to answer simple recall questions (Where, exactly, did Ivan's arrow end up? What was one insult the princess gave to a suitor?). Eventually students are asked more open-ended questions (List seven images you saw in this story. List five things that characters said. Who was your favorite character, and why?).

My favorite of all storytelling units is the one in which fourth graders become storytellers themselves. After going through exercises on language, visualization, voice, movement, dialogue, character study, personal storytelling, joke-telling, and telling the story of a wordless book, students read through a variety of stories to select the one they will tell to a small group of first or second graders. Small group coaching sessions allow me to guide the students as they learn their stories. After their experiences in storytelling, the fourth graders are unanimous in their enthusiasm.

The fifth-grade Native American unit brings an opportunity to learn about origin stories told by the Indians. Sometimes they are required to create a picture book of the story; other years they may tell the story as part of their Native American museum display.

The latest extension of storytelling has been a coordinated unit with the art teacher. After each story is told, she introduces the students to an appropriate medium and the students use the materials to create a picture of the story. I go into the art room to tell these stories, and I love to see the creations that soon appear.

It is important to remember that, as beneficial as all of these activities are, there is just as much value in just telling and listening. As storyteller Gay Ducey from California reminds us, "For every story that you tell in the service of curriculum, give one away."

Of course, telling stories does not reduce the need to read books aloud. I still want to introduce authors, writing styles, beautiful artwork, and the best of children's literature. But with storytelling my students and I have bonded in a special way. The enraptured silences and wide eyes—seeing not me, but the images in their imaginations—tell me that my students love the stories as much as I love telling them. Telling stories is a gift—of yourself as much as of the stories. Sometimes I think I'm getting the best gift of all.

Anne Shimojima has been a school library media specialist for thirty-two years and is currently at Braeside Elementary School in Highland Park, Illinois. A storyteller for over twenty years, she performed at the Exchange Place at the National Storytelling Festival in 2001. Anne has taught graduate courses in storytelling, reviewed storytelling resources for The Bulletin of the Center for Children's Books, *and for seven years was on the Board of Directors of the Wild Onion Storytelling Celebration in Chicago. She has performed in schools, libraries, museums, and festivals, and gives workshops on the use of storytelling in classrooms and library media centers.*

THE STORY BEHIND A STORYTELLING TEACHER'S JOURNEY INTO STORY
By Marni Gillard and Johanna Shogan

A smiling, curly-haired teacher walked into my in-service class in 1997. I smiled too, knowing Johanna Shogan cared deeply about children and learning. We had crossed paths often at conferences. If anyone would embrace storytelling, Johanna would.

"Back in the mid-eighties I heard 'The Girl Who Was Not Satisfied with Simple Things,' and it's never left me," Johanna said during introductions. "Stories make us look inside. Of course, I already knew that." She laughed at herself in a way I would come to love. "But a told story, it gets you right here." She pointed to her heart.

"I've wanted to introduce storytelling, but I just didn't know where to start," she continued. "But this year," she pointed to a youthful, red-haired woman, "Megan, my student teacher, and I are going to tackle it together."

Like Johanna, I too sensed the power of the oral tale when I first heard "The Cow-Tail Switch," about an African hunter whose sons bring him back to life. My father had died during my teens. That tale reminds me people still live on in our words.

I invited the class to pair up and share a memory. "Take the stance of listener," I instructed. "No interrupting." Johanna's musical laugh erupted again.

I noticed that she and Megan both teared up as they talked. Later Johanna admitted, "It feels big to be so well listened to. I walked from image to image and took Megan by the hand." The group nodded, and I knew our time together would go well.

Partnering again, participants described scenes and characters from stories they had heard or read. "I've always loved 'The Cask of Amontillado' and 'The Raven,'" Johanna told the group. She gave us glimpses of both, the teller in her coming to life.

Each person recounted a memory or summarized a tale, sounding natural yet artful. Before the next class, everyone agreed to "talk-story" and to listen for everyday storytelling in the world, as well as to choose a story to work and play with.

Reflecting on her learning, Johanna wrote, "I was skeptical when Megan chose a story illustrated by Mercer Mayer. The story is in the pictures. But Megan became a little girl with red curls making messes inside and out, oblivious to adults. She made up her own dialogue! Suddenly, we were all free to make our stories our own."

Johanna also wrote about establishing a "no violence" rule for her preteen tellers. She needed the rule for her own comfort. I told her to trust her instincts and see what happened.

At a subsequent in-service, the topic surfaced again. By then Johanna had another student teacher. "David has let in the Dark!" She shook her head and laughed. "He's brought us a huge storytelling chair and covered the windows with black paper for 'atmosphere.' He told about his friend's mother, a medic in the Philippines, who escaped a night-stalker trying to steal her soul." Johanna mimicked David's scary tone. "That blew the lid off my rule." Then she got serious. "David, like Megan, showed me that story choice matters. We have to tell what calls to us." Johanna's choices so far had been a picture book with a character like her son and an Irish tall tale that allowed her to try on her mother's brogue and get her students laughing. Although urban legends abounded in her class that year, no student used violence for its own sake, as she had feared.

The next summer, Johanna attended a storytelling institute on her own. When I heard about all she'd learned, I asked her to co-teach a class. She shared with teachers her earlier doubts and questions, as well as wonderful tales of her students' struggles and breakthroughs. "One child finally got it by telling her tale without talking!" She taught us to make masks and storyboards, strategies she'd learned at the institute. She inspired every teacher present to see him- or herself as a storyteller.

Today, Johanna presents on storytelling with me regularly. Her infectious laughter relaxes participants, and her learning is a model to us all. "We started with a three-week unit, and ended with story as the basis of everything! Our literate lives are a story. We connect story with art, and some students work their musical instruments into tales. Storytelling helps shy kids be bold, and it tames the bullies. We find ourselves as we read, write, and tell."

I asked Johanna what she understood about her own journey as a teller. "Despite all your praise and encouragement," she told me, "you were 'the storyteller'; I wasn't. Then I gave the eulogy at my father's funeral. I found a central image to describe his life—his hands. He had touched so many lives—taught the boys to play ball and use tools, and, during the war, defended the country. I introduced Dad to his nephews and grandchildren as they had never known him."

"And I wanted the eulogy to include music. I took a walk and said, 'Come on, Dad. Gimme a song.' And it came! 'Swonderful, 'smarvelous . . .'" Johanna's whole body laughed. "People wanted copies!"

Johanna also talked of turning the lead characters of "The Cask of Amantillado" into women and performing it for tellers at the summer institute she continues to attend. Poe's tale, which she deeply respects, she had made her own.

Her remarks echo what I hope for all teachers as they try on storytelling. "My stories have allowed my voice to be heard. Teachers so rarely get credit," she said with a sigh. "So much that we do is invisible. But playing with Poe and eulogizing my dad, I was heard. All along I thought I was freeing the children's voices, but I was really freeing my own."

Works Cited

Bruchac, Joseph (as told by). "The Girl Who Was Not Satisfied with Simple Things," *Iroquois Stories: Heroes and Heroines Monsters and Magic.* Trumansburg, New York: The Crossing Press, 1985.

Courlander, Harold, and George Herzog. "The Cow-Tail Switch," *The Cow-Tail Switch and Other West African Stories.* Illustrated by Madye Lee Chastain. New York: Henry Holt and Company, Inc., 1947.

Hitte, Katheryn. *Boy, Was I Mad!* Illustrated by Mercer Mayer. New York: Parents Magazine Press, 1969.

Poe, Edgar Allan. "The Raven" and "The Cask of Amontillado," *The Complete Tales and Poems of Edgar Allan Poe.* New York: Random House, 1938.

When Marni Gillard gave students the freedom to combine authentic writing and storytelling, her classroom community thrived. She published Storyteller, Storyteacher *(Stenhouse) to teach others about claiming the storyteller within. She co-edited (as Schwartz)* Give a Listen: Stories of Storytelling in School *(NCTE) and created* The Story Studio *in upstate NY to help adults find stories for life's journey. Her recording,* Without a Splash: Diving into Childhood Memories, *includes models for student memoirs. Marni has told stories with Alzheimer patients, prisoners, and pilgrims. Her new book,* Storytell Your Life, *is near completion. Reach her for workshops and performances at www.marnigillard.com.*

An English teacher for grades 7–12 in New York for thirty-four years, Johanna Shogan has taught in a mixture of private and public middle schools and high schools. She has a B.A. from State University of New York at Albany, an M.A. in English from State University of New York at Albany, and an M.S. in educational administration from State University of New York at Albany. Retired from the classroom, she now offers programs in reading, writing, speaking, listening, thinking, and storytelling.

GROWING STORIES: TOWARD A STORIES-BASED CURRICULUM
By Nancy King, Ph.D.

Part of our predicament today is due to the impoverishment of the natural images in us all. This narrow, rational awareness that we have developed has cut us off from the image-making thing in us.

Meaning comes to us in the first place, I believe, straight out of life in symbols and images, and this meaning is always greater than any concept we can consciously make of the images. It is greater than any words we can say or pictures we can paint. But these images are the source of an enormous spiritual and psychic energy, if we have access to them. When we are cut off from these images we lose the transforming energies with which we are endowed and we are poor. (Van der Post, 1961)

Imagemaking, storymaking, and storytelling are integrative activities that nourish our creativity and help us regain access to our natural images. They require us, as makers/tellers, to take disparate bits of information, internal images, and personal points of view to create something new and whole. When we make images based on a story we have heard, we learn to concretize abstract thoughts and to verbalize ideas and feelings in a coherent and articulate manner. When we tell stories we learn something about who we are, develop a sense of our authentic voice, and begin to appreciate our value as human beings in a collaborative learning community. Working with stories from around the world to develop oral and written language curricula broadens horizons, cultivates empathy, and provides the possibility for connections across time, culture, and experience. Sharing stories of our lives, both real and fantasy, helps to center us within ourselves, provides connections with others, establishes community, and makes it possible for us to appreciate our unique and common experiences.

After more than forty years, in a wide variety of classrooms, I have come to believe that the use of imagemaking and storymaking in a stories-based language curriculum is an effective and challenging way to teach native and/or foreign language. Since we know that students learn best when they are curious about, and involved in, what they are learning, why not use stories of the world and of students' lives to engage their hearts and minds when teaching reading, speech, and writing?

Imagemaking

What we know about our inner life and how we see ourselves not only affects how we understand ourselves in the world, it also impacts on the meaning we derive from what we see and hear. Because we take in more information than we consciously process, we know more than we consciously realize. An important task for educators is to enable students to discover what they know but don't know they know, in life as well as in the classroom.

When I first began to ask students to visualize, I discovered that not only did many have trouble visualizing; they also had poor access to their imaginations. Their puzzled looks in response to questions such as "What do you imagine the protagonist was wearing?" or "How do you think the house looked when he opened the door?" made me realize that many students were not used to seeing images in their mind's eye as they read a text. I explored ways to improve access to students' imaginations and creativity and discovered this could not easily be done through activities dependent on verbal acuity. My decision to use finger paints and clay came after reading a letter Albert Einstein wrote to French mathematician Jacques Hadamard (Einstein, 1957). In this letter, Einstein explained how he used "certain signs and more or less clear images which could be 'voluntarily' reproduced and combined" to discover what he knew. Einstein made it clear that it was only after he made the images and then wrote down what came to him that he began to know what he knew. Just as Einstein "doodled," I discovered that when students make spontaneous images in response to abstract concepts such as courage or an image of the protagonist at a moment of crisis, immediately followed by writing words or ideas that come to mind, they are able to learn more about what they know. The images and words in combination help them to access both feeling and thought.

The process of making an image in about one minute, with no preplanning, makes censoring more difficult. The words and ideas that become conscious often provide new insights that make it possible for students to discover and express aspects of knowing for which they may previously have had no words. Making images of particular moments in a text initially helps students to focus—to start thinking about the text at hand and to discover their unique and personal relationship to it. Imagemaking structures thought. It is the first step in the process of learning what we know. Students move from preverbal to imaginal (nonverbal) to verbal expression by tapping into their imagination, particularly important today when many are so used to seeing prepackaged images on television and in video games. Watching pre-produced images weakens one's ability to create images or visualize from one's imagination. Not only does this make it difficult for people to enter into a text to explore and connect their symbolic understanding of themselves and their world to their response to the text, it also makes it harder to feel and think about what it might be like to live as a specific character in a variety of situations and events. The process of making spontaneous images helps students regain access to their own unique imaginations because the prepackaged video images do not fit the abstraction they are asked to visualize. Imagemaking is particularly useful in EFL (English as a foreign language) classrooms because the images serve to stimulate interest in words and ideas, and to communicate these in the language being learned where the focus is on discovery and expansion of vocabulary and expression.

This paper describes some of the imagemaking and storymaking techniques that have been developed over the course of my teaching career. They are responses to events and situations where I devised activities to encourage student involvement in their study of written and oral language in first, second, and foreign language learning. These activities work with students of almost any age or ability and can be used with any text. Although some of the activities were initially designed for elementary school–age children, they work well with any group of any age beginning language study. The activities are designed to move students from feeling inadequate and uncomfortable to knowing that wherever they are is where they start and that the rest of the class, as well as the teacher, will help them learn in a safe and supportive environment.

Interactive Classroom Activities

Storypartners

In many classrooms, teachers have students of widely varying abilities. In order to encourage each student to work toward his or her potential, it becomes necessary to design activities that appropriately develop each person's language learning and usage. Storypartnering is one way for students of differing abilities to work together, with each benefiting from the experience, since each works at his or her own level without judgment or comparison.

After the teacher tells a very short folktale, myth, or legend, drawing from cultures around the world, each student paints, draws, or sculpts an image from the story. Using the image as a focal point, each student writes a short story. The length of the writing will depend on skill levels of the students, but even one sentence is encouraged, especially if partners are allowed to help each other. With students whose language is very limited, even one word can be a beginning.

For example, when working in a bilingual classroom with students whose native language was Spanish, I discovered that many children felt so uncomfortable using English they were refusing to write in either language. Given their level of fear, I asked them to write just one word that they either remembered from the story or that came to mind when they thought about the story. Going around the room, we practiced asking questions to further the story that couldn't be answered with yes or no. I asked each child to read his or her word. Two children had no words, so I asked them to write their word in Spanish, which they did. Immediately, their seatmates translated their words into English. When I told them they had written a story, most of the children giggled and shook their heads. One child said, "How can one word be a story?"

"I'll show you," I said. His question stimulated the development of collaborative learning through group questioning. To begin the development of their writing, I put the following words on the board: **description, feelings, circumstance, experience, point of view, what if.** Although these words are similar to who, what, how, why, and when, the children like learning the "big" words, and they seem to provide writers with a more focused way to enhance their writing than when using the more familiar words.

Roberto's word was "happy." The children and I read through the words, and when they understood their meaning we started to work with the first category, description. I asked him, "Who is happy?"

"The girl was happy," he answered.

When the children were asked if they could think of any more questions whose answers might enhance the description of the girl, they asked the following questions: Who is she? What is her name? What does she look like? Does she have any brothers and sisters? How old is she? When is her birthday?

I asked Roberto if the questions gave him any ideas. He nodded and laboriously wrote: Her name is Maria. She is ten years old. She lives with her grandmother and her uncle.

We moved on to the second category: feelings. "What is she feeling?"

"I already said, she was happy," he complained.

The children quickly asked: Why is she happy?

Roberto said, "I don't know."

We suggested some possibilities. "Is she happy because she got a puppy? Is she happy because her grandmother gave her something nice to eat? Is she happy because she is going to Disneyland? Is she happy because her mama is coming to visit?"

Roberto sighed and began to write. By the time we had worked our way through each of the categories, all the children had written stories that surprised and pleased them. So many of the children wanted to read their stories to the rest of the class, I decided to incorporate this into their regular reading activity.

Although these were elementary school–age children, I have used the same technique with older students who have trouble writing. Encouraging students to admit they are stuck allows the class, through the use of collaborative questioning, to create an environment that feels safe and allows students to learn and develop without criticism and/or judgment. I stress that whatever is told or written is a first draft; what matters most is to write or tell as much as they know. Subsequent revisions focus on discovery and deepening what is already told or written. As Roberto was questioned, he discovered he had much more to say than he originally knew. Writing lost its onus of punishment and became a way for him to express his feelings.

Students select a storypartner for the week by having half the class draw from a box the name of one person from the other half of the class. In order for storypartners to develop an effective working relationship, it is best that they work together for at least one week. The next week, those whose names were in the box draw names from the other half. The aim of storypartnering is to enable partners to develop a cooperative connection that enhances language development through the use of questions that cannot be answered with yes or no and through compassionate responses that connect the writer/teller's story with the listener's reactions.

Storypartners share their stories and then each partner in turn asks a question that cannot be answered with a yes or a no. The storyteller answers in any fashion she or he chooses. Because it is best to keep the structure simple, I suggest that additional questions be postponed until everyone feels comfortable with the process. Students then return to their written story to add information, addressing the issue(s) raised by the question. If the storyteller doesn't like the question, he or she is free to ask for some more questions or to add spontaneous information to the story. These stories can be shared in small groups or with the whole class on a voluntary basis to teach ways to revise written work.

With young children, or with students of any age who are learning a foreign language, this activity can become part of the daily reading/writing process if each day the teacher gives new directions. For example, the second day might focus on the main character. Paint (draw or sculpt) an image of this person. Who is this person? What does this person look like? An opportunity to further develop language occurs when students, as a group, suggest "who" questions that are written on the board for them to use as reference. The third day might involve where the action takes place. Students paint (draw or sculpt) an image of the environment in which the story occurs. The fourth day might begin with students creating an image of a "peculiar incident" or a "surprise" that they can then incorporate into their story. Each activity allows students to add to their stories, always in consultation with their storypartners. On the fifth day, students might design a cover and title for their stories before adding, editing, or honing the complete version of the story, which they then share with their storypartners as they collaborate, reading each other's stories and helping one another to smooth out any rough spots. If the course is a foreign language class, all discussion might be held in the (foreign) language as a way to practice if students' skill levels permit.

More advanced students can work more quickly and, therefore, it helps to have partners ask many questions, all of which the student writes down without comment. Later, he or she can decide which questions, if any, to address as the story is revised and developed.

The structure of the initial story and selection of a storypartner serves as the frame to explore many different aspects on which students can focus their storymaking, such as:

- Point of view;
- The story before the story—what happens before the story begins;
- A story from the story—a story evoked by the story—a memory;
- Stories between stories—what happens between one episode in the story and the next;
- The story after the story—what happens after the story ends.

Correct language usage is always an issue, yet one cannot achieve fluency and perfection simultaneously. I use the following categories to help students decide their current level of proficiency. The first level is *private*. This means students are essentially writing for or speaking to themselves. There is no interest in sharing what is expressed. The second level is *personal*. The student shares what is written or told with another person. The student is present to answer questions, clear up confusion, or explain what is missing in the narrative. The third level is *public*. The work, in this case written, is "published"; the writer is not present to explain or clarify. The work is grammatically correct and fully developed. I use the idea of publishing to include putting up work on bulletin boards outside of class, as well as hanging up written work in more public places for anyone to read or collecting stories to be made into a book.

To help hone written work, students work together in groups, reading each other's stories as if they were editors and trying to perfect a piece of writing. If there are questions, or if students miss errors, this can be the basis for further learning. The edited stories might be shared with the class, put up on a bulletin board, or collected and printed so that everyone has a copy of each classmate's stories. In one classroom, students kept a record of "writing errors" with no names attached so that students could see how to correct their own mistakes before showing their stories to a reader. While it is meaningful for teachers to talk about the importance of imagination and possibility, it is vital that the supporting structure of sharing stories and reflection be collaborative rather than with criticism. Teaching students how to ask questions that cannot be answered with yes or no, whose sole aim is to help their classmates deepen, extend, enrich, and create as the integral part of storymaking, will enhance the learning process for all students, regardless of their experience and expertise. Helpful questions are not judgmental; rather, they enable writers to revise their writing. For example: "Why did you put in the part about the donkey?" can be transformed into "Tell me how the donkey came to be in the story," a much more useful question in terms of deepening the story. Saying "That part doesn't make sense" is not nearly as helpful as "How did you decide to have your character disappear?" The extent to which students view questioning and editing as a positive process is often the extent to which students enthusiastically correct, hone, shape, and revise their work.

The Thirty-Second Hotline

Many students enjoy recording their uncensored views on books and stories. If available, tape recorders are a marvelous way to create a hotline for fellow classmates. Students read a book and then record author, title, and one or two sentences about their response to the book. The tapes can be changed weekly. Comments recorded in one middle school classroom about a variety of books ran the gamut between terse judgment and enthusiastic raves: "This one is really good because you never know until the last minute whether he is going to win the race"; "This book sucks. I hate the girl. She's so stuck up"; "This book has some hard words but don't worry, the story's great"; "This one is boring because you just know what's going to happen and it does"; "It's a really good book. I liked the way everyone has to help solve the mystery." When tape recorders were not available, students used loose-leaf notebooks, putting the name of the book, author, and title at the top of a page, and leaving room for one or two comments per student. Several notebooks were available around the room for just this purpose. Students also kept their own records of books they read and what they thought and felt about them. As a storytelling activity, students sometimes made up the "next chapter" as a way of nourishing imagination and developing writing and storytelling skills. In today's world, this could be a class blog on the Internet!

Students learning a foreign language had fun recording their ideas and impressions of stories they had read in the new language. The teacher kept the recordings, and toward the end of the semester played some of them back. Students laughed at their early attempts, yet at the same time developed an appreciation for how far they had come.

The View from Here

In the corner of the back blackboard, we hung a bulletin board for students to write on an index card—the name of the book read, its author, one or two sentences about the book, and one or two questions about their reading. We suggested that students reading the same book talk with each other, discussing their questions and sharing ideas. At the end of two weeks, the class was divided into four groups and students shared their impressions of a book they had read. They were encouraged to ask each other questions that would stimulate reading but not give away plot. For example, one student read a biography of Eleanor Roosevelt and asked, "How do you suppose she transformed herself from being a shy, retiring wife into the Eleanor Roosevelt known by the whole world?" Another student who read Nelson Mandela's autobiography asked, "What did he do to survive twenty-seven years in prison and then emerge without bitterness or wanting revenge?"

In another classroom we taped large pieces of paper to the back wall and on each we put the name of a book and its author. After students read a book, they wrote short views and reviews of the book on the paper. Each Friday, the teacher held a session called "The Critic's Corner," where students shared their ideas, discussed why there were different views of a particular book, and talked about what they liked and disliked in stories. In one classroom where students resisted most writing exercises, I asked them to write a short incident that happened to one of the characters before or after the book began or ended. This gave us a chance to talk about style, vocabulary, sensory information, dialogue, and exposition in enjoyable ways. Many of the students who felt writing was an onerous burden said this was not "really" writing because it was so much fun.

Partnering Up

In one classroom where students' reading abilities differed widely, we paired students by interest in topics such as environment, history, culture, etc.

Within these small groups students selected a partner with whom to read at least one book on a required list. Partners read out loud to each other, deciding among themselves whether to switch after a page, paragraph, or chapter. In some cases, when one student was a much better reader than the other, they apportioned out the book so the less accomplished reader read one paragraph while her partner read a page. Each pair decided how to choose their book, and sometimes each partner picked the book she or he wanted to read and the pair read two books before switching partners and topics. Students with limited reading ability benefited by reading (hearing) a book they would likely not have read, while the more advanced students said that reading out loud made them pay closer attention to the material. After the book was read, the partners collaborated on a brief report sharing the highlights and important information. Very often, the student with limited reading ability proved to have useful abilities, such as designing a poster on which to put information or creating a slide tape presentation. What students commented on most often were the benefits of partnership where each had skills and information to offer the other.

Show and Tell

One morning a week, some teachers and students come together for a book-sharing session. Students are given a minute or less to praise, pan, and/or reflect on a book. Sometimes students work in pairs so that those who feel too shy to speak have the necessary support. To increase writing skills, students make an annotated class bibliography for a semester or a year, at the end of which copies are given to each student.

Students struggling to learn a foreign language often feel shy about sharing thoughts and opinions in a language in which they are not as competent as they are in their native language. Sharing ideas informally, with an emphasis on fluency and communication of ideas and feelings, not only improved language usage but also the level of comfort when speaking.

The underlying principle that guides *all* storymaking and storytelling activity is the idea that reading, writing, and sharing stories and books is pleasurable and is an unending source and resource for learning about ourselves, our communities, and our world for our entire lives. Just as people are different, so are our responses to books and the ways we speak and write about them. As long as the speaking and writing are referenced by the text, all ideas have value.

Connecting the Story to the Storymaker

Every human being has stories to tell—of the lives we live, from our imaginations, or retelling those that have made a deep impression. Stories comfort, educate, explain, amuse, and challenge us to become our deeper selves. It is one thing, however, to be told that stories live within us but quite another experience to find and express them. The process of storymaking leads us, along our inner path, to find the places where our stories live. There are many ways to begin, and no one way works for everyone every time. What is always required is acceptance—of ourselves and of our stories. We begin where we are, with what we know and experience, however we know to tell it, with an audience that is willing to listen.

The initial story or poem, told or read, acts as the container—the issues, ideas, or feelings evoked by the text serve as our point of departure. For example, after telling a Norwegian tale about what happened when a husband and wife change places for one day, I might ask my class to imagine themselves in their families as someone other than who they are. If the class needs help thinking of ideas I offer some possibilities: becoming larger, smaller, heavier, skinnier, invisible, a family pet, an only child, one of twenty-seven. I continue to make suggestions until the group offers ideas of their own and students feel ready to select one that fascinates them. Some ideas students have suggested include becoming the family pet, a talking dining room table, the oldest rather than the youngest child, a long lost child, coming home after having lived away from home—in a foreign country, at a posh university, or working as an au pair. After choosing, they paint an image of their new self, imagine what this new existence might be like, and title their image. Sometimes, especially with beginners who are not comfortable with spontaneous writing, I ask each student to sculpt an image of this new self in relationship to their family at a particular time and place and to think about what might have happened when they interacted with their family as their new self. After doing this, the story is practically born. All they need to do now is to write about this experience. If teachers incorporate the use of a dictionary and thesaurus into the storymaking process, these books become allies as students search for ways to improve and enhance their expressive capacities.

Afterward, we share the stories, and students ask each storymaker questions that might deepen the work without negative comment or judgment. In one case, a small female student with two older, bigger brothers decided to be a giant so she could order her brothers around. One student commented, "It's easy for big people to order small people around. What would happen if you were the same size but were so much more powerful than them and they treated you the way you want them to treat you?"

The girl looked puzzled and asked, "How would I do that? It's because I'm big that they don't bother me." This stumped the class temporarily until one student offered a suggestion.

"What if you thought you were bigger and more powerful than them?" She shrugged, as if this was too silly to even consider. "But this is a story," he insisted. "You could have your character eat special food or wear clothes that give your character courage and power. I think it's much more interesting than just making yourself physically bigger."

His words got the class thinking, and soon the girl had more suggestions about how to deal with the brothers in her story than she knew what to do with. "Okay," she said, "let me think about it." In a subsequent version she wrote about a girl who devised strategies to deal with her brothers that included staring, laughter, ridicule, sarcasm, and, most important of all, learning karate so she could "deck them every time they touch me." She not only ended up writing a very funny story, she also felt personally content. As she said, "This version is much more satisfying than the first one I wrote because the girl does stuff I can really imagine doing."

Teachers have often asked me, "How do you get students to make a story when they can't find the story inside themselves?" When students have trouble imagining, it is best, in the beginning, to limit the amount they have to write. One way to stimulate writing or telling is to ask them to select a character that could be from a story they have read, one they make up, or a character they create from real life. They then write one sentence about this character. For example, during one class period a student selected a turtle as his character and wrote: "There was once a turtle that lived under an old house." He said this was his story and he had nothing more to write about this turtle.

I asked the class to ask him questions—what did they want to know about this turtle? Here were some of the questions they asked: How big is the turtle? Does the turtle live alone? Is it lonely? How does the turtle come to live under the old house? Does the turtle have any friends? Do people live in the old house? What does the turtle eat? How does the turtle get its food? How does the turtle spend its time? Is the turtle a boy or a girl turtle? What kind of turtle is it? A painted turtle? A snapping turtle? How do you know? How does this turtle behave when it's angry or when it's afraid? What adventures does the turtle have with other animals? Does the turtle have a family? Where did the turtle live before coming to live under the old house? What is most important to the turtle? What makes the turtle angry? Happy? Frustrated? Lonely? Excited? What is special about this turtle? How does this turtle come to find love?

Notice there are no "why" questions. Over the years I have found that questions asking "why?" tend to make students anxious because there is the implied assumption of a right answer. One can ask equally stimulating questions using "what if" or "how come," and these ways of asking seem not to intimidate. Also, as much as possible, encourage students to ask questions using the present tense to help writers/speakers make active choices. Of course students don't have to answer all the questions—they merely serve to stimulate thinking and to help connect storymakers with more of the story that lives inside them. Sometimes it helps to divide into small groups and to have people write down their questions for writers to use if they choose to do so. Once people get used to asking questions to help others, they realize that asking themselves questions whenever they feel stuck is a good way for anyone to get unstuck.

Another way to help students get "unstuck" is to ask them to make images, either in paint or clay, of the stuck moment, the moment just before the stuck moment, and/or the moment just after it. Spontaneous images usually stimulate the storymaker to conceive new ideas or feelings and help restart the flow of creation. Being "stuck" is often a collision between what we think should happen and what we want to happen, a time when our inner censor is dictating to our imagination, a situation that never works to our creative advantage. Rather, we have to learn to play with possibilities and regain access to our first thoughts and wonders so we can notice and discover rather than judge prematurely.

Sharing stories to create community has many benefits. Students build cooperative exchanges of information. They learn to use questioning to deepen stories and to focus on enhancement rather than judgment. Telling stories improves listening skills as storytellers connect with their audience. In the process, storytellers develop self-confidence and recognize that they are people with something to say.

In conclusion, I believe imagemaking and storymaking help students tell, write, and share stories and books. These activities stimulate informal usage such as improvisational drama, as well as the more formal usage of analysis. These participatory activities facilitate oral and written expression and language teaching at every educational level. The use of imaginative and creative interactive techniques enhances students' self-esteem, nourishes their ability to express themselves, creates a collaborative learning environment, encourages students' lifelong interest in literature, and serves to strengthen skills needed to lead productive lives.

References

Einstein, Albert. "Letter to Jacques Hadamard," *The Creative Process*. Edited by Brewster Ghiselin. New York: A Mentor Book, 1957. 43–44.

Van der Post, Laurens. *Patterns of Renewal*. Wallingford, PA: Pendle Hill Publications #121, 1961.

Nancy King holds a Ph.D. from the Union Institute and University. She has written articles, plays, and seven books, the latest of which are Storymaking and Drama and Playing Their Part: Language and Learning in the Classroom, *published by Heinemann, and* Dancing With Wonder: Self-Discovery Through Stories, *published by Champion Press. Nancy is currently a literacy, drama, and educational consultant leading workshops in the United States, Canada, and Europe. As a professor at the University of Delaware, she taught courses in theatre and drama, literacy and language development, and interdisciplinary studies, always focusing on creative and empowering approaches to learning.*

CHAPTER TWO

Pre-Kindergarten and Kindergarten

INTRODUCTION
By Jane Stenson

Ah, the little people! Let's talk first about who these children are before we write about storytelling across the curriculum. These active learners are young scientists of their physical and social worlds. They are figuring out how the world works. They move! They explore! They know the world is spirited and magical, full of life. They are bound by their kinesthetic perceptions and grounded in the Here and Now. These egocentric children know the world revolves around their desires, their whims, their problems, and their joys.

What does it mean to be a competent person in our society? What does it mean to be competent when you are two? Or five? Certainly standards for effective adults differ in degree from the two- and five-year-old, but the domains are the same: literacy and sharing a curiosity about the world. When the young child recognizes and speaks about the STOP sign or the golden arches of McDonald's, that is literacy. Speaking, listening, reading, and writing are the strands of literacy competence, and both fiction and nonfiction are equally important. Another signal of competence is curiosity about how the world works socially and physically. Why we visit Grandma on Thursdays or why the balloon floats up or why the tricycle doesn't work are questions that deserve conversation and reference to an expert and/or a book. Our twenty-first-century society demands individual effectiveness in a social context even if you are two or five. Society demands that children shape and be shaped by the world they inhabit.

What is it about telling stories that causes young children to love the teller and remember the story? When an adult looks into the eyes of the child and begins to speak in an engaging way about something important to the child, the young child feels the adult's interest and care. It's a nurturing, reciprocal environment where two great minds and hearts focus on the same idea. It's playful, a dance of recognition between the two, where difficult ideas and actions are entertained in an objective manner, so that the teacher/teller can speak and the child can participate. How many lucky children had youthful impulses disciplined with stories where an animal was constantly in trouble? Only accurate truths about people and the physical world maintain the deep and trusting relationship. Storytelling is about creating, maintaining, and building authentic relationships where language and learning happen because great minds and hearts focus on the same idea.

Storytelling and Literacy

Speaking and Listening: The young child's language is learned in relationships where speech is reciprocal—everyone gets to talk and everyone gets to listen. Discourse between young children and more competent peers is a place of language and of learning. Initially, language is holistic. "Up" can mean "I'm tired. Pick me up" or "Give me a piggyback ride." With the adult question "What happened?" the child extends her language and "Up!" becomes more specific, such as "I fell down. Pick me up!" or "Pick me up! I want to touch the sky." Those phrases begin the journey toward plot. The question "Why?" leads the young child into narrative: "Pick me up because you will make me feel safe" or "Brother is funny and will bounce me high; pick me way up!"

Reading and Language: The early years have parents snuggling with children and a good storybook or pouring intently over a picture-filled nonfiction or informational book. Reading fiction and informational books are very important in developing an intimate relationship between parent and child. Simultaneously, it promotes language development and the idea that language refers to a specific action or picture, or the idea that words create pictures in your mind. Imagination is those pictures, and language is the articulation of the pictures.

Stories of superheroes, princesses, dinosaurs, reptiles, and insects, where the youngest becomes the hero/heroine, are chosen and chosen again. The stories are active, fast paced, and value laden and help children frame how the world works. Because young children are generous and accepting and smart, they expect those values from their storybook heroes.

So, what can the teacher and storyteller do to encourage language and imagination?

- Keep the conversation going;
- Participate in the play and the language—interact;
- Ask what happened, and why;
- Listen to what children have to tell;

- As much as possible keep learning whole, that is, every learning interaction should be replete with math, science, social studies, and literacy. Note that each of our contributors emphasizes a piece of traditional curriculum. Each simultaneously keeps the knowledge in many academic domains while encouraging children to express their ideas in various ways.

Storytelling and the Sciences

Curriculum for young children should come from the teacher's/teller's knowledge of child development. If the children are active and inquisitive, then stories that emphasize the children's participation are the ones to find and tell. If the child is struggling with a particular issue, then that is a story to find and tell. Further, the curriculum/story should expand the child's awareness of the world and broaden the child's capacity to understand other people. The storytelling experience should be enjoyable. Are we having fun? Or is this only about learning a lesson? The story should be truth-filled even if all the facts aren't exactly the way "it" happened. The characters (animal or person) should behave in believable ways. The quality of the language should encourage the child to listen for the beauty of the way the words are put together as well as listening for meaning.

Contributions

Language Arts: Our contributors chose stories full of rhythm and fun. The language pulls the young child into the story and begs for participation and dramatic interpretation. Each contributor uses the oral approach first, dramatic response second, and the book as reference.

Social Studies: All of us are part of many communities. The egocentric young child widens her understanding of the communities that touch her life, learning over time that our complex society requires a division of labor.

Math: Our contributors chose stories that emphasize the playful nature of mathematical thought. Some math ideas are constant, such as number, while many are flexible and reversible, such as performing operations on those quantities.

Science: This article encapsulates the organic nature of a Best Practice preschool classroom where one serendipitous activity, listening to *Abiyoyo* on a CD, sparked the imaginations of children and teacher alike and sponsored months of activity. The three- and four-year-olds spontaneously explored physics and earth science as well as the social science of what to do when you're afraid.

A Research Project: A kindergarten teacher experimented with Milbre Burch's Storybox and developed a long-term developmental method to help children create their own stories.

MOTHER GOOSE THEATRE
By Natalie Jones

National Standards:

NCTE 12: Students use spoken, written, and visual language to accomplish their own purposes.

Objectives:

Use rhyming words, sequencing, and a variety of vocal intonation to dramatize Mother Goose rhymes.

Resources and Materials:

(Need to be collected ahead of time) Review Mother Goose collections to choose rhymes; then, collect props, costumes, puppets, musical instruments, and recordings as needed.

As much as I hate to admit it, the idea for this story lesson came from television. My children and I were spending a rainy afternoon at Grandma's. After finishing every story in Grandma's library, we turned on the television. The Teletubbies were playing a game. It went like this:

Two little Teletubbies sitting on a hill,
One named Jack, and one named Jill.
Fly away, Jack. Fly away, Jill.
Come back, Jack. Come back, Jill.

Davis, then five, and his sister, Caroline, three, were delighted. They flew away and came back, over and over again. The rest of the afternoon was spent acting out Mother Goose rhymes. The verses are full of action; plus, the kind of props needed were ordinary household items, like spoons, stuffed animals, and candlesticks. The concept of a lesson dramatizing Mother Goose rhymes was born.

Mother Goose Theatre engages children in a visual, auditory, and kinesthetic retelling of stories. While exploring the rhymes of Mother Goose, each child goes center stage to act out the story. This language arts lesson emphasizes the skills of using rhyming words, sequencing, and a variety of vocal intonation.

To begin, the teacher explains that students will take turns becoming characters in Mother Goose rhymes. The teacher recites the first rhyme, for example, "Hickory, Dickory, Dock." Two actors are called up and given props, a mouse puppet, and a paper plate clock face. The teacher leads all the students in saying the rhyme together. Then the actors say and act out the

Hickory, Dickory, Dock.

rhyme using props. A rhyme can be performed several times before a turn ends, with the teacher coaching words and actions.

Just by taking a turn, each child will have accomplished the skills objectives. Each child's turn will allow him or her to retell a rhyming story emphasizing the rhyming words, put the story events in sequence, and use different vocal intonations to express character.

One way to assess this lesson is to have students pick out rhyming words from the oral presentations or from the rhymes in their written form. Students can list other rhyming words, too. To assess sequencing, along with vocal intonation, have students perform for each other, or for other classes. They also can retell the story using their own words.

In preparation for this lesson, review Mother Goose collections to choose rhymes, and then collect props, costumes, puppets, musical instruments, and recordings. Here are some examples of items used in my lesson with individual rhymes:

"Two Little Blackbirds": two necklaces made from computer-printed blackbird images and yarn.
"Mary Had a Little Lamb": lamb toy or puppet and girl's hat
"Little Miss Muffett": spider puppet, plastic bowl and spoon
"Jack Be Nimble": unbreakable candlestick
"Little Boy Blue": party horn blower, toy cow, and toy sheep

Consider the number of characters in each rhyme and match to the participants. Have fun with group rhymes. Clap out a rhythm to "Pease, Porridge Hot," or have the class follow motions to "Teddy Bear, Teddy Bear, Turn Around." Also try recorded music. Play "London Bridge," or use listening skills to hop on the word "pop" during "Pop Goes the Weasel." "Polly Put the Kettle On" is a natural circle game. Have the group circle in one direction each time Polly puts the kettle on, and change directions when Suky takes the kettle off.

Hints for success: Dress as Mother Goose. Since my first costume, a long blue dress and bonnet, met with the comment "She doesn't look like the Mother Goose on Barney," I wear a nontraditional outfit. Each teacher can fashion just the right look for her own Mother Goose. In addition, I've found that using a large rug as a "stage" keeps the actors in place and makes it easier for the rest of the class to see and hear. Another help is to use music and musical instruments. Since it is very stimulating to act out rhymes, using a rain stick for "It's Raining, It's Pouring," or starting a steady beat on a rhythm instrument for "There was a Little Turtle," can help refocus the class.

To find other curriculum connections, check out national standards in Theatre Skills. Some standards covered in the program include interacting in improvisations and using a variety of movement and vocal techniques to assume characters.

Mother Goose Theatre is a flexible, fun lesson that can last an hour or a week. Some of my classes have gone on to perform for special parent days, or for book buddies in other grades. There are parts for everyone. Even the shyest child can pour from a watering can to help Contrary Mary's garden grow. It is a class experience your children will always remember. And you may even get the question, as I did, walking through the halls of my school, "Are you the Real Mother Goose?"

Assessments:

Have students pick out rhyming words from the oral presentations or from the rhymes in their written form. To assess sequencing, along with vocal intonation, have students perform for each other, or for other classes.

Many of the successful ideas here were road tested by the kindergarten and first-grade classes at Shelton Elementary School. I thank the students and teachers for their enthusiasm and helpful scholarly comments.

Natalie Jones inspires children to explore their imaginations through story theatre presentations using puppets, music, costumes, and audience interaction. With an eclectic résumé, including work as a park ranger, children's librarian, media specialist, and professional storyteller, Natalie uses her skills to educate and motivate reading. She has presented programs and workshops all over the southeast for librarians, teachers, parents, and students. Highlights are work with the Georgia Conference of Media Organizations; Georgia Public Libraries; Turner South Broadcasting's Education through Storytelling programs in Alabama, Georgia, North Carolina, and Tennessee; the Virginia Annual Storytelling Gathering; and South Carolina's Stone Soup Storytelling Festival. Natalie lives in Acworth, Georgia, with husband Chris, son Davis, daughter Caroline, a puppy, a cat, and a hamster. E-mail: njones69@ hotmail.com.

COMMUNITY HELPERS TO THE RESCUE!
By Betsy Doty

National Standards:

HCOF (Social Studies): Develops growing awareness of jobs and what is required to perform them. HCOF (Language Arts): Understands increasingly growing and complex vocabulary; increases ability to retell stories, to act out stories in dramatic play, to predict what happens next in a story.

Objectives:

Demonstrate knowledge of community helpers; create and retell a story using folktale pattern.

What would a preschool teacher do without "The Turnip"? That wonderful traditional tale is told to teach children that teamwork and cooperation are essential to getting the job done, and that even the smallest person is important. It's part of everyone's lesson plans, on sequencing as well as on gardening—and it can be morphed into a lesson on community helpers as well!

In my work as a freelance storyteller in Head Start classrooms throughout the Appalachian foothills of northwest Georgia, I search for ways to make stories meaningful to children whose life experience and language skills are sometimes limited, and to make relevant connections to the life experiences they can claim as their own. This story, with its cumulative plot; rhythmical, repeated phrases; and opportunities for kinesthetic, linguistic, and visual engagement, provides a perfect vehicle for helping children learn new vocabulary, grasp new information, and have fun with story!

Instructional Plan:

1. Tell *The Turnip* (Morgan Pierr, Philomel Books, 1990). Here's how I begin:
   "Once there was a farmer who loved turnips. He liked turnip French fries, he liked turnip pizza, he liked turnip ice cream." (Now the kids know this is going to be FUN!)
   "So he took a little tiny seed, dug a hole in the ground, put in the seed, and covered it up with dirt. Then he watered it.

"The next day he went out to look at it—and saw the sun shine down on it and the rain come down . . .

"The next day he went out to look at it—and saw the sun shine down on it and the rain come down . . .

"The next day he went out to look at it—and saw the sun shine down on it and the rain come down . . ." (Each time move to the planted spot, increasingly impatient/irritated. Kids certainly relate to THIS.)

2. Retell the story, inviting the kids to act out the story as you retell it. Try this method:

"... And the farmer said, 'Fe, Fi, Fo, Fum. I pulled the turnip but it wouldn't come.'

"So he called his wife to come help him." ("Who would like to come up here and be my wife?")

Make sure to wear loose clothing so that four-year-olds can hold onto a shirt-tail or a belt. Kids can hold onto each other's shoulders acceptably.

"So . . . say this part with me, too . . . the WIFE took hold of the farmer, and they . . ."

After the first time or two when the kids "get it," have each character say his or her own character name in rhythm. The kids will prompt each other!

When you reach the mouse, have them line up around the edge of the rug. After "they pulled, and they pulled," intervene with "Now wait a minute: on the next pull the turnip is going to come up. What happens to US when we are pulling really hard on something and it lets go? That's right, we fall! So, Rule #1: fall

"Pulling together" for fun and turnip ice cream at Gilmer County Head Start in Ellijay, Georgia.

this way toward the center of the rug. Rule #2: DON'T FALL ON ANYONE ELSE. Are you ready?"

"And they PULLED . . . " After the hullabaloo dies down and the giggle level is lower, the story concludes with " . . . and because the little mouse made it happen, he got the biggest piece of all."

This phase engages the whole brain, providing opportunities to watch, listen, tell in rhythm, move, and interact with others during the telling of the story. The sequence and important phrases are retained in many modalities. Add on characters if you need to—it's okay to have more than one dog!

3. Discuss the story elements: Where did it take place? Who were the characters? What was the problem? How did the problem get solved?
4. Suggest that the class make up a new story called "The Bus Got Stuck!" Where would the story take place? Who could be the characters? Lead them to call in community helpers—a fireman, a policeman, teachers and nurses and doctors and cafeteria workers, etc. What would each of these characters do to help? How does the bus finally get unstuck?
5. As you get ideas from the group, write the answers on the board.
6. Ask children to decide on an order for the characters to arrive. Refer back to "The Turnip"—was the order oldest to youngest, biggest to smallest, loudest to softest? Rearrange the written order on the board and you have a new story!
7. Tell the new story with as much audience involvement as possible.
8. Dramatize the story as in #2 above, getting the whole group involved.

I've used this lesson plan dozens of times, and the results are invariably hilarious and successful. It provides a great way to reinforce vocabulary about community helpers and knowledge about what they do. It also provides a way for teachers to authentically assess class and individual understanding of that content. Children who are normally shy surprise their teachers by participating fully; in fact, these are often the children who shine the brightest! The lesson plan is also accessible for children with learning disabilities or language deficits, as well as physical and mental disabilities. My favorite memory is of a quadriplegic child falling out of her wheelchair to be the mouse. Her full-time helper lifted her to the end of the line so that she could "almost" fall just like the rest of them. We could see her giggle silently, and we all reveled in the huge beam on her face! For children who are learning English as a second language, it's easy to learn enough key words to help them make meaning, e.g., wife = su esposa. American Sign Language works really well, too!

Kids love this activity because it's noisy and silly and they GET it. Teachers love it because it teaches content while improving vocabulary, comprehension, and understanding of story elements such as setting, character, sequencing, and cause and effect. I love it because it's so flexible; in fact, each month I adapt it to the current curriculum focus, reinforcing pattern recognition. But chiefly, I love it because it makes learning FUN!

Assessments:

Ask children to draw what happens in the new story, and then to retell the story using their picture to help. Listen for correct sequence and "community helpers" vocabulary. A classroom Big Book of the new story can be created, laminated, and kept in the classroom to remember the fun.

Betsy Doty has introduced the magic of storytelling to scores of young children and their teachers in the north Georgia mountains through her work in regional Headstart and pre-kindergarten programs. She has recently recruited, inspired, trained, and attained funding for a storytelling troupe that delivers 108 story programs to fifty-nine classrooms every week, and her own storytelling has been featured at festivals such as Corn Island, the Atlanta Winter Fest, and Magnolia Storytelling Festival. She offers workshops for teachers, parents, and religious leaders in the art of story sharing. E-mail: betsydoty@ellijay.com.

THE FAT CAT: A MATH ADVENTURE
By Karen Pillsworth

National Standards:

NCTM 2: Develop understanding of the relative position and magnitude of whole numbers and of ordinal and cardinal numbers and their connections.

Objectives:

Counting whole numbers (both cardinal and ordinal).

In many schools throughout our country, kindergarten is becoming a place where four- and five-year-olds are being asked to do tasks well beyond what is developmentally appropriate. "Earlier is better" seems to be the cry. Those of us who have been around a while know that the most important thing we can do in early childhood education is to allow children to be children; tapping into their natural curiosity allows us to make learning fun. Developmentally appropriate curriculum that engages children in meaningful activities is the most effective way to teach. Over the last twenty-five years it has become increasingly clear to me that the use of story is a most effective tool, and so, on to the adventure of the Fat Cat!

"I want to be first!" Every teacher of young children has heard this many times. The concept of "first" is easy to teach, but what about the rest of the ordinal numbers? National Math Standards tell us that we need to introduce ordinal numbers in pre-kindergarten, under Standard 2, Benchmark 5, so that students begin to understand the concept of position in sequence (e.g., first, last). At the kindergarten level, Benchmark 2, students learn to count whole numbers (both cardinal and ordinal). After a few years of trying a variety of ideas and becoming increasingly frustrated, I discovered the story of the *Fat Cat: A Danish Folktale* (Margaret Read MacDonald, August House Little

Folk, 2001). The story takes us through one day in the life of a very hungry cat. I tried reading a version to introduce the concept of ordinal numbers to my kindergarteners, but it didn't seem to capture their attention. Telling it with them involved, however—now that is another story!

All you need to tell this story is a big bed sheet and a lot of laughing. I introduce the story by telling the children I will need their help. However, if called upon they must be able to do two things. First, they have to be able to stand straight and tall, and second, they have to be able to be silent (even when they want to giggle). This sets the stage for "serious" volunteers. Next I call upon someone to be the cat. I drape the bed sheet around this child's shoulders and the story begins.

The old woman is busy cooking her gruel (porridge) when she realizes she has some business with a neighbor woman down the road. She asks the cat to stir her gruel while she is gone, and the cat agrees. The cat becomes so hungry he eats the gruel and the pot, too! When the old woman returns, she says, "My little cat, you are so fat! What have you been eating?" The cat responds, "FIRST I ate the gruel, SECOND I ate the pot, and now I am going to eat you." And he eats the old woman. I select a child from the audience and place him or her under the sheet. After a few giggles the story continues.

The cat decides to go for a walk, and on his walk he meets the following characters who always greet him with the same refrain: "My little cat, etc." The cat always responds, "FIRST I ate the gruel, SECOND I ate the pot, THIRD I ate the old woman, and now I am going to eat you!" One by one the Skottentot, the lady with the pink parasol, and the parson with the crooked staff get "eaten" by the cat. Each time the ordinal numbers are repeated. Finally, coming down the road is a mighty woodcutter (I always select the bravest child for this role). After the cat says he will eat the woodcutter, the mighty woodcutter takes his ax and chops that fat cat down the middle, and one by one the characters come out of his stomach. Then the woodcutter sews up that fat cat and he is never fat again.

For about a week I simply leave the old sheet out for the children to play with, and the story is told over and over during free time. True to the oral tradition, it is never told the same way twice, but the ordinal numbers are always included. This allows ordinal numbers to become a natural part of the kindergarten vocabulary. The next week I retell the story using simple pictures of the characters on sandwich boards so the students can wear the characters. After the story, we mix up the characters and the children have to put them in the correct order using ordinal numbers again. This activity is again left out for a week so that the students can have more hands-on interaction with the story.

The third week I give the students a long piece of paper and cutouts of the characters from the sandwich board version of the story. The students put them in order and then come and tell me the story using the ordinal numbers. This is an easy assessment tool, and all the kids get to tell a portion of the story, which makes them very happy.

It may seem like a long time to work on a single math concept; however, ordinal numbers do not come as naturally to young children as some other math concepts. Besides, why do we have to hurry everything when we are having such fun? The classroom environment should be about exploring, experimenting, and discovering. To do these things, children need time.

In many ways this story has become my signature story with young children, but the laughs received from adults participating during events only reinforce what we already know: a good story crosses all boundaries. From time to time, the mayor of the city, the principal of the school, and even some of our local religious leaders have found themselves being "eaten" by the fat cat. Who knew what fun we could all have with one simple folktale?

Assessments:

Discuss the concept of being the first one chosen to participate in an activity; use repetition to teach proper sequence of ordinal numbers; explore, experiment, and discover ordinal numbers during fun time; students place cutouts in sequential order and tell a portion of the story to the class.

In addition to being a kindergarten teacher, Karen Pillsworth has been delighting audiences with her stories for the past twenty-five years in libraries, camps, churches, schools, parks, and festivals throughout the northeast. Karen has taught "The Art of Storytelling" at Ulster County Community College and "Discovering the Stories within Us" at UPAC's Expanding Horizons Art and Education Center. She has been a keynote speaker at Early Childhood conferences, presenting her work on Sharing Stories: An Educator's Best Tool. Karen was selected as a National Arts Education Fellow for her storytelling program: There's No Place Like Home: Stories of the Hudson Valley and Catskill Mountains. In 2002, she was named the Storyteller Laureate of the city of Kingston, New York.

TOO MUCH NOISE EQUALS TWO TIMES THE FUN IN THE PRIMARY MATHEMATICS CLASSROOM
By Jennifer Whitman

National Standards:

NCTM 1: Understand numbers, ways of representing numbers, relationships among numbers, and number systems and build new mathematical knowledge through problem solving; NCTM 2: Solve problems that arise in mathematics and in other contexts.

Objectives:

Enhance students' ability to create number stories using addition and subtraction.

Materials:

• Paper cutouts of characters in story

We know that storytelling is an integral part of the literacy curriculum, but what about applications beyond reading and writing? Here is one example of taking a well-loved traditional tale and using it as the basis for a primary mathematics lesson about addition and subtraction concepts. I used this particular lesson with my kindergarten students, but it could easily be adapted for use through grade 2.

For this series of lessons, I told the familiar folktale of a man who complains there is "TOO MUCH NOISE!" in his house. He goes to the village wise person for help and is told to bring many animals into his home. In my version, the man finds dogs, cats, sheep, and horses to take home. Eventually, his home is overrun with animals and noise. The wise person then tells him to take back all of the animals. Only then does the man realize how peaceful his life was to begin with. Many variants of this tale are readily available in school libraries. Look for *Too Much Noise* by Ann McGovern (Houghton Mifflin, 1967), *It Could Always Be Worse* by Margot Zemach (Farrar, Straus, Giroux, 1976), or "What a Wonderful Life" from *Shake-It-Up Tales!* by Margaret Read MacDonald (August House, 2000).

The lessons unfolded over several days. First, I told the story to my students for fun. We just enjoyed the language of the story together. In order to use this story successfully in the context of the mathematics classroom, I needed to tailor the language of the story to the concepts of addition and subtraction. I was planning to add questions about quantity, such as "How many altogether? How many left?" This was language I would not normally use in the telling, so I added these questions only after I had told the story for pure enjoyment in its original form. We then used the narrative structure of the tale for math activities throughout the week.

The next day, we acted out the story with children taking the roles of the animals. The man now brought different numbers of each animal home. I asked my students, "How many cats did the wise woman tell him to get?" The children answered, "TWO!" So two children then came up front to be the cats. In this telling, I began to add questions using mathematical language. Each time we added a new set of animals, I asked, "How many animals did the man have altogether now?" Eventually, there were 10 children mooing, barking, meowing, and bleating up front. When we finally sent the animals away, one group at a time, I asked, "How many animals did he have left now?" after each group sat back down. The children counted the actors to be certain. I was careful in my questioning to use the same mathematical language I wanted the students to explore in their work with addition and subtraction. The students loved playing with the story in this way, so we told it twice, giving everyone a chance to be the loud animals.

During our next math session, I presented paper cutouts of the animals as storytelling props. There were four images of each animal to use in the telling.

We sat in a circle and told the story once again, this time using the props. We went around the circle and each child told a bit of the story. The children again decided how many of each animal the man needed. He brought two cats home, so we put two paper cats into the center of the circle. Then he brought three dogs home, so we added three paper dogs to the cats, and so on. Each time we put more animals into the center, I asked the same question as the day before: "How many animals did the man have altogether now?" Some children counted each of the props, others knew just by looking at the set, but all were engaged in finding the answer. Students then shared their strategies for finding the solution.

The following day, we reviewed the story quickly and then I gave the children their own set of storytelling props to cut and color. When the props were ready, the students paired up with a classmate and told the story to each other. The children enjoyed manipulating the props while telling the story and also benefited from hearing their partner's version of the story. I had an opportunity to assess their understanding of and ability to make word sentences. And we all had fun—there were many lively and inventive variations of the tale!

That evening, the students packed up their props and took them home to tell the story to their parents. Copies of the storytelling props were also put in a math center for students to revisit on their own. I left an option for students to use their white boards to try writing the number sentences as they were telling the story if they needed an additional challenge.

I introduced this story after we had spent numerous math sessions telling number stories with concrete objects. Students had experienced manipulating blocks to tell their own number stories. For example, one student's story went like this: "There were five people taking their blanket out for a picnic and then a big monster tree came and scared them all away and then there were none." She showed five blocks marching along and then whisked them away. She then drew a picture and accompanied her story with a number sentence: $5 - 5 = 0$.

During our work with "Too Much Noise," children quickly made connections between the storytelling sessions and the number stories and number sentences we had been playing with in earlier math lessons. When we had two paper cats and three paper dogs and I asked, "How many animals did the man have altogether now?" One student shouted out, "It's just like $2 + 3 = 5!$" The other students reveled in that discovery. They had made a fast leap from the concrete to the abstract.

The enthusiasm the students showed throughout this week of storytelling math was tremendous. Isn't it wonderful what a good story can do for a math lesson? It's just TOO MUCH FUN!

Assessments:

Using the storytelling props already created, ask children to create their own number problems.

Jen Whitman teaches kindergarten at Hong Kong International School. She has been a storyteller and educator for over ten years. Jen holds National Board Certification as an Early Childhood Generalist. She uses storytelling daily with her students, and she enjoys giving workshops for colleagues on the power of storytelling in the classroom. Jen and her husband, Nat, perform together for family audiences as a tandem storytelling team.

ABIYOYO: ONE GIANT LESSON
By Sherelyn Rubin Kaufman

National Standards:

NAS 1: Science as inquiry: ask a question about an event in the environment; plan and conduct a simple investigation; employ equipment and tools to gather data; use data to construct a reasonable explanation.

Objectives:

Keeping knowledge whole and connected and relevant is important for young children who are trying to figure out how the world works; extending units of study based on children's continued interest; addressing children's fears in a way that helps them manage their fear; meeting national curricular standards in science.

Storytelling in the preschool classroom gives us a few moments to gather together, take a breath, imagine, and problem-solve in a world that isn't real, but isn't unlike the children's world in some important way. With storytelling, I like to say that I'm exercising the child's brain: encouraging children to make connections and to think in sometimes parallel and in sometimes divergent ways about certain characters or situations. All the while, we're meeting national curriculum and content area standards across the disciplinary spectrum. In this long, serendipitous project, the integrating "thread" of storytelling meets standards for the English language arts, social studies, and arts education, as well as the science standard stated above.

This school year, my class of eighteen three- to five-year-olds listened to Pete Seeger, on CD, tell the story of Abiyoyo. Seeger adapted "Abiyoyo," a South African lullaby/folktale, as a story for his own small children. He later recorded it and published it in picture book form as *Abiyoyo*, illustrated by Michael Hays (Simon & Schuster Children's Publishing Division, 1963). In Seeger's version, a small boy and his father save their village from the threatening giant, Abiyoyo, by using their unique gifts of music and magic to exhaust the giant and make him disappear.

The children realized they needed to listen intently, since the CD format didn't allow them to ask Seeger to immediately repeat! They sang along when appropriate, and occasionally guessed out loud at what was coming. The children who already knew the story shared their excitement about "knowing that already." Their familiarity served only to increase their excitement and made the other children want to hear the story too.

At the children's insistence, I also read the book, showed the illustrations, and again they sang the song and "played" imaginary ukuleles. We compared the two versions.

I read *Abiyoyo Returns*, by Pete Seeger and Paul Dubois (Simon & Schuster Children's Publishing Division, 2001), illustrated by Michael Hays, a few days later. One little boy pointed to the illustration and asked if Abiyoyo was made of metal. I told him that this was the illustrator's version of Abiyoyo and that they might each have a different picture of him in their heads. We pondered this for a while.

At the children's request, we shared the story of *Abiyoyo Returns* with our second-grade buddies. The story became a bonding experience, since sharing a story with a friend forms a connection. We found that the words alone didn't help us understand how Abiyoyo helped to build a dam to keep back the water from flooding the town. Rather, the story led to a need to experiment with materials. You've never seen so much enthusiasm for a science lesson that exposed them to physical properties of clay, water, and rock. And the cooperation amongst almost forty children in two classes was impressive, too.

Professional storyteller Jennifer Armstrong visited our school to tell stories during the Betty Weeks Storytelling Conference. Imagine our surprise when she announced from the stage that she would be telling a story about a giant. It was serendipitous, and the class was engaged, appropriately interactive, joyous, and proud. A few minutes into her introduction, the same little boy who had asked if Abiyoyo was made of metal turned to me and whispered, "Abiyoyo's still not real, right?" I assured him it was still a story, and he settled in for the fun.

Over the next few months, the children built rivers and dams in various physical substances in the sensory tables. They drew a huge Abiyoyo on butcher paper. And they built a towering Abiyoyo by "recycling" large pieces of Styrofoam packing material. At unpredictable times, they burst into chorus with "Abiyoyo, Abiyoyo." One little boy, about a month later, with no immediate provocation, approached with a smile and presented me with a hand-drawn representation of Abiyoyo "with stinky teeth."

When a new student arrived in our class late in the school year, the children took turns at the rug telling the story of Abiyoyo so that she, too, could share what had become part of our class culture.

I wrote to Pete Seeger to share how he had inspired such experiential learning in our classroom, and much to my delight and the children's wonder he responded. Pete asked me to share with the boy who asked if Abiyoyo was made of metal that he "purposely made the giant a little like Frankenstein's monster." And, because he is truly a teacher at heart, Pete also suggested that I read *Pete Seeger's Storytelling Book*, by Pete Seeger and Paul Dubois (Jacobs, Harcourt, 2000). It was a privilege to share with the children that the author of *Abiyoyo* knew about them and their experiences, for the underlying message is that authors are real and caring people, and that each of us is an author and storyteller, too!

The giant Abiyoyo is sometimes scary, and sometimes helpful with his strength. Our own Styrofoam Abiyoyo was fearsome, yet fragile. The boy with the ukulele is small, but can effect change. The dad in the second tale is the boy from the first story, all grown. These stories provide multiple opportunities/assessments to think about and process choices, growth, opposites, ironies, taking risks, and using your talents.

I find that the best lessons of a story are never instantaneous. Stories need to settle, and be repeated, by me and by the children in, as educator Loris Malaguzzi of Reggio Emilia, Italy, suggested, "a hundred different languages." It is only then that the children connect them to their own experiences in infinite and valuable ways, thereby making their world meaningful. The repetition of these stories serves to deepen each child's understanding in some small way, since every telling is unique in detail or inflection, and in timing within the child's life. Words travel from lips, to hearts, to hands, and on to brains. Storytelling inspires young children to think for themselves, to ask meaningful questions, and to take control of their own interdisciplinary learning.

Assessments:

Authentic assessment of student learning shows throughout this organic project in the children's artwork, science questions, and play. It shows in their generosity with their friends, and in their sustaining of the project. Further, it is shown in the repeated reading of and listening to the story, so that the structure and meaning are known and played out in the classroom.

Sherry Kaufman earned her B.A. in English Honors from the University of Massachusetts, Amherst, and graduated from University of Michigan Law School with a J.D. in 1983. She practiced school law and was an attorney with the U. S. Department of Education, Office for Civil Rights. Her interest in education and experience with her own three children led Sherry to National-Louis University to learn more about how children learn. After earning her M.A.T. in Elementary Education, Sherry taught at Ravinia Nursery School, where she discovered the excitement of engaging young children in conversation and exploration. There she was introduced to Abiyoyo, *and the joys of observing children making connections between wonderful stories and their own experiences. Sherry also taught pre-kindergarten at Baker Demonstration*

School, where the art of storytelling is a highly valued shared "culture." She is currently Director of Winnetka Public School Nursery, a Reggio Emilia-inspired preschool. E-mail: skauf300@yahoo.com.

STORYBOX RESEARCH IN THE EARLY CHILDHOOD CLASSROOM
By Jane Stenson

National Standards:

NCTE 2: Students read a wide range of literature from many periods; NCTE 4: Students adjust their use of spoken, written, and visual language to communicate effectively with a variety of audiences; NCTE 5: Students employ a wide range of strategies as they write and use different writing elements; NCTE 6: Students apply knowledge of language structure and language conventions to create and critique print and non-print texts; NCTE 11: Students participate as knowledgeable, reflective, creative, and critical members of literacy communities.

I am a teacher and a storyteller. Most of my professional development in the last decade has concerned my interest in integrating these avocations/professions. Then, Milbre Burch presented her storybox idea (Chapter Three) at a storytelling conference for educators that I produce. I was smitten! I had to put a storybox in my classroom! Could kindergarten students practice and play with story structure and construct their own stories from a tableau? Burch recommended storyboxes for first through fifth grades; I teach kindergarten. Over the school year, would children's stories change substantively if they used the storybox? Would I need to directly teach story conventions to accompany the storybox? What children's picture books should accompany this long-range endeavor? I was ready for an experiment, a teacher action research project, full of questions that might change and improve my practice . . . and children's stories.

I made a storybox, purchased white sand and miniatures, and put the box on its own small table with two chairs, one for a child and one for a teacher. Initially, the children treated the storybox like a sandbox. I was uncompromising about saying, "This is only for <u>stories</u>, playing with stories. You can play with sand in the sandbox."

I asked one child at a time to arrange several miniatures in the sand in a way that made sense and then tell me a story. "I will write it down and you have to speak slowly." This is based on Vivian Paley's story dictation work, so the children were familiar with the scribing aspect. They loved my concentrated attention! They loved the personal conversation about their story, and they liked

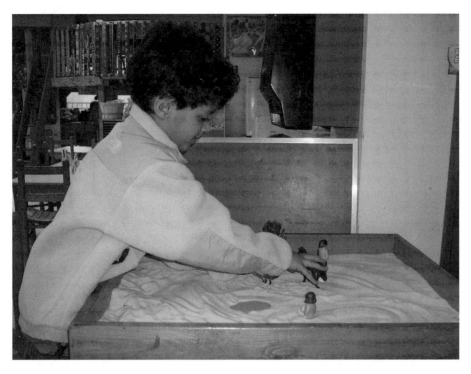

Kindergartner sets up his tableau in the Storybox: children tell stories that are scribed each month and compiled in a book of stories at the end of the school year.

The Storybox in Kindergarten: individual attention, telling a story from a picture, and a permanent record of the story are part of the storybox experience.

the sensory nature of the storybox. If I did not understand something, I asked clarifying questions, scaffolding questions! As the year progressed, I learned the stumbling places of each child and could ask increasingly specific questions to help the child discover what she needed to learn about story structure. Children were eager to tell and often waited in line, listening to their friends' stories. I read the story out loud later that day at Rug Time to hushed and proud children. Sometimes we acted out the story, a most revered activity.

Knowing the children found this to be a wonderful activity, I thought about how to frame a year's worth of their stories. That was it: one story per month, per child, or ten stories per year to be made into a book at the end of the school year so families could enjoy their child's work. Each child would have the benefit of his or her own story and the benefit of every other child's story, every month. I would discuss story structure in direct teaching time (Rug Time), and I would read traditional tales where the structure was easily accessible for kindergartners. Further, we would storyboard, breaking stories into six parts, much the way Elizabeth Ellis describes in her article (Chapter Four).

When tellers and teachers combine their best ideas and efforts, the children win. Because Milbre Burch and Elizabeth Ellis discuss their art and their methods and because I, the teacher, am constantly looking for ways to integrate children's interest with stories, this activity was realized. The professional storyteller doesn't stay in the school with the children, but her ideas can be harnessed and adapted for long-term use in the storytelling classroom.

Jane Stenson teaches kindergarten at the Baker Demonstration School, affiliated with National-Louis University, Evanston, Illinois. She is a professional storyteller and is one of the authors of The Storytelling Classroom: Applications Across the Curriculum. *E-mail: jane@janestenson.com.*

CHAPTER THREE

Grades One and Two

INTRODUCTION
By Diane Williams

When students reach elementary school they are prepared to continue exploring the learning process. First and second graders will interact and react to stories in a more elaborate way than students in pre-kindergarten and kindergarten, if they are allowed to explore the story elements first. For example, do you recall the story about the "Tortoise and the Hare"? Well, as you well know, no one is calling a turtle a tortoise anymore and a rabbit by any other name is still a rabbit. Therefore, you might want to engage the students in a comparative discussion about turtles' and rabbits' names, lifestyles, and habits.

Some of the stories in this chapter will relate to classic and traditional stories. Sharing stories about families is a great way for students to value relationships. Students get to look at family traits in a positive manner and learn that we are all very much alike, even though we look a little bit different or come from a different part of the world. Exploring a variety of themes through folktales can help students learn a lot about comparing and contrasting. There are many lessons to be learned that can help students know and grow.

First and second graders enjoy learning what the story characters will or will not do. Discovering what the student would have done differently from the characters in folktales is rewarding for everyone involved in the process. What causes something to happen? How many different ways can we experience an adventure? These are important elements to the first- and second-grade world. That's why the story of Jack and the Beanstalk and other Jack tales will never go out of style.

This is the best time in a child's life to participate in the telling of a tale. Songs, music, sounds, and movement enhance the learning experience for life. Stories incorporating visual arts support the learning experience and help to leave lasting impressions in the minds of students. This is also a great time to focus on the learning styles of the students in your classroom. Modeling storytelling should be presented to first and second graders and then get them involved in an interactive way. What's the best way to engage students? Twenty or more years ago, we simply called on any students who raised their hands. Invariably, once invited to the front of the class, the student may or may not follow through and participate. The experienced teacher and story-teller have learned the importance of getting to know students well enough to make decisions on how to involve the ones who will best portray a portion of the story. But beware! No one will want to be left out.

In the classroom, Gardner's theory of multiple intelligences is a help-ful tool for observing the learning styles of students. Dr. Howard Gardner, Hobbs Professor of Cognition and Education at the Harvard Graduate School of Education, developed his theory of multiple intelligences in 1983 (*Frames of Mind: The Theory of Multiple Intelligences,* Basic Books, 1993). Basically, it honors the different learning styles of human potential in children and adults. Many sites on the Internet discuss multiple intelligences, and some even offer lesson plans.

Essentially, the learning styles include: linguistic intelligence (words), logical-mathematical intelligence (numbers and reasoning), spatial intelli-gence (pictures), bodily-kinesthetic intelligence (movement), interpersonal intelligence (relating to others), intrapersonal intelligence (relating to self), and naturalist intelligence (nature smarts). Many of the stories in this book will incorporate most of the aforementioned learning styles, if not all of them. Understanding their students from the perspective of multiple intelligences will help teachers and storytellers determine how to best involve the individual student learner.

The lesson plans embedded in this chapter include ways to evaluate knowledge and learning that will help you assess the effects of the story con-tent. The connection to standards for comprehensive learning and classroom best practices makes the contributors' work a valuable tool that you can incor-porate into your classroom activities.

Strategies that Work by Stephanie Harvey and Anne Goudvis (Stenhouse Publisher, 2000) explores teaching comprehension to enhance understanding. This text would be a great companion and resource based on cur-rent research. It includes strategies for instruction in context. It also includes visualization and inference strategies for understanding. Based on current research, making text-to-self, text-to-text, and text-to-world connections greatly enhances a child's ability to know and grow in understanding story.

There are other great resources that guide understanding of story-telling across the curriculum. The important concept to remember is that finding stories that are interesting, fun, engaging, and relevant should be first and foremost. The stories selected for this chapter include all of these points and more.

THE TORTOISE AND THE HARE
By Lyn Ford

National Standards:

NCTE 1: Students read a wide range of print and non-print texts to build an understanding of texts, of themselves, and of the cultures of the United States and the world; NCTE 5: Students employ a wide range of strategies as they write and use different writing process elements appropriately to communicate with different audiences for a variety of purposes.

Objectives:

Nurturing listening skills and appreciation of stories from various cultures; understanding of the basic elements of "story" (beginning, middle, and end; characters and their characterization; visual, physical, and linguistic expression; setting; problem and solution in plot); use of these elements in spoken, visual, and written presentation; contrast and comparison of similar characters in similar stories; and recognition of the moral lessons these folktales can provide.

I use two versions of the fable "The Tortoise and the Hare" to provide lessons in character education, and to effectively encourage first- and second-grade students to follow and comprehend the path and pattern of "story."

First, I tell the fable attributed to Aesop: Hare challenges Tortoise to a footrace; Hare, confident that he will win, rests, giving Tortoise a chance to pass him; Tortoise wins the race. To encourage and reinforce word recognition, I make the story interactive; we pat on our legs for the action sounds of Hare's *speeding* and *racing*, and Tortoise's *plodding* and *trudging*. This tale's lesson is "Slow and steady wins the race," which I explain and then express by posting one word on the board, "persistence," and gathering definitions from the students: "Doing your best"; "Don't just quit"; "Taking our time with the work is okay; we don't have to be fast all the time."

The students answer questions; I write their answers on the board. Some questions I ask, and some answers I've received, are:

- Who are the characters? (Tortoise and Hare)
- Could we add characters to the story? ("We could, but we don't need 'em." "Yes, other animals, to cheer.")
- Where do you think the story happened? ("In the woods." "In the jungle." "On a road.")

- What problem did Tortoise have? ("Hare thought he was faster and better." "Hare was teasing Tortoise." "Hare was a bully.")
- What happened? ("Tortoise won!" "Hare got lazy, and he lost the race." "Tortoise was proud, and Hare was sad.")
- Why did Tortoise win? ("Because he didn't give up!" "Because he just kept on goin'.")
- Did Hare learn anything from this race? ("Yes! Don't go to sleep when you're in a race!" "Don't be mean." "Be friends, and don't brag.")

All these new "morals" can lead to new endings for the story, in writing projects after our session.

Next, we map the story together. I draw a line on the board for the path of the race. At the left end of the line, I print the words "Beginning" and "Starting Line," since this is the beginning of both the story and the race. At the middle, I draw a tree where Hare can stop and rest; I mark this as the "middle" of the race and the story. At the right end, I print the words "finish line" and "end." Note that the beginning words use capital letters, and the last word ends with a period; the left-to-right progression also reinforces sentence structure and reading skills.

Beginning/Starting Line   Middle/Tree   Finish Line/End.

As I point to the important locations on our map, the students give details of events. I emphasize that Tortoise faces a problem at the beginning of his adventure; boasting Hare has challenged Tortoise to race because Hare thinks Tortoise can't win. The solution is also the moral of the story: persistence.

To extend and enhance the student's experience, and to add cultural awareness and diversity to the storytelling, I share an adaptation of a similar "Tortoise and Hare" fable that is rooted in several African versions (in addition to the tale from Aesop, I have found versions from Zimbabwe, South Africa, and Nigeria, with the help of librarians at the Columbus Metropolitan and Delaware County Public Library Systems in Ohio). Tortoise's problem is the same, but his solution leads to a different lesson: Hare challenges Tortoise to a footrace; Hare stops to rest, and sees Tortoise ahead of him; each time Hare rests, he sees Tortoise in the lead; exhausted Hare finally approaches the finish line, where Tortoise is already the winner. What Hare doesn't know is that Tortoise's family has helped; relatives waited along the footpath, and the Tortoise at the finish line is not the Tortoise who started the race. The lesson from this story is that unity brings strength.

The ending in this version leads to a discussion of cooperation, community, and whether Tortoise's family is simply tricky or cheats to win.

According to Connie Pottle, Youth Services Coordinator for the Delaware County District Library, "I think it's just the African versions that have the turtle tricking the hare by having his relatives stationed along the way."

The point of our discussion is the gathering of ideas for further writing. We again chart the path of the story: Tortoise's problem at the beginning, the places where Hare rested and other tortoises waited (the solution), and the ending of the story. We compare this to Aesop's cautionary tale.

Each student then selects a moral and creates a story to share. Students make their own maps on large, heavy white paper, illustrating the path, labeling the important places, and drawing the actions of the main characters. After sharing the illustrations, students write their stories on lined paper, which is attached to the back of the illustrations, so that they can now read their stories to others. These pictures are put on display, or laminated and bound into a big book. The pictures, writing, and presentation by students as they share their stories can be used as an assessment of whether participants understand both the story and the story concepts, and if language arts skills meet benchmarks for the grade level.

This experience can lead to scientific study of the characters in the stories: Where do they live? How fast do they move? Who might really win the race?

One source for teachers, for the story as retold from West African folktales, is "The Elephant, The Tortoise, and the Hare," in *West African Folktales*, collected and translated by Jack Berry, edited by Richard Spears (Northwestern University Press, 1991).

Assessments:

The pictures, writing, and presentation by students as they share their stories can be used as an assessment of participants' understanding of the story and the story concepts, and whether their language arts skills meet grade level benchmarks.

Lynette Ford is a fourth-generation storyteller, and a member of the Greater Columbus (Ohio) Arts Council's Artists-in-Schools program. Lyn shares an interactive, rhythmic style and stories rooted in her family's multicultural African American oral traditions. Lyn has encouraged young people to understand and utilize the basic elements of "story" since 1993, when she began providing performances and workshops in schools, libraries, and other venues, including the Thurber Center in Columbus. Lyn has enjoyed being Herbert Mills Elementary School's resident storyteller, in Reynoldsburg, Ohio, since 1995. Lyn also facilitates interactive workshops for storytellers, educators, and other mentors. E-mail: friedtales@aol.com.

MAKING SAND TRAY STORIES
By Milbre Burch

National Standards:

NCTE 4: Students adjust their use of spoken, written, and visual language to communicate effectively with a wide variety of audiences; NCTE 5: Students employ a wide range of strategies as they write; NCTE 6: Students apply knowledge of language structure and language conventions; NCTE 11: Students participate as knowledgeable, reflective, creative, and critical members of a literacy community; NCTE 12: Students use spoken, written, and visual language to accomplish their own pursuits for learning, enjoyment, persuasion, and the exchange of information.

A veteran teaching artist, I developed the use of sand trays as oral story prompts first at the Walden School in Pasadena, California, and then at Hillsborough Elementary School in Hillsborough, North Carolina, with first- through fifth-grade students. I have come to call this five-day residency experience for primary- and elementary-age students **Sand to Stories** ... **Tableaux to Tales.**

Objectives:

Engaging students in a multifaceted language arts experience; increasing their ability to recognize and use the component parts of oral narrative; and building their confidence in "talking story" as a precursor to individual or group writing.

My sand trays are made of wood and measure $23\frac{1}{4}$ inches by $29\frac{3}{4}$ inches. For the duration of the residency, they are "carpeted" with white sand. The floor and interior walls of each tray are painted blue, so sand can be swept away to create a lake, a river, or a shoreline. Blue walls evoke the horizon. Similar trays can be made by anyone who is a woodworker.

I have also used large kitty litter pans or plastic storage containers as trays. The latter are sold with lids that come in handy to contain the sand when the trays aren't being used. These are available at neighborhood discount stores.

From yard sales, toy stores, teacher supply houses, and toy box attrition, I have collected an array of miniatures: males and females of varying ages, skin tones, and occupational dress; domestic and wild animals; reptiles, insects, fish, and fowl; mythological creatures and "magical objects"; household furnishings, trees, shrubs, houses, barns, bridges, boulders, volcanoes, etc. I fill plastic shoeboxes with these assorted objects for participants to use in the sand trays.

The sand stabilizes objects in the tray and begs to be handled, shaped into a mountain range or a spiraling confluence of rivers. Patterns can be pressed into it. Things can be hidden in it.

Teaching Tray.

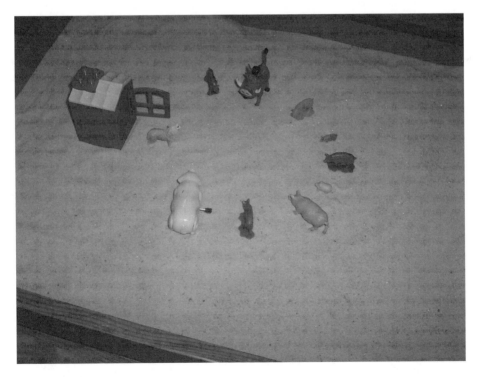

The Wolf in the Land of the Pigs.

The Troll's Dilemma.

Objects in the tray can be used literally: I place a cat next to a child and dub them "A Girl and Her Pet." Or they can be used metaphorically: I balance a row of four cars on end and call it "A Mysterious Forest." Both approaches work—even in the same story.

Placing three trays side by side can suggest Beginning, Middle, and End. "Reading" the objects in a tray from left to right results in one tale. "Reading" the same objects from right to left results in another. Trays can also be "read" top to bottom. In other words, every story can be seen from many perspectives, depending on one's "starting place."

My toy figures include characters from popular culture, like Barbie or Batman. I ask the students to name these something else, like The Princess with the Flowing Hair or The Man in the Gray Cape. Fresh ideas deserve primacy over what is packaged and sold on TV.

If students create a story about groups or individuals at war, I ask them to say what's at stake, why the people or nations are fighting, and what will be gained in the resolution of the battle. Bang, bang, boom by itself does not a story make.

Storymakers get their ideas from dreams, wishes, imagining, family and cultural history, everyday experiences, myths, legends, objects, images, and other storymakers. But it is up to the individual to weave these threads into a story of her own.

Sand tray etiquette includes (1) keeping the sand in the tray; (2) brushing excess sand off hands; and (3) shaking off toys before returning them to the toy boxes. Even so, there will be spills; a vacuum cleaner and more sand come in handy. The tactile sensation of sifting sand through fingers is one of the joys of this work. Since the students must wait till the second session to get their hands in the sand, they are full of anticipation.

Each class begins with students seated around a central tray. During the orientation, I tell or read several versions of "Goldilocks and the Three Bears." We examine the variations from story to story. Students note that characters from this old tale can be seen in the tray along with unrelated objects and figures. The children brainstorm about who and what they see. Then I improvise a tale using their ideas and mine. Afterward we discuss this new story made from old cloth.

I create a new tableau for each session, improvising a tale that stresses different narrative elements every day. The students are reminded to pay attention to these story elements as they adjourn to work in their own trays. Toy boxes are rotated around the room to offer fresh story prompts. The children are welcome to hold over ideas from day to day or to start anew each time.

Many load the tray with everything available from the toy box. Others spend their time arranging an empty expanse of sand. Some construct, and then deconstruct, scene after scene. Some are ready to recount a chapter book within minutes. A very young or very shy child may need to be interviewed about the contents of her tray to realize there's a story there. Almost all eventually bury or hide an object for discovery.

Students clean up their trays with fifteen minutes to spare so we can reconvene and talk about the process. All the children have something to say. Some ideas they'll keep for tomorrow. Others they'll forget or discard. In the heat of the exchange, embers are lit in the group's imagination. A teacher need only fan the flames to make the children burn with desire to capture their stories on paper. Making sand tray stories teaches them that literacy isn't work. It's child's play.

Assessments:

Teachers can assess the efficacy of this teaching model by evaluating their students' oral and written storymaking skills before and after the residency activities.

Kudos to Linda Cary, Carol Per Lee, Kathy Garrison, Kelly Sharpe, Carol Ford, Julia Workman, Sarah Chestnut, and Mary Beth Giles for inspiration and support in this work.

Milbre has been an artist in residence since 1978, working for state and local arts councils in Utah, North Carolina, South Carolina, Georgia, Rhode Island, and California. Her students have been mainstream pre-kindergarten to twelfth grades as well as ESL, hearing impaired, and developmentally disabled children of all ages, at-risk teens, well elders, mentally challenged adults, mini-mum and maximum security prison inmates, college students, conference attend-ees, fellow tellers, family business owners, therapists, ministers, rabbis and lay people, and countless teachers earning CEUs. Her work in designing and imple-menting a three-year residency at the Walden School in Pasadena has been fea-tured as a national model at education conferences across the country. E-mail: kindcrone@aol.com.

SHOE STORIES: A STEP-BY-STEP APPROACH TO STORYTELLING IN PRIMARY GRADES
By Denise Berry-Hanna

National Standards:

NCTE 4: Students adjust their use of spoken, written, and visual lan-guage to communicate effectively with a variety of audiences; NCTE 5: Students employ a wide range of strategies as they write; NCTE 6: Students apply knowledge of language structure language conventions; NCTE 11: Students participate as knowledgeable, reflective, creative, and critical members of a literacy community; NCTE 12: Students use spoken, written, and visual language to accompany their own purposes for learning, enjoyment, persua-sion, and the exchange of information.

Objectives:

Learn familiar shoe stories and songs; create and tell individual sto-ries; explore the idea of shoes in several domains (story, visual art projects, and song); and learn about various types of footwear.

Countless pairs of shoes have walked listeners into the world of story-telling and imaginative play. Mention "ruby slippers" to everyone familiar with Frank L. Baum's *The Wizard of Oz* and they will tell you they were magic and held the power to fight wicked witches and to transport young girls home. Say "glass slippers" in a primary classroom and the children will chorus "Cinderella!" The slightest mention of Air Jordans makes kids jump higher and turns them into basketball superstars.

Shoes are a great catalyst for creating stories, especially with younger students, pre-kindergarten to first grade. Shoes can take you to wonderful pla-ces, keep you dry in the rain, warm in the snow, and help you dance. Children love shoes! They know that different shoes have different jobs and different adventures waiting inside them.

I begin a Shoe Story Unit with an old favorite shoe tale such as "Cinderella," "Puss in Boots," "The Red Shoes," or "The Elves and the

Shoemaker," some of my personal favorites. I bring in various types of shoes, allowing the children time to try them on and experience the differences. I talk about the shoes and where they might go and what jobs they might have. When James, a shy, reserved five-year-old, pulled on a pair of Puss's big leather boots, his voice got big and deep, and then he began to strut! Matthew wore magic dance shoes that made him turn until he was dizzy.

Next, I pick a specific pair of shoes. I like to begin with rain or snow boots. Gathering the students in a circle, I have the shoes in a secret box with an opening big enough to peek through. I pass the box around and let each child look in and make an observation about the shoes. After all students have made their observations, I ask them to guess what kind of shoe they think it is and where it might go. I take the shoes out. Did you identify the right kind of shoe?

Gather the students in a circle. You are now ready to create a shoe story inspired by the traditional American folksong "Jim Along Josie" (a version of this song may be found in Ruth Crawford Seeger's *American Folksongs for Children*, Doubleday & Co., 1948). Jim Along walks, hops, and runs to different places. Using the chorus of the song, have the students move around the circle dramatizing Jim Along's actions. The simple structure of this story makes it very accessible to young listeners. Change what Jim Along sees and does on his adventure based on the different shoes he wears.

Jim Along got up and went to the window.
It was a snowy day.
Jim Along went to his closet and put on his warmest clothes.
He got his big thick winter boots.
Downstairs Jim Along's mom had breakfast ready.
Jim ate his breakfast and outside to play.
    Chorus:
    Walk along, Jim Along Josie,
    Walk along, Jim Along Joe
Jim walked until he came to a small pile of snow.
He jumped right into that snow. There was snow up to his ankles.
Jim Along began to skip in the snow.
    Chorus:
    Skip along, Jim Along Josie
    Skip along, Jim Along Joe.
Jim skipped until he came to a medium size pile of snow. He jumped right into
it. There was snow to his knees!
Jim Along began to hop in the snow.
    Chorus:
    Hop along, Jim Along Josie
    Hop along, Jim Along Joe
Jim hopped till he came to a giant pile of snow! He jumped in. There is snow to
his belly button. He had to dig his way out.
Jim Along heard his mom calling.
Time for lunch.

Jim turned around and went past the big pile of snow
   Chorus
Past the medium size pile of snow.
   Chorus
Past the small pile of snow.
   Chorus
Until he got home.
Jim Along took off his snow boots, sat down, and fell asleep.
   Chorus
   Sleep along, Jim Along Josie
   Sleep along, Jim Along Joe
   Shh.

Try doing this exercise two or three times with different types of shoes. Then small groups of four or five students can create new stories. Give each group a pair of shoes and have them create a "Jim Along Josie" story about a day in those shoes. These stories can then be shared with the class.

The final activity is to create a gallery of shoe sculptures, each with its own story. Each student brings in a shoe. (Canvas shoes work well because glue sticks better to the cloth than to manmade or leather shoes.) Set out a variety of decorating supplies. I have found including an assortment of foam cutouts, leftover little toy animals, dinosaurs, butterflies, and bugs to be great motivators. Larger objects may need an adult with a hot glue gun. Limit each student to three objects per shoe. As students decorate, encourage them to develop the story of their shoe. Where did it go? How did it get a butterfly on its back? How did it change? When the design is complete, have students dictate or write a final version of their story.

Assessments:

Although the process is at the heart of the residency, the best part is always a day of shoe stories. Students display their completed shoe sculptures with their written stories for parents or other classes to see. As visitors view the sculptures students tell their original tales. Each shoe becomes a story prompt and a three-dimensional illustration of the child's ideas. Each telling of their story inspires more confidence and develops their skills in oral presentation. At our last shoe gallery, one little girl proudly exclaimed how she had told her story twenty times and . . . could she tell it some more!

Storytelling is a natural activity for students in primary grades. Keeping on track and giving focus to a story is not as easy. Using shoes as a story motivator allows the students to walk into a story and actually follow a path. The combination of designing the shoe sculptures and writing, telling, and finally sharing shoe stories leads children on a creative, fun road of literacy and learning.

Denise Berry-Hanna is a professional storyteller, writer, and artist in residence. A two-time National Parenting Publications award-winning performer, Denise delights audiences across the country with her unique blend of words, mime, and imagination. Performances and workshops focus on the love of language, engaging participants in a contagious blend of rhythm, words, and imagination. Denise has conducted over fifty artist residencies across America and is currently a selected artist with the Illinois Arts Council Artist in Education program. For more information about performance or residency work, you may contact Denise at berryhanna@aol.com.

CINDERELLA'S SHOES
By Darlene Neumann

National Standards:

NCTE 2: Students read a wide range of literature from many periods in many genres to build an understanding of the many dimensions (e.g., philosophical, ethical, aesthetic) of human experience; NCTE 4: Students adjust their use of spoken, written, and visual language (e.g., conventions, style, vocabulary) to communicate effectively with a variety of audiences and for different purposes.

Objectives:

Read many versions of Cinderella; listen to versions of Cinderella; discuss the structure of the Cinderella tale; create and tell your own version of Cinderella.

The fairy tale every American child knows is "Cinderella"; how can we extend students' understanding of this universal story? In the library a child can find the very same story in many cultures! Simultaneously, the librarian can reinforce basic story structure for students listening to a storyteller and reading a variety of Cinderella stories. Because young children have a strong sense of justice and a need for belonging, Cinderella stories are greatly enjoyed by first and second graders. Perhaps it is from the needs and longings that human beings share that hundreds of Cinderella stories have emerged. Students can become the storyteller and the reader using a clear and pleasant voice in order to communicate with their peers.

Materials:

- At least twelve picture book versions of Cinderella stories are essential. My favorites include *The Irish Cinderlad* (Shirley Climo, HarperTrophy, 2000), *The Rough-Faced Girl* (Rafe Martin, Putnam, 1992), and *Yeh-Shen* (Ai-Ling Louie, Philomel Books, 1982).

- A selection of shoes is required
- A chart of story elements

Instructional Plan:

The Cinderella unit began as I told "The Little Glass Slipper" and "Little Scarface" in the library media center. Second graders discussed each story as I recorded story fundamentals on a large chart. In response to the stories and the chart, students filled out individual charts that requested: Title of story; Country; Name of Cinderella character; What the character wanted to do, Where the character wanted to go, or What the character wanted to be; Magic person, animal, or object; Magic that happened to Cinderella character; and the Type of shoe.

Partners chose another Cinderella version to read from the available stack of Cinderella tales and added information to their chart for that story. After experiencing three versions, students had a clear understanding of the Cinderella elements.

I brought in a suitcase filled with shoes collected from travels, garage sales, and thrift shops to the library. When opened, it revealed woven grass shoes, wooden shoes, basketball high-tops, baby Nikes, shoes with turned-up toes from India, red cloth slippers from China, glittery high heels, moccasins, hiking and cowboy boots, two ruby slipper pins, a blue-sequined, lace-up Victorian shoe coin purse, and horseshoes.

Partners pored over the assortment of shoes and chose a favorite pair. Reviewing their charts, they found the variety of shoes fit with the variety of stories, and their imaginations soared! Their assignment or assessment was to make up a brand-new Cinderella story using the chosen shoes. Amid squeals of laughter, story elements began to emerge. Partners did not write their stories but practiced telling their new story using their chart of story elements. They shared stories in small groups, asking questions about each other's stories and offering suggestions.

Assessments:

Students' understanding of the structure and themes of the Cinderella tale was demonstrated in the retelling or creating of a Cinderella story. Each second grader told a Cinderella story that reflected the unique interests and talents of its teller. Stories were heartbreaking, funny, or inspiring. Some examples were that Franken-Poodle's iron shoes rust before she could even get to the ball, and long ago when people lived on the moon, a basketball coach flew to the moon. He really wanted to be a basketball player. Because of the difference in gravity, he could really jump. Moonjumper became the most famous basketball player in the history of the moon.

"The Deaf Cinderella" was signed by a deaf child while her partner did voice interpretation. This Cinderella wanted to be a hearing angel. A good fairy gave her a choice: either she could begin to hear or she could become a kinder person. The deaf Cinderella decided that it was more important for her to be a good person who helped others than to be able to hear the other angels singing.

Darlene Neumann is a storyteller and a library media specialist. With her clear, pleasing voice and her engaging facial expressions, she paints compelling pictures, inviting children and adults to laugh and cry and revel in the joy of stories. Darlene tells world folktales and shares bittersweet stories about growing up on a southern Illinois farm. She has told at festivals, international schools, and public libraries, and has conducted storytelling workshops at library conferences, educational conferences, and universities. She coordinates an annual storytelling festival at her school in which each fourth and fifth grader, and some younger students, tells a story. Darlene helps the students choose, learn, and tell their stories. She is also an adjunct professor in storytelling at National-Louis University in Evanston, Illinois. E-mail: ldneu@tds.net.

HELPING SHY CHILDREN TELL CINDERELLA
By Jeanne Haynes

National Standards:

NCTE 1: Using classic fiction to better understand themselves and society; NCTE 2: Building an understanding of the human experience; NCTE 3: Drawing on prior experience to increase knowledge of word meanings; NCTE 4: Adjusting use of spoken language to communicate effectively; NCTE 5: Employing a wide range of strategies; NCTE 6: Applying knowledge of media techniques and figurative language; NCTE 7: Generating questions to synthesize data to discover ways that suit their purpose and audience; NCTE 9: Developing an understanding for diversity in language use, patterns, and social roles; NCTE 10: Making use of first language to develop understanding of content across the curriculum; NCTE 11: Participating as knowledgeable, reflective, creative, and critical members of a variety of literacy communities; and especially NCTE 12: Using spoken and visual language.

Objectives:

The primary objective of my residencies is participation, or having all children on stage for the culminating performance; all children practice skills in dialogue, gesture, story detail, demonstrating emotional content, and sound effects.

Instructional Plan:

In my residencies, this one being appropriate for first through eighth grades, I am committed to having all students on stage for the culminating performance. But what to do with the really shy ones? I've discovered a type of Storytelling Theatre, with Cinderella being a favorite choice. Since practically all children know this story, it's easy to encourage their participation. With students clustered around me, I ask if they will help supply the basic storytelling elements we've discussed during the residency: dialogue, gestures, details, emotions, and sound effects. Generally eager to participate, they nod their heads and move in closer as I begin to narrate and feed them questions. Examples follow.

<u>Dialogue and Gestures</u>: Speaking in an ominous voice, I say: "The mean stepmother was always ordering Cinderella to do something!" Then, placing the mike in front of a child, I ask, "What was the stepmother's favorite command?" In the beginning, they tend to respond in a wee small voice with eyes glued on me, something like "Sweep the floor?" I jump on whatever they say and enthuse: "Yes! Exactly! The mean stepmother was *always* ordering Cinderella to sweep the floor! Show the audience just how she said that." This playful buildup and coaching usually leads the child to face the audience and repeat the chore with a waggle of a finger or hands on the hips. Often they are rewarded with delighted laughter from the audience that does wonders for building their confidence. I ask the next child, "What else did the mean stepmother say?" If a student responds to me, but not to the audience, and I feel he or she is ready (this is key!), I gently steer him or her face forward while whispering, "Show and tell the audience."

<u>Details</u>: Encouraging them to reach from the general to the specific, I ask for "the delicious details," while quickly moving the mike among them to create an upbeat tempo. For example, in a voice filled with wonder, I ask, "When the doors of the castle opened, what did Cinderella see?" Whatever the child says, I repeat it with great enthusiasm and dig further. "Food," one will say. "Yes indeed! What kind of food?" Child responds, "Cake." I say, "Yes indeed! What kind of cake?" Next child says, "Chocolate!" Thrilled, I say, "Yes, a chocolate cake! What else did Cinderella see?" Another time for details is in the creation of Cinderella's dress. While enacting the Fairy Godmother as a sassy, no-nonsense personality, I prod the young tellers to describe this dress, repeating each suggestion and totaling them up as I frenetically wave my imaginary wand. Soon a picture—*their* picture—begins to blossom. "Yes, it will be a blue dress, kind of shiny, with lots of sparkles!" When they stall, I demand more. "Well, do you want this dress long or short? Full or slinky? High-necked or low-cut?" This can be a good time for audience participation, calling on children just itching to contribute.

Preparing for the Ball.

Emotions: Among the many opportunities, here's one example: Grief-stricken, I ask, "When Cinderella ran away, how did the Prince feel?" Predictably, the first response is "Sad." The second response is often "Very sad." In an agitated state, I challenge them to come up with more emotions. Finally, I get "Upset," "Mad," "Angry," "Confused." My favorite response to date came from an especially shy youngster at the end of the line. I nearly let him off the hook, when suddenly he cried out, "Heart attack!"

Group Sound Effects: Here's a good opportunity for woefully shy children. Rather than relying on the improv responses of the foregoing, I instruct them beforehand on exactly what to do, such as: "Whenever the Fairy God-mother performs her magic, wave an imaginary wand and say 'twang.' When the horses pull the coach to the castle, make the sound of their hoofs, 'clip-clop, clip-clop,' and prance in place like a horse. When the clock strikes midnight, repeat twelve loud 'bongs' and punch the air with both fists." I keep the sound effects group to one side of me if I have large number of young performers. For smaller groups, I may instruct all of the children to do these effects.

Character Assignments: Another variation is to select specific children to play the main characters while standing on stage in a single storytelling line. But in golden moments, they can get so carried away that they interact with one another. On one such occasion, when I said, "The Prince danced with

Cinderella and her Prince.

Cinderella," the boy Prince Charming encircled his Cinderella and began to twirl her around. The rest of my young tellers covered their faces with embarrassed giggles. But the audience whooped their delight, as the fairy-tale couple continued to twirl. As the narrator, all I could say was, "And they danced and they danced and they danced." It was pure magic. In conclusion, note that children will often ask to use props. Generally I hold fast to the classic tradition, relying on good storytelling techniques to create pictures in listeners' imaginations.

Assessments:

Like much of the best educational work with young children, the process is often more affirming than a particular product. Over time, with a variety of positive experiences, the young child can feel "good enough" to participate in a meaningful way. Assessment can be based on children's willingness to participate and ultimate enjoyment in telling a compelling story in their own words, which is a goal to which this author is committed!

Jeanne Haynes's goal is to give students the desire, tools, and opportunity to stand before a group, tell a compelling story in their own words, be acknowledged with applause, and respond as a respectful, active listener while other students perform. With a degree in journalism, she is a former news reporter and media relations consultant. A resident artist with Young Audiences of Northern California and Stagebridge, Oakland, and as a guest lecturer at Diablo Valley College and Cal State of the East Bay, she has taught 1,250+ students in eighteen schools and colleges. Her stories air on KPFA FM Berkeley Public Radio, and original monologues (Those Telling Moments) are performed in San Francisco and East Bay. E-mail: jhaynestory@sbcglobal.net.

THE GREAT PLOP
By Janice Butt

National Standards:

NCTE 4: Students adjust their use of spoken, written, and visual language (e.g., conventions, style, vocabulary) to communicate effectively with a variety of audiences and for different purposes; NCTE 6: Students apply knowledge of language structure, language conventions (e.g., spelling and punctuation), media techniques, figurative language, and genre to create, critique, and discuss print and non-print texts; NCSS 3 (Physical Systems): Students should understand the characteristics and spatial distribution of ecosystems on Earth's surface.

Objectives:

Create and write original story with correct story structure that demonstrates knowledge of the animals that live in specific habitats.

In science class, my students have learned habitats using puppets or masks to act out my original story "The Great Plop." Inspired by the traditional Jewish tale "The Lion of Judah," this story is like "Chicken Little," because one animal hears a scary noise (Plop!) and runs away from it, chanting, "The Great Plop is coming." This animal meets other animals who inquire, "Why are you running?" Upon hearing that the Great Plop is coming, each animal joins the fleeing group. They finally come to a tree where Wise Old Owl is sleeping, and he asks, "What is a Plop?"

None of the animals knows, so Owl asks them to take him back to where the Plop was heard, only to find that the loud sound is something falling into the stream and making a loud plop! This story can easily be set in most habitats just by changing the animals involved. Students have a wonderful time speaking in the "language" of their animals and being found in their "homes."

The lesson begins with my telling of the story. Students then act out the story using animal masks or puppets from the particular habitat you choose. The class can then do a prewriting exercise, in which students will examine each scene of the story from the story map, changing or keeping the setting and characters of "The Great Plop," which in turn will change the habitat. Older students can use these new elements to create their own individual stories.

This exercise works in preschool as well as in primary grades. Preschoolers use puppets to act out the story, while older students create written stories or plays based on the elements of "The Great Plop." Students at all levels create both written and oral stories that use correct sequence and, by sharing their stories with classmates, develop their editing skills. They successfully identify habitats on post tests, as well!

When using this storytelling approach, I have seen students succeed in writing for the first time. They have gone on to create books out of these stories with book jackets, and have performed their stories for other students as well as parents and other teachers.

Assessments:

Embedded assessment occurs during creative drama and prewriting sessions, providing an opportunity to identify children who need more help in understanding and applying the concepts. Writing samples are assessed for sequence, conceptual understanding, and use of appropriate animals for chosen habitats.

Janice Butt's stories weave a comfortable quilt that wraps around listeners and brings them in close. She draws on more than thirty years' experience as an educator to teach children and adults how to tell folktales and personal stories. She has spent ten years helping teachers use stories to teach the curriculum. Her performances include her original creations "In Love with JFK" and "Not So Scary Stories." In August 2005, she completed her first CD entitled Livin' Above Her Raisin', *stories about growing up around the Blue Ridge Mountains. Founder of Women's Imaginative Guild of Storytellers, Janice dreams of new ways and places people can tell stories. She has produced three successful "Days of Discovery for Women" at Callanwolde Fine Arts Center and has organized ten performances at the Royal in Historic Norcross (GA) to celebrate Women's History Month. E-mail: teachtale@mindspring.com.*

TICKY-PICKY BOOM-BOOM
By Marilyn Kinsella

National Standards:

Language Arts, Math, Science, Social Studies, Physical Education, Fine Arts. See below.

Objectives:

Use the multiple intelligences to explore numerous aspects of a story.

Nineteen eighty-one was a banner year for me. I was going to begin a second-grade teaching assignment. I had just returned from Jonesborough, Tennessee, where I took a class offered by NAPPS on creative storytelling with Jackie Torrence. As I walked into the classroom that first day, I had something new in my arsenal of teaching techniques to try with my class—storytelling! Sometimes, we closed the shades and I lit a candle. It was storytelling time! I still have former students come up and tell me about those stories.

It naturally evolved that I began developing some lessons and activities from the stories I told. After I heard Elizabeth Ellis tell "Ticky-Picky Boom-Boom," I started to tell it and eventually wrote a lesson/activity for each subject in my classroom. I only did this for one story. I truly feel that most stories are best told and left to the imagination of the child. Kids are savvy to hearing a story, only for it to then be used in lessons. So, I caution to use this idea sparingly, maybe once a year.

I no longer teach school, but I often go to schools for assemblies. I use the same idea for my study guides. First, I look at the story and pick out any outstanding word or words that I know can be extended into a lesson. In this story it is "yam" and "Jamaica." From those words I extrapolate lessons. Some ideas spring from existing lessons found in the texts, others are from fellow storytellers (see reference below), and others are from my imagination.

In front of every subject is a reference for national standards in the related field. I have given a sketchy outline for the following activities. More extensive directions and other ideas are online at www.marilynkinsella.org, under "Teacher/Teller" – "Study Guides."

<u>Language Arts</u>

NCTE 3: Students apply a wide range of strategies to comprehend, interpret, evaluate, and appreciate texts.

By asking questions about the story, the student will understand the main idea and supporting details. Example: Why didn't Anansi dig up the yams himself?

NCTE 6. Students apply knowledge of language structure, language conventions (e.g., spelling and punctuation), media techniques, figurative language, and genre to create, critique, and discuss print and non-print texts.

By adding nouns, verbs, adjectives, and adverbs to Mad-Libs, the student uses grammatical conventions. Make up some Mad-Libs using sentences from the story.

By making his or her own "Ticky-Picky Boom-Boom" book, each student will write in a variety of forms. This is an extended activity, requiring a copy machine. Elicit from the class every scene in the story and write it on the chalkboard (there are over twenty of them). Assign one scene to each child to pencil draw and then outline with a thin-tipped black marker. Write a sentence or two about the scene at the bottom of the page. Photocopy each picture times the number of children in the class. Compile. While they are waiting for the copies, they can work on the title page.

Math

NCTM 2.2: Understand meanings of operations and how they relate to one another.

Make up word problems using characters from the story. As a result of this activity, students will be able to understand the inverse relationship between addition and subtraction. Example: Anansi had four rows of yams in his garden. Each row had ten yams. How many yams were in Anansi's garden? Tiger came along and took fifteen ran away. Now how many yams?

Science

NAS K-4.3 Life Sciences: Students should develop understanding of characteristics of organisms, life cycles of organisms, organisms and environments.

By noting the differences between yams and sweet potatoes, the student will know that living things are found almost everywhere in the world and that distinct environments support the life of different types of plants. In America, the two words are used to mean the same, but yams are a different vegetable and are primarily grown in other countries. Try to find real yams and compare them to sweet potatoes (size, color, texture, taste, weight, smell, etc.). What countries grow yams? For information on yams from different countries, see http://www.foodsubs.com/Sweetpotatoes.htm.

By growing a sweet potato plant, the student will learn that plants need certain resources of energy and growth. Try this Web site: http://www.urbanext.uiuc.edu/gpe/case5/c5hgi.html.

Social Studies/Geography

NSS I: The World in Spatial Terms: Understand how to use maps and other geographic representations, tools, and technologies to acquire, process, and report information from a spatial perspective.

By looking up Jamaica on the globe, the student will begin to understand a globe as a representation of our world. Jamaica is an island country.

Find it on the globe. What other islands are close to Jamaica? How far is it to Jamaica? How big is the island?

Physical Education

> NASPE K-12.2 Movement concepts: Applies movement concepts and principles to the learning and development of motor skills.

By participating in the following game, the student will use concepts of space awareness and movement control with a variety of basic skills: "Tiger-Tiger-Yam" (Adapt the game "Duck-Duck-Goose.")

Pulling the movement from the story—Discuss a movement in the story: For example, Tiger digging the yams. Have one child come forward and show what that looks like. Have everyone in the circle do the same action four times. Discuss another movement: Tiger running (in place). Have everyone in the circle run in place to the count of four, plus digging four times. Keep adding new movements and repeating the others. It can be a real workout. If you add music (Jamaican music) and do the movement, it can add to the fun.

Fine Arts

> CNAEA (Visual Arts) 1: Understanding and applying media, techniques, and processes.

By making potato prints, the student will know the similarities and differences in the meaning of common terms used in the arts, such as form, line, and contrast. For details, see http://www.amazingmoms.com/htm/artpaintnprint.htm.

> CNAEA (Theatre) 2: Acting by assuming roles and interacting in improvisations.

By actively participating in the following activities, the student will select interrelated characters, environments, and situations for simple dramatization and improvised dialogue. Ask two children to do a scene from the story, for example: Tiger talking to Sister Goose.

References:

- "Ticky-Picky Boom-Boom" in *Anansi the Spider Man* by Philip M. Sherlock (Crowell, 1954) or on my Web site at: www.marilynkinsella.org
- "Fabulous Folktales" in *Beyond the Beanstalk: Interdisciplinary Learning through Storytelling* by Lynn Rubright (Heinemann, 1996.) Lynn was my first teacher and reference for developing my own lessons from stories. See my Web site for a complete list of references.

Assessments:

Exploration of a story through a variety of modes allows assessment of students' best learning styles and provides insight into the way each individual processes and applies knowledge.

Marilyn Kinsella, from Fairview Heights, Illinois, has been telling stories since 1981. As an elementary teacher at the time, she found ways to implement stories into her curriculum. She has presented many workshops for teachers on these techniques and now, as a full-time storyteller, uses the ideas in the study guides she gives to the teachers. Many of these ideas are on her Web pages under "Teacher/Teller." Marilyn travels the Midwest and beyond telling stories and presenting workshops. For a complete picture of "Taleypo the Storyteller," visit her Web site, www.marilynkinsella.org.

A BUS OF OUR OWN
By Freddi Williams Evans

National Standards:

NCTE 5: Communication strategies (using grammatical and mechanical convention in written composition); NCTM 3: Compute fluently and make reasonable estimates; CNAEA (Visual Arts) 2: Using knowledge of structure and functions; NSS-USH.K-4.1: Living and working together in families and communities, now and long ago; NSS-USH.K-4.2: The history of student's own state or region. Understand the people, events, problems, and ideas that were significant in creating the history of their state.

Objectives:

Recall facts from *A Bus of Our Own* and create a story sequence with illustrations and summarizing sentences; relate this event to community events in your community; solve math problems using background information and facts from *A Bus of Our Own*.

All families have stories. Usually these stories are passed from person to person in the oral tradition. Such was the case with this story from my family until I wrote it down and submitted it for publication. *A Bus of Our Own*, set in Madison, Mississippi, during the late 1940s and early 1950s, tells how African American families bonded together to provide a school bus for their children. Based on real events, this story celebrates the spirit of the community and demonstrates the value placed on children and education.

The main character, young Mable Jean, provides an opportunity for students to witness conditions of segregation and the hardships encountered by many African American children when walking to school. Mable Jean's determination to attend school influenced her Cousin Smith, her family, and ultimately her community to provide a school bus and inevitably ensure a better life for all the children.

Preparing for the Story:

Prepare students for the story by engaging them in the following math exercise and discussion: The first incident in the story took place in 1949. The last incident took place in 1954. Have students round those numbers to the nearest ten. Next, ask students to use that number to calculate how long ago the story took place.

When this story was set, educational opportunities and conditions for African American children, especially those in rural areas, were quite different than they are today. During the 1940s and '50s, African Americans and whites in the South lived separately and unequally. Segregation laws, also known as "Jim Crow," mandated separate neighborhoods, schools, public facilities (i.e., parks, water fountains, bathrooms, waiting rooms, etc.), jobs, restaurants, etc. The provisions and accommodations for African Americans were also inferior to those for whites. Allow students to share their knowledge and other books about segregation. Additional books on the subject include: *White Socks Only* by Evelyn Coleman (A. Whitman, 1996), *Going Someplace Special* by Patricia McKissack (Atheneum, 2001), and *Roll of Thunder, Hear My Cry* by Mildred Taylor (Dial Press, 1976).

Classrooms in rural areas were not decorated with beautiful posters and colorful bulletin boards when the story was set. If anything at all, there may have been a portrait of a significant person. Ask students whose portrait may have been on the wall of a classroom for African American students in the 1940s and '50s. Usual answers include Martin Luther King and Rosa Parks. However, the Civil Rights movement had not begun during this time. The answer is President Abraham Lincoln. Students will be able to identify his portrait in the illustration.

Presenting the Story:

It is important to read the story before presenting it to students. Allow them to view each illustration during the presentation.

Processing the Story:

Language Arts: Allow each student to create a story sequence by first folding a sheet of legal size typing paper into fourths. Have students number the upper left-hand corner of each section with small numbers—1, 2, 3, 4. Students will illustrate four events from the story in sequential order and write a summarizing sentence at the bottom of each section. Students do not have to begin with the first incident in the story. They may begin with: Mabel Jean and Jeff rode in Cousin Smith's car. The remaining illustrations should follow in sequential order.

Math: Allow students to work in groups to solve the following word problems.

- How many miles did Mable Jean walk to school per week? (5 miles × 5 days = 25 miles)
- How many miles did she walk to school per month? (5 miles × 20 days = 100 miles) or (4 weeks × 25 miles = 100 miles)
- How much did Mable Jean pay to ride the bus each week? (5 cents × 5 days = 25 cents)
- How much did Mable Jean and Jeff pay to ride the bus each week? (2 × 25 cents each = 50 cents)
- How much did Mable Jean pay to ride the bus each month? (5 × 20 days = $1.00) or (4 × 25 cents = $1.00)
- What amount did Mable Jean and Jeff pay each month? (2 × $1.00 = $2.00) or (4 × 50 cents = $2.00)

Conclusion:

A Bus of Our Own offers wonderful subject matter for generating classroom discussions, which lead to meaningful conclusions for the story.

- In the book, Cousin Smith told Mable Jean's parents that they would have to pay twice for their children to get a good learning. When the bus was completed, everyone agreed it was a sight worth paying twice to see. How did they pay twice? Why did they have to pay twice?
- The people in this book did not see themselves as heroes or heroines. They saw themselves as ordinary people who did what they could to make life better for their children. Do you think they were heroes or heroines? What makes a hero or heroine? Do you have to be an adult to do something heroic? Tell something heroic that you can do as a student.
- *A Bus of Our Own* is a family narrative that is based on real events. I began this story by interviewing family members and people in my neighborhood who either rode the bus or knew about the bus. Students may also write a narrative based on an event, an experience, a special object, a place, or a memorable person in their family. They may also begin the process by talking to family members.

Assessments:

Recall and depict facts from the story in sequential order and write sentence synopsis of the plot; compare and contrast setting; compare and contrast this story with other stories about segregation; discuss economics and correctly solve math problems.

Resources and Materials:

- Evans, Freddi Williams. *A Bus of Our Own*. Morton Grove, IL: Albert Whitman & Company, 2001. ISBN 0-8075-0970-1.
- Legal size (11″ × 14″) unlined copy paper
- Pencils

Freddi Williams Evans is an artist, educator, and author. Her books for children include The Battle of New Orleans: The Drummer's Story *and* A Bus of Our Own, *which received the 2004 Mississippi Library Association Juvenile Book Award, 2003 Living the Dream Book Award, and 2002 Oppenheim Toy Portfolio Platinum Book Award, and is a 2002 Notable Social Studies Trade Book for Young People. Freddi has written for local newspapers, and her poems are published in several anthologies, including* From a Bend in the River: 100 New Orleans Poets. *Originally from Madison, Mississippi, she now resides in New Orleans. E-mail: freddiwevans@aol.com.*

GATHERING FAMILY STORIES
By Thom Bristow, Ph.D.

National Standards:

NCSS IV: Individual Development and Identity; NCSS I: Culture; NCSS V: Individuals, Groups and Institutions; NCSS X: Civic Ideals and Practices. (May be adapted to other lessons.)

Objectives:

Experience various ways to collect family stories; share oral and written forms.

Required Materials:

- Form included for the student to take home
- Students' imagination and sense of humor

A clever line states, "The shortest distance between two people is a story." I have seen this many times while helping students gather stories from their families. Family stories, in centuries past, served to support society and teach values. We can do it again! The National Council for the Social Studies states that the primary purpose of social studies is to develop the ability to make informed and reasoned decisions for the public good in a culturally diverse yet interdependent world. U.S. Secretary of Education Richard Riley made the statement that civics is one of the most important subjects children can learn in school because it enables them to contribute to our survival as a people. This critical knowledge should begin early.

This can be done through storytelling. Kieran Egan presents an alternative approach to teaching in the elementary school in his book *Teaching as Story Telling* (University of Chicago Press, 1986). His concept of "imaginative education" emphasizes the absolute necessity of oral communication to stimulate the brain. (See his Web site: http://www.ierg.net.)

A page using the following format might be used to gather family stories:

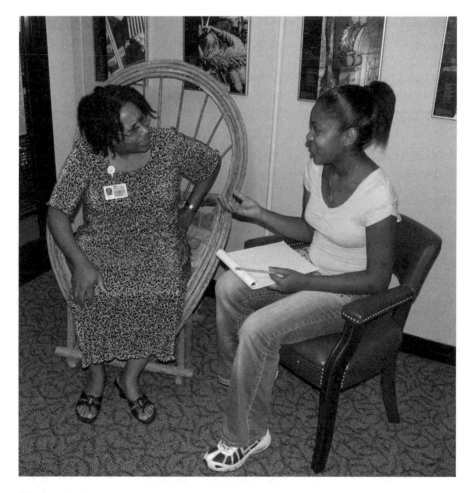

Sharing Stories.

Gathering Stories at _____ Elementary School

  Hello, Families! We need your help to teach some important lessons. We need you to tell some stories! With stories, we can have fun and learn at the same time, and families need to tell more stories. Stories can help children understand the world.

  This week we are studying (Underline). We are asking you to take a few minutes and share a story with your child about this subject. It can be any kind of story, for example: What I remember about growing up; The time Mom/Dad/Grand was a hero; The dumbest thing I ever did! The story that taught me a lesson; The time I told a lie/got caught/etc. Tell it, help your child tell it, and write it down so he or she can bring it to school and tell it to us.

Most Important! Have Fun!

The Story?

_____

_____

_____

_____

_____

_____

_____

_____

_____

_____

_____

_____

_____

_____

_____

_____

_____

_____

_____

Process:

Prior to the homework assignment, the children need to become comfortable with simply telling a story and having some fun with it. We began with mixed-up fairy tales. We might use a deep voice for Red Riding Hood, a sweet, soft voice for a giant, or perhaps have three bears eating pizza. These are to illustrate the importance of using your imagination when telling a story. Students are encouraged to change stories, get a laugh, and work together to spice them up.

This is important later, when the students are asked to gather stories from their families. Family stories offered for classroom perusal can be rather bland. We want to keep the truth but improve the story. After all, this is how all history was created! Students will be encouraged to share stories with classmates and get and give feedback to make the stories more interesting, entertaining, and informative. In their classroom banter, they are not making fun or belittling but are learning to listen and create. They are making history!

Conclusion:

Let me share a few examples based on the lesson plan described here. A second-grade boy related a beach vacation and enumerated how he went swimming, fishing, shopping, and ate pancakes, with few other details except it was a cold weekend. We came up with this story: "Last summer we went to the beach on vacation. We went swimming and fishing; we went to a toy store and had pancakes at the best pancake place in the world. (Pause) It was awful! I almost froze in the water and we didn't catch any fish. Then Dad said the toys were too expensive and I ate so many pancakes, I threw up in the back seat! I don't ever want to go on another vacation!"

Another first grader told how his father tried to teach him the danger of fire with a book of matches in the front yard and accidentally burned up the whole yard. The final line of his story was, "So don't play with matches!" We changed it to, "So if you find some matches, keep them away from my dad!" This ending taught the lesson but got a laugh, even from his father.

There is humor in these stories, and they relate good times and bad. They make some fun but keep the truth. Many stories end with "It was awful at the time, but it's funny now." One such story was told by a first-grade girl concerning her mother's recent pregnancy. (The mother okayed the telling of the story!) The mother's water broke, in public, and the little girl screamed, "Mommy, the baby's throwing up!"

One final note on the gathering of stories: There are some painful stories that need telling. Stories of poverty, prison, and abuse are not easily shared. "Being broke ain't no joke" could start a whole series of stories in some classes. Leading children and their families gently and slowly into exploring tough stories and how they impact the family and community is important. If we challenge creative young minds to find new endings to these stories, we will do well.

Assessments:

The assessment may be done in two ways. First, the student tells the story in class and then takes it home to share with the families. Finally, the story is transferred to written form and is perhaps put in a class journal.

Thom C. Bristow, Jr., Ph.D., has been a professional storyteller for over twenty years. Holding a Ph.D. with a concentration in Developmental and Educational Psychology, he has been a marriage and family therapist and college professor for forty-three years. He has always used storytelling in his work. In addition to being fun, he sees storytelling as a magic springboard to all learning. He believes that storytelling is for all ages and is especially interested in getting high school students more involved in telling. He does workshops for teachers and therapists on the use of storytelling in their work. E-mail: tcbristow@thomtells.com.

GRANDPARENT'S AND GRAND FRIEND'S DAY
By Angela Lloyd and Margie Brown

National Standards:

NCTE 1: Students read and listen to a wide range of print and non-print texts to build an understanding of the human experience; NCTE 4: Students adjust their use of spoken, written, and visual language to communicate effectively for different purposes; NCTE 6: Students apply knowledge of language structure, language conventions to create, critique, and discuss print and non-print texts; NCTE 12: Students use spoken, written, and visual language to accomplish their own purposes; NCSS I: Social Studies programs should include experiences that provide for the study of culture and cultural diversity.

Objectives:

Create an interactive presence where invited elders and students share life experiences; storyteller shares folktales, biographies, and personal tales; students tell stories they learn from relatives.

The grandfather chuckled. "Where did I go for holidays when I was nine? I went to Africa!" He spun a wild tale of riding on an elephant's back through treacherous landscapes and terrifying weather, and then he burst out laughing. "I have never been to Africa!"

The students howled with delight. The storyteller exclaimed, "Oh, yes, you have! You just went there and took us with you, and now we are all back home!"

Grandparent's/Grand Friend's Day is an annual event at The Walden School (kindergarten through grade six) in Pasadena, California. The celebration is usually scheduled on the last day before spring break because relatives are often in town for family holidays. The school is in its tenth year of commitment to having a storyteller in residence work throughout the year with all grade levels and classroom subjects. This social studies storytelling project has involved kindergarten through fifth grade over the years. The objective is to create an interactive presence where invited elders and schoolchildren share life experiences, rather than guests being observers for the day.

A six-week curriculum of twice-weekly sessions entitled "I've Got Wisdom. I've Got Magic" prefaced the event. The storyteller told world folktales, biographies, and personal tales featuring elders in mentoring relationships with children. Activities included students telling stories they knew about their elders and wondering aloud what they would ask their relatives (living or deceased) if they had the opportunity.

A sample activity was my bringing my mother's collection of gloves and my own childhood cache of white and wool gloves. I told a story about my mother's hands, and the students were invited to choose a glove and tell a story about their mothers' hands.

The students were then encouraged to develop specific questions. Sometimes the students asked questions at home as homework. On other occasions, some wrote letters or were able to make a phone call and report back during class.

Here is a sample list of questions developed by the students: What toys or books or games did you have? What did you like to do in your spare time? Did you get to swim when you were six? Where? Did you have a lot of friends when you were seven? What form of transportation did your mom have when you were six? Was it a rough life for you when you were nine? Please describe how you dressed. Tell us about your entire wardrobe! Did the tooth fairy ever come to your house? What was the highest amount of money you got? Where did you get your shoes when you were a child? What was your favorite thing to draw when you were eighteen? Did you ever fall on rough times? When did you fall in love? How did you fall? What made you feel like marrying your husband or wife? What was the daily newspaper called? What was your principal's name in school? What did they wear? What kind of school supplies did you use in fifth grade? Did you have any pets when you were five? Were you musical? What was the most popular sport around when you were in the ninth grade? What was your favorite class in college, and why? What job did you have at the age of thirty-five? What was it like during World War II? Did your mom or dad serve in World War I?

On Grandparent's/Grand Friend's Day, teachers crafted their own way to present the questions. One made a Jeopardy!-style board; elders chose a

Answering the Question.

The Elders are in the Building.

Austin with his Grandparents.

category such as Childhood, Education, History, Adventure, Travel, Fashion, Mistakes and Experiences, or Triumphs and "Try-Agains." The teacher turned the requested category card over, and the student who had developed that question would read it aloud. Another teacher passed a basket around and guests withdrew a child's query. Again, the child who had written the question read it aloud, and his or her own elder answered.

The anticipation of never knowing when it was going to be your turn helped move beyond reporting answers to spontaneous storytelling. The opportunity for the child's voice and the elder's voice to be heard together added to the story's texture. Everybody had a chance to hear and to be heard.

The social studies standards that were addressed encouraged children to explore their unique place in time and space by comparing and contrasting everyday life in different times and places. Students were assessed by their ability to format interesting questions for their elders, recognizing that some aspects of life change over time while others stay the same.

Students were encouraged to explore how living in the United States and/or abroad provides continuity and community across time. They were assessed in their ability to use the globe and map in describing the varied backgrounds of American citizens and residents in those places.

Students were encouraged to appreciate people who make a difference. They differentiated between things that happened long ago and things that happened yesterday. They explored biographies to investigate the importance of individual action and character. They were assessed in their ability to explain how famous heroes and their own everyday heroes have made a difference in people's lives.

The next step would be for students to write out their elder's or another elder's story, and then tell it in their own storytelling voice. This echoes the storyteller's invitation to the elders: "We are so looking forward to what you have to say. If, perchance, you cannot remember the answer to the question, please make it up!" We re-create in the classroom the age-old magic akin to four generations gathered on a hot summer porch cloaked in the hum of cicadas and the home sweet home of stories.

Assessments:

Develop specific questions and craft interesting ways to present them; explore, compare/contrast everyday life in different time periods; format interesting questions to pose to relatives with recognition of life changes; use globe and map to identify places where relatives have lived; explore biographies to investigate important action and character of relatives and to learn how famous heroes made a difference.

Resources:

Fox, Mem. *Wilfred Gordon McDonald Partridge*. Brooklyn, New York: Kane/Miller Book Publishers, 1984.

Martin, Bill. *Knots on the Counting Rope*. New York: Henry Holt, 1987.

Nye, Naomi Shihab. *Sitti's Secrets*. New York: Simon & Schuster, 1994.

Yolen, Jane. *Gray Heroes*. New York: Penguin, 1999.

Angela Lloyd tells stories in English and Spanish. She incorporates rhythm, music, poetry, and whimsy. A virtuoso on washboard, Angela's performance partners also include autoharp, tenor guitar, spoons, and bell. Her stories come from traditional world folktales, oral tradition, personal experience, and the best in children's literature. She earned her M.F.A. at the Florida State/Asolo Conservatory for Professional Actor Training, and criss-crosses the country for performances, residencies, tutorials, and as featured teller for regional and national festivals. Since 2000 she has been storyteller in residence at The Walden School in Pasadena, California. Go to http://www.angelalloyd. com/ for information on her calendar and on her award-winning recordings.

Margie Brown has been a storyteller and story educator since the mid-seventies and has told and taught in ten countries. She specializes in intercultural stories of the Holy Fool, holds a Ph.D. in biblical humor from the Graduate Theological Union in Berkeley, California, and has authored numerous articles and several books, most recently co-authoring The Storyteller's Companion to the Bible: Acts of the Apostles *by Abingdon Press. She is available in central California as a master coach, and nationally as an editor to storytellers as they create articles, grant proposals, evaluations, and other writing projects. Contact her at himargieb@sbcglobal.net.*

A STORY USING TANGRAMS
By Chris Summerhayes

National Standards:

NCTM 1: Understands basic properties of (e.g., number of sides, corners, square corners) and similarities and differences between simple geometric shapes; NCTM 3: Understands that geometric shapes are useful for representing and describing real world situations; NCTM 4: Understands that patterns can be made by putting different shapes together or taking them apart.

Objectives:

Review names and definitions of shapes; introduce tangrams and history of tangrams; tell tangram story and allow students to explore by telling their own tangram stories.

Resources and Materials:

- Tompert, Ann. *Grandfather Tang's Story: A Story Told with Tangrams*. New York: Crown Publishers, 1990.
- Ellison die-cut tangrams (if available) for each student
- Preprinted cardboard/paper tangrams in color
- Tangram sheets with letters and animals
- Construction paper
- Scissors and glue

Introduction:

Grandfather Tang's Story by Ann Tompert is a tale told with tangrams. I use this story as a fun way of introducing sides, corners, and shape names to first and second graders. In the story, Grandfather Tang is telling a story to his granddaughter, Little Soo, about two fairy foxes while using tangrams. The fairy foxes are able to change into other animals. They are the best of friends, but always try to outdo each other by becoming different animals. They chase each other through the story until a hunter's arrow makes them realize that the game should end.

This story is very effective when told in small groups of five to eight students. I have found the best way to tell it is at a small table with the students facing me. I tell the story with the tangrams facing the students. Telling a story with tangrams takes practice. Add to that the arranging of the tangrams upside down, and this is a story that will take some preparation time. (For larger groups, I have used an overhead projector successfully.)

Over the years, I have found that some students want to know where the original tangram came from. After reading various versions available on the Internet, I made up my own version as a preface to telling Grandfather Tang's story:

Once upon a time, although not so very long ago, in a place not so very far from here, there lived a great tile maker named Tang. One day, the king asked Tang to create a new tile floor for the palace. It was such a great honor that Tang immediately said yes. Tang worked night and day and day and night. First, he made the pattern for the floor and then he made the individual tiles. One by one, he carefully wrapped and carried the tiles to the palace and fit them into place on the floor. At last, there was only one more tile. Tang wrapped the tile with care and walked to the palace. But just as he got to the palace door, he tripped and the last tile slipped out of his hands, breaking into seven pieces. Tang knew that the king would never be happy with a broken tile, so he quickly began to clean it up. Just then, the king came into the room. Instead of being upset, the king was delighted. The seven pieces of the broken tile had fallen onto the floor in the shape of a dancing girl. The king asked Tang what other pictures he could make with these wonderful tiles of his. Tang quickly rearranged the tiles into the shape of a man. The king was so pleased with the tiles and the shapes that they made that he invited Tang to come and live in the palace. And for every new shape that Tang could make with the tiles, the king said he would pay him one dollar. Tang agreed. He finished the floor and every day, he made a new shape with his tiles.

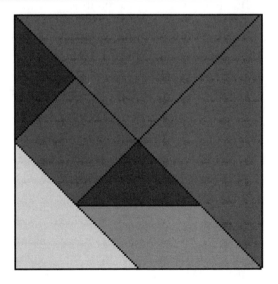

Tangram.

> It is now many years later, and Tang is a grandfather. He is in the garden of the palace with his granddaughter. This story is called *Grandfather Tang's Story*.

Using this introduction gives me the opportunity to introduce the tangrams and to have Little Soo and the grandfather already on the table before beginning the "real story."

Process:

After telling the story, I arrange the students in groups of two. Each student is given his or her own set of tangrams. There are many ways to make sure each student has the tangram shapes. For example, they could cut them out of preprinted cards or trace them. I have found using an Ellison die cut that precuts the shapes works best when the students are introduced to tangrams. This way, the students have their own set with little confusion, especially if you use a variety of colors to make the set of tangrams. The students are then asked to retell the story to their partner with their tangrams. I always have a sheet with the shapes from the story (as well as a few others) for the students who need them. Most students enjoy trying to make the animals and retelling the story. They often want to add extra animals. Other students like to branch off and make their own stories with robots and fantastic animals. After some experimentation time, I ask the students to choose one animal from the story to make and glue to a piece of paper. I remind the student that they must use all seven tangram shapes in their animal. The students then write a short story to go with their animals.

The next day, I give the students two preprinted cards with the tangrams on them so that they can cut them out. It is best to make sure that they get cards that are different colors. The goal on this day will be for the students to make their initials with the tangrams. It may be necessary to be very direct with the students, as almost all will want to go back to making stories. And that, of course, is the carrot to get the initials done. "When you have finished your initials, you may add your favorite animal from the story." I remind the students to use all seven shapes in each letter. As always, I allow the students to experiment, but I also have a sheet with the tangram letter shapes available. The students then glue their initials to a piece of construction paper.

The next step, of course, is to explore the relationships between triangles, squares, sides, corners, and so on. This mini two-day lesson really gets the students having fun with math, and when math is fun...

Assessments:

Retell story using tangrams; experiment and contrast by adding other animals and things such as robots to create tangrams; explore the relationship between triangles, squares, sides, corners, etc.; write new tangram stories. Additionally, parquetry blocks and/or Froebel blocks offer children free play experiences with combining shapes in beautiful, symmetrical, and geometric ways.

Chris Summerhayes is originally from Winnepeg, Manitoba. His parents moved to Ontario when Chris was just a year old. He wisely decided to go with them. Since that time, Chris has tried everything from life guarding to being a garbage man before settling on becoming a teacher. "Teaching is just putting the stories in the right order," he says. Chris is a teacher/storyteller in Wainfleet, Ontario, Canada, where he lives with his beautiful wife, Sandra, two cats, and a dog named Archie, in a train station. E-mail: cshayes@iaw.on.ca.

WHY ARE RIVER ROCKS SMOOTH?
By DWe Williams

National Standards:

NS 4.4: Students should develop an understanding of properties of earth materials and changes in the earth; NCTE 12: Students use spoken, written, and visual language to accomplish their own purposes for learning, enjoyment, persuasion, and the exchange of information; CNAEA 1: Students improvise dialogue to tell stories and formalize improvisations; CNAEA 2: Students use variations of locomotor and nonlocomotor movement and vocal pitch, tempo, and tone for different characters.

Objectives:

Experience learning earth science through a variety of artistic teaching methods; understanding the rock cycle is the science objective that is embedded in visual arts and descriptive writing required in this residency; understanding and enjoying how several cultures use rocks in artistic and playful ways.

Children learn and experience learning in many ways. Howard Gardner encourages us to consider educational possibilities through exploration of the multiple intelligences children exhibit. When we tell stories, a holistic endeavor, we leave the way open for children to access the experience and the knowledge of the story in their own way. Curricular knowledge becomes integrated with artistic expressions that children imagine in a story. This act sets the stage for children to show their science knowledge through visual art, movement, music and song, dialogue, experimentation, and other forms of concrete expression. Clearly, the main objective of the residency is the integration of art and science.

"Why Are River Rocks Smooth?"
By DWe Williams

The children live happily in the sky with their guardian the wind. Often the guardian warns the children against going down to the earth. In time their inquisitive nature lures them to explore the earth. Flying down from the sky and landing on the river water, the children are pulled to the floor of the river, where their feet are bruised and cut on the sharp rocks. The wind rushes down to the earth to save the children. His frantic blowing rushes the water and sand against the sharp rocks, smoothing them. Once the stones are worn and smooth, the children can walk in the river bed and play with the beautiful and smooth river rocks.

The River Rock Project: In this school residency the students, teachers, and I explore stones through science, culture, and art. The story is the basis for art projects that reinforce the science, the beauty, and the cultural uses of stones. Cultures have gathered and played with stones since the beginning of time. Stones hold the stories of past civilizations, the wonders of nature, and the evidence of the rock cycle or what geologic activity occurred in that particular area. The project encourages so many ways for children to experience rocks and therefore provides many opportunities for authentic assessment. Science activities include identifying stones by color, size, shape, content, and weight, as well as defining and sequencing the rock cycle, particularly erosion. Art activities support the science objectives through guided sensory exercises, making sedimentary rock, increased observation skills, dancing the rock cycle, visual arts experiences, and descriptive writing activities (rock ID cards).

The Guided Sensory Process: Students are seated in a circle with a pile of small river rocks in the center. Each student is asked to focus on one stone in the pile. One at a time they are invited to go to the center and pick out their stone. After all students have selected a stone, students are taken through a guided sensory. How does your stone feel? What does your stone look like? What colors are in your stone? Does your stone have a "birth mark"? Students are then guided through the sensory with eyes closed. After the closed-eye sensory, students briefly open their eyes to reacquaint themselves with their stones. They are asked to close their eyes again while the teacher collects all the stones and places them in a circle around the remaining pile of stones. Students then retrieve their original stone.

At this point, students begin to recognize the importance of being able to identify their stones by color, shape, texture, and size. Each student now creates an ID card for his or her stone. Kindergarten and first-grade students draw their stone and write color words on the card. Second-grade students describe their stone in complete sentences along with their drawing. Once the ID cards are completed, the teacher is asked to match the stones with their ID cards. During the matching process the teacher is able to assess the student penmanship, descriptive writing, and ability to reproduce the details of the stone visually. Stones are returned to their original owner and placed in a circle.

The story "Why Are River Rocks Smooth?" is then layered on this sensory activity. Students are asked to close their eyes and create pictures of the story, to imagine the story. After the story, I ask, "What did you see?" Students offer a variety of pictures that inevitably include strong knowledge of erosion.

Assessments:

Students create a dance of the story, with their variations focused on "bound" and "free" movement. First, students create different shapes to resemble stones. Then they experiment with free movement such as gliding, soaring, and floating. Then students are partnered in order that one is the stone and the other the water. The water will move around and (erode) reshape the stone into a new formation.

Make Your Own Books: The children's versions of the story and the dance "Why Are River Rocks Smooth?" can be written out and illustrated individually or made into a big book for the classroom. The following activities are story sources as well.

Family Stones: Using West African Adinkra symbols and personal symbols, students draw designs representative of their family strengths and values. Stones are then embellished with feathers, trinkets, and other small items.

Family Stones.

Family Stones.

Rock Passing Game: This is based on Native American stone-passing games. Students place a stone in their right hand. The teacher sets the steady and not-too-fast tempo for the rhyme. On the first beat of River Rock, all stones are passed at the same time to the student seated to their right. Older students repeat this pattern of passing the stones while keeping the beat to the River Rock Chant.

River Rock, River Rock
Cool and smooth
River Rock, River Rock
Reflect the moon
River Rock, River Rock
How old are you?
Now count by ten to one hundred
10, 20, 30, 40, 50, 60, 70, 80, 90, 100

Long after the River Rock project is over, students remember the fanciful story and the classroom culture that loved each stone they gathered. On the back of a thank-you note, a student wrote, "When the rushing water and the sand smooth the rocks they call that EROSION." Because the story is coupled with the ability to gather, handle, organize, and create artistically, the River Rock Project is highly successful in terms of knowledge acquisition and in terms of emotional satisfaction.

Ms. DWe is a native of Durham, North Carolina. She holds a master's degree in speech and theatre from SIU Carbondale with a focus on creative drama and children's theatre. Ms. DWe is a popular storyteller who weaves stories for the enjoyment and education of her audiences. Williams appears in libraries and schools, and at festivals, community events, and conferences. She is well known for the use of drama in integrated curriculum and cultural awareness. Ms. DWe is the lead mentoring teaching artist for special populations with the Oklahoma City Arts Council. The Oklahoma City Metropolitan Library System frequently uses Ms. Williams as a storyteller, playwright, and workshop presenter. E-mail: ewdwms@sbcglobal.net.

CHAPTER FOUR

Grades Three, Four, and Five

INTRODUCTION
By Sherry Norfolk

Enter a third-, fourth-, or fifth-grade classroom, and you feel the buzz of energy: movement and talk and rhythm and animation. All of that humming, thrilling, keyed-up agitation can be channeled into learning!

Storytelling is the ideal teaching method to engage the attention, emotion, and imagination of upper-elementary students, allowing learning to take place. By third grade, children have developed a sense of self and find it important to gain social acceptance and experience achievement. Students have begun to identify themselves as smart or stupid, winners or losers, successful learners or constant failures. They have either remained absorbed in the school environment, or have begun to disassociate themselves from it.

For many children, the information being presented in the classroom seems totally irrelevant to their interests, their lives, their futures—and without the ability to make connections between what they are supposed to learn and what they care about, students begin to tune out. The buzz in the classroom is the dial tone.

When the teacher finds ways to make learning relevant for everyone in the classroom—and make it holistic (relating to lots of other things that students are learning about)—well, that's when all children have access to academic, artistic, and social learning.

Learning is enhanced through developmentally appropriate teaching methods, as well. Third- through fifth-grade students are in Piaget's age of "concrete operations," learning effectively through multiple representations of concepts, including concrete/pictorial, verbal/written, reference/data-based, and graphical/symbolic. This age group is particularly well served when concepts are introduced and used in the context of the real world: when the learning is made relevant.

Eight- to ten-year-olds are beginning to learn that others have ideas and views that are different from their own. They are able to work together within social and cooperative groups. Lesson plans that incorporate opportunities for cooperative learning maximize that potential by increasing the opportunity for peer teaching, providing platforms for oral and written communication, and converting a boring classroom into an exciting learning environment.

Our contributing authors tap into all of these models in their lesson plans. They include lots of humor, plenty of "real," meaningful adventure, opportunities for both interpersonal and intrapersonal experiences, and, most importantly, fun!

This chapter is about latency—an emotionally quiet period where lots of leaps can occur in skills and content, and kids can practice negotiating with peers and adults. Stories give children a framework and options on their way through the forest. That's why we need to use stories: the children are listening, so let's let them listen to stories!

GARGANTUAN FUCHSIA STOMPING BOOTS
By Willy Claflin

National Standards:

NCTE 4: Students adjust their use of spoken, written, and visual language to communicate effectively with a variety of audiences; NCTE 5: Students employ a wide range of strategies as they write and use different writing elements appropriately to communicate with different audiences for a variety of purposes.

Objectives:

In learning to define parody, students will play with language and ideas; students will maintain a story's structure while substituting new characters; students will understand that the organization or story structure is the basis of good writing and telling.

Children love parodies. Making up parodies is one of kids' favorite activities. Who doesn't remember singing, "Jingle bells, Batman smells/Robin laid an egg," or "On top of spaghetti, all covered with cheese," or (in a slightly darker vein, from my own childhood) "Mine eyes have seen the glory of the burning of the school"?

Parodies are relatively easy to make up—the original form is already in place. And the thrill of irreverence adds extra zing to the pleasures of "saying it wrong on purpose." With this in mind, I decided some years ago to teach creative writing/storytelling through parody exercises. By far the most popular of these exercises has been one called Gargantuan Fuchsia Stomping Boots. I still use this exercise regularly in second- to sixth-grade classrooms (and in adult storytelling classes as well). It never fails to produce fascinating, unpredictable, humorous tales.

I usually begin by telling the class a standard version of the Little Red Riding Hood tale. This was not necessary even twenty years ago, but by now very few classic fairy tales are widely known, and even popular stories like Little Red Riding Hood exist in so many contemporary altered versions that the original outline has been obscured. Once I've told the tale, we make up a parody together as a group exercise. For homework, or in follow-up classes, each student makes up his or her own original parody of the story.

We begin by giving the heroine a new name, one word at a time. Little is changed to another adjective describing size, Red to another adjective describing color, Riding to another verb of locomotion, and Hood to another article of clothing. To make her name as interesting as possible, I ask the students to choose words that are somewhat unusual words that they do not hear every day. This helps us avoid relatively boring names like Big Blue Walking Hat. Sometimes, especially if the kids are having a hard time loosening up, I'll suggest that the first word in her name refer to a character trait, such as Lazy, Angry, Whiny, Cheerful, etc. This often leads to the creation of a more interesting protagonist.

Having chosen a new name—say, Gargantuan Fuchsia Stomping Boots—we then change all the main characters in the story. Again, I may suggest to the class that they choose somewhat unusual characters that might make the story more compelling. At the end of this process we have a new cast. Perhaps (to use some student examples) she lives with Barney, who sends her to visit stepsister Penguin, and tells her to look out for the Big Bad Gerbil. Perhaps in the end a brave, handsome Moose rescues them. The possibilities, of course, are endless.

It is very important to remind the students that the new story must follow the original plot, step by step, all the way through. This is what makes it a parody, not just a weird, funny story. There are many important elements to consider as we journey along: What is she carrying in the basket? What does she see or hear in the forest that makes her forget her promise to (Barney) and leave the path? What does the big bad (Gerbil) say or do when it meets her? What does it do when it gets to (the Penguin's) house first? What does the big bad (Gerbil) do to (the Penguin), remembering that it must be alive at the end, so that it can be rescued by the brave, handsome (Moose)? And, perhaps most difficult—how does that final, famous conversation go in the end? Suppose you stepped into a very dark cabin, and the Penguin, in those pajamas, looked really odd—like a . . . Gerbil? "Why Penguin, what soft and fuzzy fur you have!" "The better to stay warm in the winter, my dear . . . come closer."

Assessments:

Because it is easy for students to get sidetracked, I always provide a handout (below) of the story—an outline of the plot, with blanks for the new names, characters, and altered conversations. This turns out to be very important, as it helps students keep the parody on track.

The hidden agenda here, besides allowing the imagination comic expression, is teaching story structure. This tale has lasted because its structure is so strong. When students use that structure to write their own story, it teaches them techniques that they can use in telling future tales as well.

Willy Claflin grew up in Wolfeboro, New Hampshire, where he spent his childhood daydreaming, wandering through the woods, and worrying about the wolf under his bed. He became a storyteller in 1972, after a truck drove through his living room on Christmas morning. Willy has received three Parents' Choice Gold Awards and two ALA Notable Awards. He is a frequently featured teller at the National Storytelling Festival, and has appeared at dozens of other storytelling festivals in the United States and abroad. Willy is frequently accompanied by his faithful sidekick, Maynard Moose, teller of ancient Mother Moose Tales. Maynard and Willy currently make their home in San Francisco. Web site: www.willyclaflin.com; E-mail: claflin@willyclaflin.com.

FRACTURING FOLK AND FAIRY TALES

How to Write and Tell Original Parodies

1. Name of main character: _____

2. How did she get her name? _____

   _____

   _____

3. Who does she live with? _____

4. Who is she told to visit at the other end of the forest? _____

5. What does she bring in her basket for her/him/it? _____

   _____

   _____

6. Why does she leave the path? _____

   _____

   _____

7. What/who is the Big Bad _____

8. What does the Big Bad _____ do when it gets to the house first?

9. How does the conversation go?

   "Why _____, what _____ _____ you have!"

   "The better to _____ you!"

   "Why _____, what _____ _____ you have!"

   "The better to _____ you!"

   "Why _____, what _____ _____ you have!"

   "The better to _____ you!"

10. Who rescues everyone at the end, and how do they do it?

   _____

   _____

   _____

   _____

   _____

ANANSI'S ADVENTURE
By Lynn Rubright

National Standards:

NCTE 8: Listening and speaking (including storytelling); NCTE 6: Applying knowledge of language structure to create text.

Objectives:

Develop literacy skills: listening, thinking, speaking, writing, reading, and performing; get to know the trickster, Anansi.

I love to tell and work with Anansi stories in the classroom, and this lesson plan provides one example of what happens when Anansi comes to school! It's based on *Anansi the Spider: A Tale from the Ashanti*, adapted and illustrated by Gerald McDermott (Holt, Rinehart and Winston, 1972), and "How the Moon Got into the Sky" retold by Joyce Arkhurst in *More Adventures of Spider* (Scholastic Book Services, 1964). By introducing the story to children through storytelling rather than story reading, everyone learns the story structure (bones)—setting, characters, sequence of events, conflict, crisis, and resolution—without having to read it. This takes great pressure off poor or nonreaders, and allows all the children to participate in the creative drama activities that follow.

These "lessons" are designed to develop language arts skills: listening, thinking, speaking, writing, reading, and performing. The role play also helps children become more orally expressive and articulate as they reinforce their understanding of all the components of story.

Instructional Plan:

1. Tell "Anansi's Adventure." Consult the McDermott or Arkhurst texts to learn the story bones, and then tell your own version, up to the point where Anansi decides to give the light to the son who rescued him.
2. Choose an audience member to play son See Trouble, and "join in" the dialogue. Finish the tale by involving a bit of improvisational story theater:

    Storyteller/Papa Anansi asks: "But why do you think you deserve the prize, See Trouble? Tell me."

    With this minimum of cueing, the person playing See Trouble pleads for Anansi to give the globe of light to him (or her), saying something like, "I deserve the prize because I saw you in the belly of the fish. Without me you would still be there."

    Storyteller/Anansi asks audience, "Do you think I should give See Trouble the great globe of light as a prize?"

Audience, cued by Anansi, yells, "NO! NO! NO!"

Storyteller then asks for volunteers to repeat the sequence with each of the sons.

When Papa gives the globe of light to Nyame, who takes it into the sky, the spider sons and daughters realize that Papa Anansi is very wise, for the light of the great globe now shines down upon all of them. The prize of the MOON has been shared with everyone.

3. Review the story bones and outline some of the children's favorite scenes on the board.

4. Ask children to act out some of the scenes. Provide suggestions: one might become the storyteller/narrator as others act out the scene, another might give a monologue from the point of view of a character, others could present a dialogue between two characters, as modeled during the telling of the story to the large group. Get all children involved.

In re-creating these scenes, children are working in all modalities, processing meaning through aural, kinesthetic, linguistic, and spatial intelligences. They have internalized the story structure, demonstrated a grasp of plot and sequence, and, most important, they comprehend the story. This provides an authentic assessment while creating a fun environment that promotes learning.

Recently, I taught this lesson plan at a St. Louis public school. The first two third-grade classes with whom I worked were highly motivated and successfully completed the entire lesson. But in the third classroom, one child was clearly not engaged with this process. Ryan sat in the back with his head on the desk covered with his leather jacket, apparently sleeping. I worked with the children who were interested, but was bothered that all my energy and enthusiasm did not engage this child. Then, as I was packing up to leave, there was Ryan by my side. He whispered, "Mrs. Rubright, do you think we could turn this Anansi story into a rap?"

"Of course," I said, not having a clue how to do this, but delighted that Ryan had actually been listening! The teacher gave us permission to work in the hall, and two other boys perked up and asked to join us. Soon we were lounging on bean bag "chairs" in the hall, me with yellow pad and pen in hand.

Suddenly, Ryan was up and performing a rap he had memorized (with moves) word for word. The other two boys were very impressed. But how to turn our Anansi story into something like THAT?

We wrote phrases about Anansi's rain forest adventures, falling into the water and getting swallowed by a fish. The boys gave me some ideas, but nothing hung together, sounded rhythmical or rhymed, or even made much sense. But they obviously knew the story, having heard it told. I was overwhelmed by a sense of frustration and felt totally inept as to how to shape Anansi into a rap. I promised them I would take their ideas, work on them, and return with a rap the next week. They smiled.

With help from Ellen Eliceiri, head of the reference library at Webster University, and trying to be respectful of a poetic cultural art form about which I knew nothing and for which I didn't have an ear, I struggled to come up with something based on ideas, words, and phrases that Ryan and his friends had come up with. Here is the result:

Anansi the Spider, RAP
By Ryan, Donovan, Terrence,
   Third-Grade Rappers
With Lynn Rubright

One morning Anansi
Woke up quick.
He felt his bones.
He didn't feel sick.

His sons were sleeping
In a heap.
Anansi was quiet.
He didn't make a peep.

He crawled over, under,
In between,
Careful not to wake them,
So he wouldn't be seen.

Papa Anansi
Went for a walk.
It was quiet in the jungle.
There was no talk.

Light as a feather,
Papa flew through the sky

On a thread of silk!
My! Oh my!

Chorus:
Hey! Papa!
Papa Anansi!
You gonna get in trouble
If you don't watch out!

Just like Tarzan
Swinging vine to vine,
Until the wind snatched him
And broke his line.

Chorus (repeat)

Papa Anansi
Fell into the river.
In the belly of a fish
He started to shiver.

Papa Anansi
Began to shout:
"See Trouble, See Trouble!
Get me OUT!"

The most gratifying moment came when I presented a copy of *Anansi's Rap* to each child in Ryan's room. As I read it, Ryan just looked at me and smiled. It wasn't until we had read it through several times that he began to join in—he had started to memorize it. I also knew that once Ryan had memorized the rap, he might have enough confidence to really work on decoding the text, word for word.

I had copies made for children in the other third-grade classes. They were impressed that Ryan, Donovan, Terrence, and I had written the rap together. They, too, delighted in reading over and over until they could read it smoothly, with expression. The children were encouraged to take their rap home and read it to their families, which many of them did enthusiastically.

This cycle of storytelling to "get the story" to poorly reading or non-reading children, working on "lessons" like creating the rap with the children, and having them read, memorize, and perform it from text, is a much-needed link in the process of becoming literate. My two months of work with Anansi tales with the third graders in this St. Louis public school was over. I do not know to what degree Ryan's teachers used the rap to further develop his literacy skills. I do know he took a copy home. I bet he learned to read it!

Assessments:

Creative drama segments allow assessment of how well children comprehend the story and its sequence, and each student's ability to use oral language to retell the story.

For more information on Lynn Rubright's years of working with cross-curricular applications of Anansi the spider from the Ashanti people of Ghana, West Africa, see Chapter 9, "Anansi the Spider, Storytelling African Style," *Beyond the Beanstalk: Interdisciplinary Learning through Storytelling* (Heinemann, 1996). Available through http://www.heinemann.com.

A complete reader's theatre script of "Anansi's Adventure" (grades three through eight) is available on Lynn's Web site.

Lynn Rubright, professor emerita, Webster University, St. Louis, Missouri, is an award-winning educator, storyteller, and author of Mama's Window *(Lee and Low Books, 2005) and co-producer of the EMMY Award-winning video documentary,* Oh Freedom After While: Sharecropper Protest in SE Missouri in 1939. *Recipient of a National Storytelling Network Circle of Excellence Award, and Distinguished Alumna Award, Webster University, she presently designs and teaches storytelling and literacy for the Center for Contemporary Arts in St. Louis public schools, continues to teach Storytelling Across the Curriculum in the MAT program at Webster University as a summer institute, and is adjunct professor at University of Missouri, St. Louis. Lynn co-founded the award-winning Metro Theater Company and the St. Louis Storytelling Festival. For Lynn: www.lynnrubright.com; for* Mama's Window: *www.leeandlow.com/booktalk/rubright.html.*

PICTURE THIS: STORYBOARDING IN THE CLASSROOM
By Elizabeth Ellis

National Standards:

NCTE 4: Students adjust their use of spoken, written, and visual language to communicate effectively with a variety of audiences; NCTE 5: Students employ a wide range of strategies as they write and use different elements appropriately to communicate with different audiences for a variety of purposes; NCTE 11: Students participate as knowledgeable, reflective, creative, and critical members of literacy communities.

Objectives:

In order to emphasize the importance of story structure, students will draw their story in six simple drawings called a storyboard; students will learn story conventions: main character, setting, types of conflict, beginning-middle-end, and extended ending; students will explore sensory imagery for inclusion in their stories.

After telling a story about getting into trouble as a child, I ask the fourth graders, "When I was telling the story, could you see anything in your mind?" All hands shoot up. "Well," I tell them, "when we want to write, we have pictures inside our heads that go with the story. Sometimes it is difficult to get our pictures out so that other people can enjoy them. We have to turn them into words to help others *see what we are saying.*

"I am going to show you a process that will help you turn your story ideas into a great piece of writing that people will really want to read.

"How many of you like to watch television?" I ask. "Movies? Playing video games?" There is lots of response. "Everything you have ever watched on the screen was once a ***storyboard***. A storyboard is a set of pictures that tells the story, like the Sunday comic strips. There is one picture for each major thing that happens.

"Here are the pictures I want you to put in your storyboard. Picture One will tell us when and where the story takes place. That is called the ***setting***. It will also tell us whom the story is about. That's the ***main character***.

"Picture Two gives us the ***problem*** or the ***conflict***. Put your fists together. Now push! That's conflict: two forces pushing against each other. If you don't have any conflict, there won't be much story.

"There are two kinds of conflict: internal and external. You break a lamp. That's an ***external conflict***. It is happening outside you. Your mother asks, 'Who broke the lamp?' You say, 'I dunno.' You told a lie. Now the conflict is ***internal***, inside you. The conflict is between you and the person you really want to be." I push my fists together. "I don't want to get in trouble. I want to tell the truth." The students join in, pushing their fists together and chanting, "I want to tell the truth! I don't want to get in trouble!"

"Picture Three shows us how things get worse before they get better. Sometimes people say, 'The plot thickens.' If your conflict was breaking the lamp, Picture Three might be of your mother arriving home to find the lamp broken. Things just got worse, didn't they?

"In Picture Four you begin to think about a way to solve your problem or a way to get out of your difficulty. Maybe help arrives. In the movies this is when the cavalry arrives.

"Picture Five is the ***conclusion***. What happened? How did it end?

Storyboard.

"We still have a picture left over. Picture Six is for the ***extended ending***. Tell us what you learned from the experience, or how you grew. Tell us what you wished or dreamed. Or tell us how things changed after the conflict. If your story is about the broken lamp, perhaps your extended ending is about learning to tell the truth."

I ask them to draw around their hands on a piece of paper. I ask, "What are the five senses?" They yell them out. "Please write one of your five senses on each of the fingers on your paper." Then we brainstorm words that go with each of the five senses.

"When we write our stories, we are going to give them a High Five." The students all give one another a high five. "We want our readers to feel like they are there when the story is taking place, so we include words to help them use their five senses in the story. This is called ***sensory imagery***."

Smell is my favorite to play with. I write the words "fragrance" and "odor" on the board. We talk about how words that mean almost the same thing give us a different feeling when we hear them. Kids write on the board by the two terms. It starts simply: "roses," "cookies," "new-cut grass." It soon balloons into an all-out gross-out. "Dirty socks," "wet dogs," "three-day-old garbage." Each student tries to come up with the grossest odor he or she can imagine. The classroom dissolves in laughter, but they remember High Five.

I introduce a story prompt: "Tell us about a time you got into trouble." Nearly everyone has something to say at this point.

"Make a storyboard of a time you got into trouble. Give me six pictures. After you draw the pictures, please use a second piece of paper. Divide it into six sections. Then I want you to High Five each of your pictures. Imagine each picture and write words about the five senses that you could use when you write your story."

When we meet for our second session together, I have placed a comic strip on each desk. "I want you to share the comic strip with a partner—but don't let them see it."

There is much consternation. Finally a boy asks, "How can we share it with them if they can't see the pictures?"

It only takes a moment before a girl says, "We could tell them what is happening." "Right," I say. "If you don't have pictures, you will have to use words." So they tell the comic strips.

I ask them to look at their storyboards. "You are going to write your story. It will be easy to do because your storyboard is a *visual outline* of the story. Each picture is a *paragraph*. What's a paragraph?"

A student tells me, "A paragraph is three to five sentences."

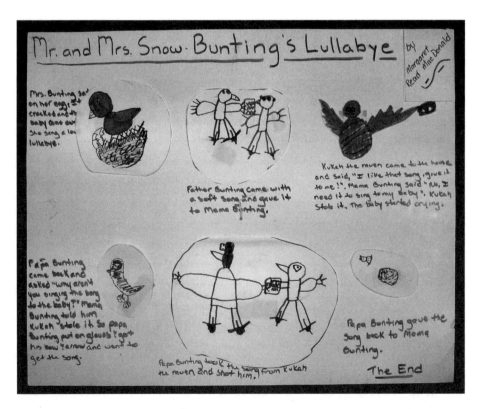

Kindergarten Storyboard Adaptation: children draw pictures that show the plot and teachers scribe the children's words.

Papa Bunting took the song from Kukah the raven and shot him.

Close-up.

"Good!" I say. "My cat has big teeth. Our house is on Wofford Street. I have lived in Dallas for thirty-five years. Is that a paragraph?"

"No," they say, but no one can tell me why until a boy says, "If you drew it, you would have to draw three separate pictures!" Now everyone is sure of the problem. To be a paragraph it has to be about one idea.

"My cat's teeth are too big for his mouth. He cannot close his lips around them. He drools a lot. It's disgusting, but I love him anyway." Everyone agrees this is a paragraph because they proclaim with excitement, "You can draw it in just one picture."

They settle into the writing process, using the High Five list of sensory words and their storyboards. The writing residency is off to a great start.

Assessments:

Students can be graded on their ability to first draw and then write their stories using clearly defined conventions as well as images.

Elizabeth Ellis has been a professional storyteller for more than a quarter of a century. A nurturing teacher, she shares Appalachian tales and stories of heroic American women, but her personal stories are arguably her best. A repeated favorite at the National Storytelling Festival, she is the recipient of the Circle of Excellence Award from the National Storytelling Network. Elizabeth's writing residencies and storytelling workshops are in great demand. With Loren Niemi, she co-authored Inviting the Wolf In: Thinking about Difficult Stories, *published by August House. She currently lives in Dallas, Texas. For further information, visit www.elizabethellis.com.*

STORYTELLING IN THE WRITING WORKSHOP
By Paige Tighe

National Standards:

NCTE 3: Evaluation Strategies; NCTE 6: Applying Knowledge; NCTE 9: Multicultural Understanding; NCTE 12: Applying Language Skills.

Objectives:

Employ basic elements of story in an engaging way, to create a positive and non-threatening atmosphere for writing; accept, value, and challenge; edit sentences for content; review prescribed method for process writing; rewrite sentences into paragraph form; publish student work

It is my job to walk away from a writing session having taught young writers the process and mechanics of effective writing. It is my joy to stagger away from a writing session dizzy with rich, juicy images and full-bodied words, feeling like I've just ridden the Tilt-a-Whirl.

Story is a wonderful vehicle for teaching and reinforcing mandated writing skills in the elementary and middle grades, as well as in the special education classroom. By employing basic elements of story in an engaging way, the teacher creates a positive and non-threatening atmosphere where students free themselves to take risks without the fear of being wrong.

In the 1990s, I developed a program called BERP: Brainstorm, Edit, Rewrite, and Publish. A basic approach works with younger students, as well as with the student who struggles with his or her writing. The class must already be familiar and comfortable with a prescribed method for process writing. While we incorporate the same steps taken in a more formal program and devote much energy to publishing a truly polished end product, the brainstorm is just that, a *brain storm*.

Any meaty lesson involves effective modeling and direction. As teacher and class create a piece together, the teacher's role is that of an encourager, rather than a lecturer. The teacher's function is to accept, value, and challenge the vulnerability and creativity offered, and to do it with gusto. Ray Bradbury states in his essay "The Joy of Writing" (*Zen in the Art of Writing and the Joy of Writing:*

Two Essays. Capra Press, 1973), "Zest. Gusto. How rarely one hears these words used. How rarely do we see people living, or for that matter, creating by them? Yet, if I were asked to name the most important items in a writer's make-up, the things which shape his material and rushes him along the road to where he wants to go, I could only warn him to look to his zest and see to his gusto." A story, well-told, will usher both zest and gusto into the writing workshop.

To begin, the teacher chooses a story element to be taught. An excellent choice for a first attempt would be *setting*. As such, the class should become completely immersed in the whys and wherefores of *setting*, examining it from every direction, inside out, upside down, and sideways. Students and teacher discuss their own setting as well as those from familiar stories (books, movies, and plays). How do things feel, smell, taste, appear, and sound in the Arabels' barn, where Wilbur and Charlotte live (*Charlotte's Web*, E. B. White)? Is the air heavy and the scent sweet?

When every student is comfortable with *setting*, the teacher chooses a story illustrating it in a multi-sensory way. It should contain imagery, from the setting, that is vivid enough to pique the interest of even the most reluctant writer. While teaching setting, I have had great success with the Old Testament story of Jonah and the big fish. Elementary school students belly-laugh at the thought of poor Jonah spending three days in the slimy, slippery, stinky belly of a fish! Another good story for setting is the ancient Greek tale "Damon and Pitheus," best friends whose friendship lands one in a dungeon and the other on a tempest-tossed sea. What settings!

But finding the right story can be difficult. Some stories jump onto our laps begging to be told. Some lie in the corner and sleep. Some sleeping stories just need to be prodded a little, and they will spring to action. The school librarian or local children's librarian, fellow teachers, and the Internet are valuable resources for stories.

Once found, the story must be learned so that its presentation is spontaneous, alive, and captivating. Once learned, the story must be told, boldly and confidently, with zest and gusto. And then comes the brainstorming part. Wild and wonderful heights are reached by quickly listing, and then organizing, the brainstormed ideas. As students and teacher begin the process of describing the story's setting, they fall inside the world of the story, where characters move and breathe. They can describe it because they are walking through it. Together, they write meaty sentences that describe where they have found themselves.

By using the five-sentence paragraph model, students and teacher develop one topic sentence, three detail sentences, and one clincher sentence describing the story's setting. After editing the sentences for content, students rewrite them into paragraph form, edit (proofread), rewrite, and finally publish by illustrating their work (which can be just as graphic as their verbal descriptors).

Also, the teacher may tailor the writing part of this lesson to suit the academic needs of the students involved. It can be as simple as a standard five-sentence paragraph or as complex as an analysis of the story's setting and its effect on the characters. The lesson is also easily adapted to meet the needs of a multi-level classroom. Assessment is made using a cumulative writing folder.

As described, storytelling in the writing workshop covers national standards, a multitude of language arts objectives, and curriculum requirements as they relate to both process writing and works of literature. And, while many teachers see storytelling as a treat, something to use as a culminating activity, I say a loud, resounding, emphatic no!

Storytelling is a wonderful way to slide into writing that drips with zest and gusto. Miracles happen! The moment will come when you will jump up and down, spin around, arms outstretched, repeating to no one in particular: THEY GET IT! THEY GET IT!

Recently, a fourth grader with Attention Deficit Hyperactivity Disorder (ADHD) and an aversion for writing offered to tell a story in class. I granted his request, although I didn't expect much. (Shame on me!) What followed left me utterly amazed. He told a well-ordered story with tons of excitement and breath-holding suspense. He held us all captive for a few moments and then blew us out of the water with the story's conclusion. When he finished, I took a deep breath. "Will you write that for me?" I whispered. And he did.

Assessments:

Use the five-sentence paragraph model for assessment; assessment is made over time, using a cumulative writing folder; written stories will be told with zest and gusto.

Open Hand Storytelling's Paige Tighe, married, mother of six, resides in southern New Jersey, but passionately craves full-time life on Open Hand Farm near Paw Paw, West Virginia. Following the completion of an undergraduate degree in English (Towson University), Tighe found herself teaching special education and doing graduate coursework to obtain certification. In 1997, she left the classroom to be a full-time mommy, and thereafter discovered the world of professional storytelling. "It is an amazing integration of my talents," she says. Although Tighe tells regularly and conducts storytelling workshops for children and adults, her current professional focus is biblical storytelling. E-mail: pjtighe@verizon.net.

WHAT IS A FOLKTALE?
By Susan A. Selk

National Standards:

NCTE 1: Students read a wide range of print and non-print texts to build understanding; NCTE 2: Students read a wide range of

literature from many periods in many genres to build an understanding of the many dimensions of human experience; NCTE 4:
Students adjust their use of spoken, written, and visual language
to communicate effectively with a variety of audiences and for different purposes; NCTE 9: Students develop an understanding of
and respect for diversity in language use, patterns, and dialects
across cultures, ethnic groups, geographic regions, and social roles;
NCTE 12: Students use spoken, written, and visual language to accomplish their own purposes; NSS 2: Understand the physical and
human characteristics of places. Understand that people create
regions to interpret Earth's complexity. Understand how culture
and experience influence people's perceptions of places and
regions; NSS 4: Understand the characteristics, distribution, and
migration of human populations on Earth's surface. Understand
the characteristics, distribution, and complexity of Earth's cultural
mosaics; NSS 4: Understand family life now and in the past and
family life in various places long ago, understand the folklore and
cultural contributions from various regions of the United States
and how they helped to form a national heritage. Understand
selected attributes and historical development of societies in
Africa, the Americas, Asia, and Europe.

Objectives:

Understand that different cultures across the globe have similar needs,
practices, and beliefs; understand why individual cultures can also possess
unique needs, practices, and beliefs; determine the main idea (nonfiction) or
theme (fiction) within a written work; identify or infer important characters,
settings, problems, events, relationships, and details within a written work;
select and use relevant information from a written work in order to summarize; orally compose and present a folktale; organize information and ideas;
respond to written/spoken text; practice verbal and nonverbal communication;
practice the writing process.

As a school library media specialist, I am always looking for ways to
get both students and teachers excited about coming to the library. One way
that I keep them coming is through story.

I begin this particular unit later in the year. Students come with a beginning understanding of culture, and they have heard several folktales during
earlier visits to the library. We have talked about folktales briefly, identifying
them as stories that have been passed down orally from generation to generation, and are often used to teach a lesson or to explain something. We have
also briefly discussed that different cultures have different tales, and that
sometimes tales have similar characters, plots, or motifs.

During the first week, I inform the students that they will be reading,
listening to, and telling stories over the next several visits, and that they will

also be writing stories and writing about stories. After hearing two stories from different cultures, each student receives a journal and is encouraged to decorate it creatively. Some of the students decorate their journals with pictures relating to the stories they've heard.

A folktale "bingo" is introduced as an incentive for reading folktales. The bingo card consists of nine squares, each representing folktales from different cultures. Students are allowed to explore a variety of classic folktales through picture books. There is an opportunity to select a folktale to read during each visit. Students get to identify, with help, the culture the story comes from, and then they briefly describe, in writing, what the story is about and identify something they especially liked or disliked about it. This is my way of making sure they have actually read the story. Each student who gets bingo receives a small token prize like a bookmark or pencil.

We begin our second session with a folktale, followed by the pre-project writing prompt "What is folktale?" Students are asked to tell me whatever they can about folktales, referring back to what we have talked about, what they read during the week, and what they heard.

Each week, I begin with a folktale from another culture. The students may read a folktale themselves, listen to a recording or watch a video of someone telling a tale, or listen to a live reading or performance, so long as they select something different each week. I appeal to as many different learning styles as possible.

After each story, there is a retelling, and then a writing activity where students respond, individually, to the story. One week, we use a round robin during which each child retells one part of the story orally. You may have to prompt some of the students with questions to keep the proper sequence. Then students rewrite the story with as much detail as they can remember about the story and its meaning. The next week, they practice retelling the entire story to one other person and then rewrite the ending. The week after that, they draw the story as a mural or a storyboard, and then write their own folktale variant.

One session, after a character visualization exercise, focuses on describing the main character through words and picture. Each week a different folktale from a different culture is presented, with a different activity and a different writing exercise in the journals.

I keep the stories short, no more than five to seven minutes, and the activity is held to the same time limit. Then I give students ten minutes to write. This leaves us a few minutes at the end to discuss, as a group, any changes to our definition of a folktale, and to identify and acknowledge any bingos they may have. Some weeks there is even time for volunteers to read something they have written.

Students are given a hard copy of our final definition of a folktale. Using their definition, students complete a post-project writing prompt, "What is folktale?" They refer to the definition and also give examples from the stories they have read and heard over the past weeks. After the prompt is complete, we talk about the final aspect of the project—writing and telling their folktale.

Over the next few sessions, students write their own folktales using the definition they created of what a folktale is and why it is important. They create a story map with a problem, three or four events, and a solution. Then they write a rough draft of the story. I ask them to show me what folktale elements they are using to make sure they understand and can apply what we have been talking about the last few weeks. Examples of folktale elements would be development of the leading character; a quick introduction to conflict or a problem to be faced; time/place (once upon a time, back in the day, etc.); setting (on a road, on a bridge, in the forest); development (sequential action that moves toward the climax); hero and/or heroine who faces conflict; conclusions that end with short and sweet resolutions. I stress that the story is just a rough draft, and that spelling and grammar are not as important. Getting the plot written down is important. Reading the story to a critical friend is the next step.

Students create a storyboard from their story and use it to practice telling their folktales in small groups. We practice adding appropriate tone to the story and voice to the characters. For further practice, they can tell their story to a different group of students.

Students really enjoyed this part of the project. Most of the children were able to add some detail to their written stories that would enhance it for verbal telling, and they came away with a good tale to tell. We culminated the project with a class storytelling festival, and anyone who wanted to tell was invited to tell his or her story.

Collaborating on the Story.

Small Miracles:

Students definitely responded to and enjoyed this project. The folktale bingo was a great incentive to get the children to read. It was not part of their regular reading assignments, but instead took the place of their reading for pleasure. All the students read enough folktales to get two bingos, and many read nine tales in order to get their third bingo. It gave them a sampling of different types of folktales from different cultures, which tied into their study of culture in social studies.

The students' attention spans, specifically the boys', increased over the course of the unit. By the end of the unit, boys who could not sit still for a seven-minute story at the beginning of the project were able to stay focused and engaged throughout the story. I was very impressed with their interest in reading folktales and their obvious understanding of what a folktale is.

Their original stories were creative and definitely showcased what the students learned during the unit. They enjoyed telling the stories to each other, and they discovered some strategies that they can use to become better listeners.

Assessments:

Pre- and post-writing prompts are scored using a rubric; weekly journal writings are scored using a rubric to evaluate comprehension; weekly oral discussions.

Susan Selk has worked in the education field for over twenty years. She has been a school library media specialist for over ten years, has taught high school and middle school, and presently teaches at the elementary level. While working as the director of a school district television studio, she had the opportunity to meet many professional storytellers, and fell in love with the idea of becoming one. As a library media specialist, she has had the opportunity to incorporate storytelling into the classroom on a regular basis. Susan has a master's degree in library science, and in the art of the oral tradition, and is presently teaching a graduate course on incorporating storytelling into the kindergarten through eighth-grade curriculum. E-mail: sselk@fairfield.K12.ct.us.

A STORY WITHOUT WORDS
By Lizanne Wilson

> *"I hope that there will be many more days like today."*
>
> —Andrea D, age 10

National Standards:

NAS 4: Students should develop an understanding of the earth in the solar system; NAS 7: Students develop an understanding of the history of science; CNAEA (Theater) 1: Students should understand script writing by planning and recording improvisations, based on personal experience and heritage, imagination, literature and history; CNAEA (Theater) 3: Students should understand design by visualization and arranging environments for classroom dramatizations; CNAEA (Dance) 1: Students should identify and demonstrate movement elements and skills in performing dance; NCSS III: Students should be able to explain why individuals and groups respond differently to their physical and social environments.

Objectives:

Students will create scenes using characters from myths; understand and use drama terms; understand the tools of drama—mind, voice, body, and imagination; understand and identify the parts of a story; work together cooperatively in large and small groups to create ideas; express ideas non-verbally using the mind, the body, and the imagination; explore another culture through myth.

Resources and Materials:

- A space where students can move about freely
- A variety of recorded music
- Simple expressionless masks for each adult and child in the room
- Paper and pencil or notebook for journaling
- Sturdy chairs
- Access to mirrors
- Chart paper and markers
- Exercises for exploration and skill building are adapted or are from:

Appel, Libby. Mask Characterization: An Acting Process. Carbondale and Edwardsville: Southern Illinois University Press, 1982. Board of Trustees, Southern Illinois University. Used with permission.

McCaughrean, Geraldine. "The Bat and the Basket, A Kono Myth from Sierra Leone," Starry Tales. Margaret K. McElderry, 2001. Ages 9–12. ISBN: 0689830157.

- *For masks: Comfortable cotton-covered neutral masks. Tom Thumb Crafts, 1026 Davis St., Evanston, IL 60201. 847-869-9575.*

Instructional Plan:

In the spring of 2004 our school was invited to pilot the program *Sky Tellers, the Myths, the Magic, and the Mysteries of the Universe.* The National Science Foundation and the International Storytelling Center, wanting to connect science concepts and storytelling, developed this program to research how using folktales might inform student understanding of the same astronomical event. Thinking ahead to the solar system unit the next fall, the fourth-grade classroom teachers recognized the value of this model for using myths, legends, and folktales to explore the sun, moon, stars, and seasons. Eager to enrich our unit, the classroom teachers and the drama teacher decided to synthesize a previously taught mask unit with a focus of myths explaining the sun, moon, stars, and seasons.

Phase I—Exploration and Skill Building Have a neutral full-face mask for each child and each teacher in the class. The drama teacher presents mask workshops based on the work of Appel's *Mask Characterization: An Acting Process*. The mask work frees the students to develop a variety of movement styles and to explore movement first, without the constraints of story or character. Everyone should practice with a mirror to demonstrate how the mask takes away the ability to use facial expressions and demands physical expression. In mask, only the body is the tool for expression, and expansive movements allow the children to "read" the emotions expressed.

"You're nothing, but you are everybody."

—Cathy, age 10

A Sample Day
Warm-up: To prevent injuries and to focus the group, always begin class with movement (without the mask) where the students stretch and warm up their bodies.

Getting to know the mask: Through your attitude, and by following a set protocol to put on the mask and begin the workshop, students learn to respect the mask and their work in the mask. Sequential directions that the teacher demonstrates and in which children participate are:

1. Prepare to don the mask.
2. Stand still, tall, with focus.
3. Take time to regulate the breath (in for a count of four, out for a count of four).
4. Remain silent from now until the end of the exercise. Put your energy into movement and exploration instead of talking.
5. Cradle the mask in your hands.
6. Turn the face of the mask toward you.
7. Study the mask for a moment.
8. When you are still and your mind is focused, put on the mask.

Exploring the Room (20–30 minutes): The teacher must allow enough time for the students to move beyond the (inevitable) silliness that lasts about ten to fifteen minutes and to fall into a deep exploration. When students realize that they have time to explore, they will shed their preconceptions, their imaginations will open up, and they will begin to explore.

After introductory exercises, the children work in mask in the room. Play different qualities of music without lyrics for thirty-second to two-minute intervals and give the following directions: "Explore the room in your mask. You must keep your focus on the mask. If you need to lift the mask to breathe, do so, but stay focused on your assignment." Guidelines from Appel include: 1. Work alone. 2. Devise no stories. 3. Do not pretend to be anyone else. 4. Create no sensory illusions. 5. Do not touch anyone or their personal belongings. 6. Inspect the room. 7. Live in the moment.

The teacher's job is to maintain a safe environment for the students to explore. To maintain focus and expand the sense of freedom, students and teachers should remain free of value judgments about the students' work. Give vocal direction regularly to move them to explore more thoroughly. The teacher sets the tone for the entire class. If the teacher remains focused and has the courage to expect students to work deeply for fifteen to thirty minutes, they will do so.

"My face is expressionless, but yet alive."

—Cate, age 10

After every class students reflect in an open-ended manner in their journal.

"I took care of another body. I was the body."

—Terry, age 10

Phase II—Applying the Skills in Small Ensemble Work and Creating an Outline for Performance Introduce the myth: Read or tell the myth "The Bat and the Basket" from Sierra Leone and have the students orally retell the myth. Summarize the myth and list the characters, beginning, middle, and ending. Mark the conflict or "trouble, trouble, trouble" in the developing outline of the myth.

Managing the students to work on the myth: Have the class divide the story into three scenes (beginning, middle, end). Encourage students to outline the action in the story. Break the class into groups of four or five; each group creates a tableau—a frozen moment from the story using all the actors in the group where actors do not speak or move. Someone can take a picture of the tableau to help clarify the concept and allow for further reflection. Students create a headline or title for their group's frozen picture. The frozen pictures/ tableaux and their respective headlines provide the rough draft of the piece.

Phase III—Putting it Together—Rehearsal and Casting The entire piece was cast and rehearsed for four to six class periods, with actors in mask and narrators connecting the threads of the story. Students chose their roles through a child-driven democratic process. By the time the students finished the outline, they had a collective vision for the finished performance. Students also acted as stage managers, assistant stage managers, and script supervisor. Participation in the ensemble work is mandatory, but the way students participate is limited only by the group's imagination.

Finally, students worked on the sections of the story that most excited them. By the time we sequenced the story and shaped transitions for performance, the class had enough skills and had a "muscle memory" of the story. When it came time to share our work, the children had done almost all of the creative work.

Assessments:

Videotaping at intervals throughout the process, anecdotal records, journal entries, and still photography. We taped our debriefing session and self-evaluations at the end of the unit.

An actor, teacher, and educational consultant, Lizanne Wilson has worked as the drama specialist at Baker Demonstration School since 1995. Along with her work with elementary and middle school students, her teaching ranges from the university to the creation of the Performing Apprentice Program at the Children's Theatre Company in Minneapolis to working as a resident artist in Chicago Public Schools. Her essays on teaching and motherhood are featured on public radio stations across the country on Mombo: A Radio Resource for Mothers. *In 2002, the Illinois Theatre Association recognized her with an award for Outstanding Contribution in Creative Drama. E-mail: lizannewilson@sbcglobal.net.*

HISTORIC ARTIFACTS ARE DOORWAYS INTO THE STORIES OF THE PAST
By Brian "Fox" Ellis

National Standards:

NCTE 4: Students adjust their use of spoken, written, and visual language to communicate effectively with a variety of audiences; NCTE 5: Students employ a wide range of strategies as they write and use different writing elements appropriately to communicate with different audiences for a variety of purposes; NCTE 6: Students apply knowledge of language structure, language conventions, media techniques, figurative language, and genre to create, critique print and non-print texts; NCTE 11: Students participate as knowledgeable, reflective, creative, and critical members of literacy communities; NCSS 2: Time, Continuity, and Change—Learners gain experience with sequencing to establish a sense of order and time; students enjoy hearing stories of the past as well as of long ago; NCSS 3: People, Places, and Environment—Learners draw upon immediate personal experiences as a basis for exploring geographic concepts and skills; NCSS 4: Individual Development and

Identity—Learners develop their persona; identities in the context of families, peers, schools, and communities; central to this development are the exploration, identification, and analysis of how individuals relate to others.

Objectives:

Using basic research skills, write historically accurate fiction; have hands-on experience with museum artifacts (anthropology and archaeology); use storytelling to improve writing and rewriting skills.

Materials:

- A suitcase, trunk, box, or trade blanket of historical artifacts, beads, arrowheads, furs, spoons, old glasses, tools, and assorted historical bric-a-brac. (These are easily acquired from a local historical society, museum, library, or nature center that has an educational loan program. It could even be a collection of old junk from your grandma's attic or grandpa's garage!)
- Writing materials such as pen and paper or word processors

Perhaps this oversimplifies, but I like to think of a museum as a large box full of stories. Archaeologists, paleontologists, and anthropologists are all professional storytellers at heart, who collect and study interesting artifacts and objects. In this hands-on active lesson, you will learn to turn historic artifacts into a dynamic writing exercise and a storytelling opportunity for children.

Historical objects are vessels for stories, doorways into tales of the past. Students' intrinsic curiosity and excitement are easily sparked when they have a really cool object to talk about. With an object in hand, the student becomes active and interactive, an optimum learning situation. Their stories flow naturally and can be shaped into both solid writing and entertaining storytelling.

Instructional Plan:

Whatever history is being taught, about the French Explorers, Lewis and Clark, sod-busting prairie farmers on the Oregon Trail, WWII, the Civil War, or the poverty of the Great Depression, it is important to begin with stories. Dramatically tell or read aloud stories of the type that you want students to write and tell. Stories give students solid models of good historical fiction.

During an artist-in-residence program, I begin with a large assembly. After the performance, I visit each classroom and help the students write their own historical fiction. Spreading a fur trapper's trade blanket filled with accurate reproductions of historical artifacts, I model the process: I pick up an object, hold it to my ear, and, in a comic fashion, move it away, saying, "No," hold it back to my ear, and then say, "Really, You don't say? Listen, this artifact just told me this wonderful story … " Then, I tell them the tale. It is best if the teacher invents a story based on an artifact he has in his hands.

After the story, we discuss what questions students should ask and answer in their stories. Every artifact actually tells several stories: what the materials are, how it was made, how it was used, and how it got here, but right now we are acquiring information about the artifact and ideas for stories.

Students line up and walk past the artifacts, perhaps arrowheads, beads, furs, antique toys, cattail dolls, bark rattles, miniature canoes, claw necklaces, musket balls, horn spoons, Jefferson Peace Medals, and other historic artifacts. They pick up one object that catches their attention. They are not to linger at the table. Grab something and go!

Back at their seats, students choose a partner to discuss their artifact. Partners help each other focus on the questions and the artifacts. In their conversation, they discuss the following questions, which are written out.

- What is it?
- What is it made from or what is the raw material?
- How was this material acquired?
- Who made it?
- Step by step, how was it made?
- Why did they make it? How did they use it?
- Where was it found? And how did it get here?

Students need to answer one question well, but not with a short phrase or a strictly factual answer; the response should turn into a story. After the initial telling to a partner, students write their story in a narrative. Because this is historical fiction, it is important and appropriate to guess, to imagine, to make up part of the story, but researching the object will produce more interesting, accurate details to include. So, it's off to the library to flesh out details and discover what else can be included without turning the story into a report.

Telling and Listening: I review active listening behavior and good telling techniques. Students choose a new partner and retell the story. Retelling is a way of reshaping, reworking, rewriting their story. I challenge them to watch their partner watch the story. If they look confused, explain it. If they look excited or scared, stretch this part out and build on the strengths. If they look bored, then make something happen! Based on this telling, students may add to their research and adjust the story before they write a final draft.

Assessments:

Because this is a holistic activity, research and writing and telling may be assessed. A pre- and post-test of children's writing can be administered, aimed at the use of writing conventions, grammar, details, historical accuracy, and general appeal. Over the next week, encourage students to tell their story to the class each day. Exceptional stories, well told, can be allowed to travel. Students can perform for other classes. Students can even host a school-wide assembly or parent night!

Having an object in hand to talk about, motivate research, and share with their friends makes it easy for students to see themselves as storytellers. The artifact invites a story. Telling stories makes it easier to write. The whole process makes history visceral and alive!

I am often amazed at the imaginative quality of the writing and the evocative nature of the performance. At a recent residency, the fifth-grade students who performed at the end of the week were confident and engaging. A visiting scholar from a local museum asked about recruiting students to interpret at the museum!

An energetic and experienced storyteller, Brian "Fox" Ellis emphasizes the natural and historical environment. In the field of outdoor education, Brian is often invited as a keynoter or workshop presenter at major conferences. As teller, he performs regularly at festivals, conferences, and schools. He has books, CDs, and magazine articles to his credit. He is a founder and performer at the Prairie Folklore Theatre. Web site: http://www.foxtalesint.com.

TEACHING THE WORLD WE LIVE IN: COLLECTING AND TELLING ETHNOGRAPHIC STORIES
By Mark Wagler

National Standards:

NCTE 3: Apply a wide range of strategies to comprehend, interpret, and evaluate texts; NCTE 4: Adjust spoken, written, and visual language to communicate effectively and accomplish a purpose; NCTE 7: Gather, evaluate, and synthesize data; NCTE 12: Use spoken, written, and visual language to accomplish their own purposes; NCSS I: Interact with other students, some of whom are like the student and some different; NCSS II: Begin to recognize that individuals may hold different views about the past and to understand the linkages between human decisions and consequences; NCSS III: Draw upon immediate personal experiences as a basis for exploring geographic concepts and skills; NCSS X: Develop their personal identities in the context of families, peers, schools, and communities.

Objectives:

Find, record, and present ethnographic stories; increase understanding and acceptance of other cultures; use ethnographic techniques to find and create stories in every academic domain.

Ethnographic stories are accounts of everyday life, told with everyday language, with an awareness of cultural context. Ethnography, the hands-on and in-depth study of contemporary culture, uses interviews and observations to describe a person or group. These descriptions are often learned and reported at least partially as stories. Storytelling and ethnography are ideally braided together in the classroom. *We live in a world of stories*, and indeed experience our lives as stories. Culture is most commonly explained and transmitted through accounts of how and why things are the way they are. *Storytelling is our native language*. All of us heard and told narratives long before we read and wrote expositions. The most efficient way for students to learn language arts and social studies is in a mutual context where form and content, language and local culture, are learned simultaneously—with ethnographic stories.

During the years I worked as a full-time storyteller and folklorist, I directed ethnographic projects with students ranging from primary grades

During an immigrant simulation, an associate teacher tells of her escape from Saigon to Malaysia by boat in 1968. From Malaysia, Mrs. Truong and her husband immigrated to Chicago, the "Land of Freedom."

through graduate school. Here, I will focus on projects in my fourth- and fifth-grade classrooms at Randall School in Madison, Wisconsin, from as simple as a single homework assignment to as complicated as a yearlong investigation of communities, but the strategies described can be adapted for all grade levels. I will give examples of the ethnographic stories we find, record, and present in the course of our conscious study of local culture and show how "story" structures the classroom introductory lessons, the "field work" assignments, and the reports students give of their inquiries.

Every year my students investigate family home remedies—as an introduction to the study of health beliefs and institutions. Typically I begin the lesson with an anecdote about regularly losing my voice while performing stories until I went to an ear, nose, and throat specialist who suggested I gargle with warm salt water, exactly what my mother prescribed when I was young. *Stories beget stories.* Soon our whole class is begging to tell brief accounts of remedies for everything from hiccups to headaches. At that point I give them their homework: a list of common health symptoms with the assignment to interview a parent or grandparent about remedies for each symptom. The next day, students have many more short stories as they tell their favorite remedies.

This same format (a beginning example and discussion, a homework assignment, and reports from students the following day) can be used for every cultural element, from music, foodways, and rites of passage to occupations, transportation, and decision-making. Sometimes a short lesson can expand to a longer project. Last fall, for example, I introduced a lesson on family storytelling by asking, "Who tells the best stories in your family?"

I illustrated with several humorous stories my Uncle Dave used to tell that reflected on our Amish heritage. As he sat in our Ohio farm kitchen getting his hair cut by my dad, he told this story in our German dialect.

> There was an Amishman in a horse and buggy going to market along Route 8, with a crate of eggs between his feet. Back then there was a trolley car line in the middle of the road going between Canton and Akron. Well, the trolley came along, spooked his horse. He planted his feet, pulled back hard on the reins, but it took him half a mile to stop the horse. When he looked down, he saw he had his boots in the crate of eggs; he looked back up the road, "'*S waar Oyer-Dutch der ganzser Weeg zrick*" ("It was scrambled eggs all the way back").

Many students raised their hands with their favorite storytellers and their stories. Next I asked, "What makes these stories excellent?" and "When and where are these stories most often told in your family?" Their homework assignment followed: to make a list of "some of the most important stories in your family" and the tellers and occasions for each story. The next day, many complete family stories were told in our class. The students asked to be allowed to write out family stories for homework that evening, an assignment they asked to be continued every night for more than three weeks, with family storytelling in class nearly every day. At the end of the project, each student wrote an eight-page essay, telling some of their favorite family stories, with introductions to each so that readers would understand the culture expressed in these narratives.

Rosa began her essay, "The stories are organized by time, starting with my great-great-great-great-grandmother to my mom and then me." Danny wrote, "When my Grandma lived in Chicago things were much different. ... My Grandma would always go down to the organ grinder and give a penny to the monkey to hear a song from the grinder. ... The ragman ... would always come outside and start saying, 'Rags and old iron, rags and old iron.'" Giulia told the story of her grandparents meeting in a *favela* in Brazil and getting married with the governor of Rio de Janeiro as their best man. And Sam concluded, "These stories have brought me much closer to my family."

We spent all of last year studying neighborhood cultures along nearby Park Street, the most diverse community in Madison—and told ethnographic stories during every step of our process. In the beginning, to spark their curiosity, I told anecdotes about some of my favorite Park Street neighbors and places: the shoe repair man, the world-class jazz bassist, the families of former students, and the fishermen along Wingra Creek. Soon the students in my class who lived near Park Street joined in by saying, "Oh, I know him!" or "I've been there!" Fourth-grade students caught the fever for doing ethnographic study by looking at the Web sites from previous classroom cultural tours and by hearing the stories returning fifth graders told about documenting Hmong culture the year before in seven cities throughout Wisconsin.

On our cultural tours, students take photos, make drawings, and write lots of notes, typically five to twenty pages in a day. As Nikki wrote, "You look for things when you're taking notes." When we return to the classroom, students use their notes and visual images to write articles for a student journal, create Web pages, make videos, design museum exhibits, and participate in international classroom networks. Along the way, students use every language art, explore most of the national social studies and arts education standards, and change the way they see the world. "It's a rich cultural area, seriously diverse," Izzy wrote. "Before we went on this tour, Park Street was a black box of secrets. But after the cultural tour, I felt like a detective who just solved the mystery." Alexandra echoed, "I felt like a whole new world had opened up for me."

Ethnographic stories show up briefly anytime in our classroom: as examples in math story problems, reflections on doing scientific investigations, instances examined in social studies, connections to books we read, illustrations of writing strategies, and processes in building classroom community. Whether improvised to grab attention in other content areas, or planned as a short assignment or a long-term project, ethnographic stories in our classroom, just like in the real world, bring us to the center of the universe—where people learn with stories.

To sample the ethnographic stories students recorded and retold about Park Street, go to http://csumc.wisc.edu/cmct/ParkStreetCT/index.htm. Detailed lesson plans on doing classroom ethnography (*Teacher's Guide to Local Culture*) with accompanying student materials (*Kids' Field Guide to Local Culture*) are available as pdf files at http://csumc.wisc.edu/cmct/ HmongTour/howwedidit/index.htm.

Assessments:

Assessment is ongoing during the school year: oral and written narratives demonstrate students' current depth of understanding; over time, a developing ability to relate these stories to everyday life or to the literature, history, and science being studied demonstrates deepening understanding and cultural acceptance.

Mark Wagler (mwagler@wisc.edu) has told stories, taught storytelling, and guided folklore projects in more than 700 schools and in hundreds of other educational settings. Recipient of a Presidential Award for Excellence in Mathematics and Science Teaching, he weaves narrative pedagogy into his entire curriculum at Randall School in Madison, Wisconsin. He was the first president of Northlands Storytelling Network; co-director of Heads & Tales, an international conference on storytelling in education; director of two year-long teacher-training programs with the University of Wisconsin on storytelling in the language arts and social studies; and is co-author of Kids' Field Guide to Local Culture.

KINDRED KEEPSAKES: INSPIRING CHILDREN TO WRITE THROUGH ORAL HISTORY STORYTELLING
By Lainie Levin and Yvonne Healy

National Standards:

NCTE 4: Using language to communicate effectively; NCTE 5: Communicating with different audiences; NCTE 6: Creating, critiquing, and discussing texts; NCTE 7: Conducting research; NCTE 9: Respecting diversity in language use; Participating in literacy communities; NCTE 12: Using language to accomplish a purpose; NCSS: All strands.

Objectives:

Learn active listening, questioning, and interviewing techniques; learn story structure; develop a story from an elder's anecdote; learn peer coaching methods; transition between oral and written story; learn written story revision through peer editing; present story orally; publish story in written form.

"Reluctant writer" was Dominic's middle name. Asked to compose a journal entry, he stared into space for twenty minutes, complaining, "I have nothing to say."

Dominic's typical final product averaged eighteen disjointed words. After completing the program outlined below, he emerged with a nine-sentence story, averaging fifteen words per sentence. Dominic's comment: "I didn't know I was a writer!"

Kindred Keepsakes is the family history experience of teaching writing through storytelling and oral history. Children realize they have "something to say," and teachers discover how important it is to incorporate oral storytelling into the writing curriculum.

The full unit as developed by a classroom teacher and a professional storyteller, Lainie Levin and Yvonne Healy, spans three months, averaging ninety minutes of class time weekly. It streamlines successfully to fit twelve-hour artist residencies. While Kindred Keepsakes works best as a whole, each component is valuable in its own context. Interviewing elders and playing additional games increases both the time needed and students' development.

Resources and Materials:

- Required: Professional storytellers (live or recorded), TV, senior citizens (preferably family)
- Optional: Audiotape recorder, video camera, adult assistance

Instructional Process:

1. Interviewing. Students learn from masters by observing professional storytellers sharing family stories and watching television talk shows. Children learn interview skills and practice creating questions that elicit stories before arranging interviews with family elders.

   One game invented to develop interviewing skills is called "Mother, May I?" because students play by saying "magic words." In pairs, one student makes observations about the room using the senses of sight, smell, touch, and sound. The listener repeats the observations exactly. Switch.

   After learning basic question starters, students learn kinesthetic cues for questioning. Counting each of five fingers, the child's "Handy Outline" reveals story elements: Someone / Wants / Something / But / Then. Counting the five senses on the second hand, students discover that sensory prompts encourage subjects to talk and to remember overlooked details ("What did it smell/look/feel/sound like?").

2. Recording. Each child records a thirty- to sixty-minute interview with an elder. Ideally, this is recorded on audio- or videotape. For families, this step is invaluable, providing a priceless keepsake. Regardless of access to equipment, this step is possible. Students can conduct interviews in another language, over the phone, even with written notes or drawings.

3. Storytelling. In this most intensive stage, students reshape anecdotes from their interviews into stories. One method is to compose story "skeletons" by drawing or writing comic strips called storyboards. In the "Touch and Tell" game, students tell stories orally while touching each picture and explaining its action.

   Students play the "Three Bears Game" for supportive peer coaching and editing. Rather than waiting for a teacher's critique, students revise in response to a partner's immediate feedback. The coach/editor does not "fix what's wrong," but lets the teller/writer know what is likable. In both oral and writing coaching, feedback is given by offering:
   Twin Baby Bears: two things that are "just right" with the story.
   Mama Bear: what is "too little" in the story?
   Papa Bear: what is "too much" in the story?
   Begin peer coaching by teaching how to offer "Baby Bears." When students can easily offer supportive advice, the class can be taught to offer "Mama and Papa Bears."

4. Transitioning from oral to written story. If our brains are the cheetahs of our body, and our mouths are the rabbits, our hands are the snails. When teachers ask students to write, they essentially tell students that the cheetah and the snail must keep pace! Oral language levels the playing field by helping children organize thoughts effectively. Reluctant writers excitedly discover the connection between their thoughts and written language.

   Students record stories onto audiotape, then transcribe them using pencil or keyboard. While not critical, adult assistance expedites transcription. Using the "Three Bears" model, students peer-edit written work.

5. Showcasing. Students publish for families and community via hand, computer or copy machine printouts, local newspapers, Web site posting, or by entering a contest. Students perform stories in family or school concerts.

Assessments:

Rubrics are the ideal assessment for the interview, performance, and written story. They document measurable progress and specifically address curricular expectations. Ideally, teachers allow students to help create rubrics and share them before each step is completed (See following samples). Students find greater success because they know what they need to accomplish.

Conclusion:

Kindred Keepsakes affected our students in very real ways. Maya was a painfully shy girl. Never speaking above a whisper or seeking companionship, she endured school alone, unnoticed. Not once did she smile. Her parents didn't realize the depth of Maya's unease in social situations. Teachers' reports were incompatible with the energetic sprite they knew. Inspired by love for her grandfather and pride in her work, Maya willingly volunteered to perform publicly at a springtime concert. Perched on folding chairs in the gym, her parents saw Maya as she was at school—a scared child retreating

KID DESIGNED RUBRIC SAMPLES

INTERVIEWING RUBRIC

The interviewer... _____
                                        Name

_____	**Sat still.**
_____	**Did not play with papers, etc.**
_____	**Looked at the person s/he interviewed.**
_____	**Appeared interested and respectful.**
_____	**Spoke loudly.**
_____	**Spoke clearly.**
_____	**Gave the other person a chance to speak without interruption.**
_____	**Had questions organized.**
_____	**Gave meaningful responses.**
_____	**Asked questions to follow up on stories and ideas.**

Score: _____/10

Comments/suggestions: _____

Story Telling Rubric

The storyteller... _____
                                        Name

_____	**Remembered a strong entrance & closing.**
_____	**Was loud enough to be heard, even in back.**
_____	**Spoke clearly enough to be understood.**
_____	**Created mental images in the story.**
_____	**Controlled volume, pitch and speed.**
_____	**Made the audience feel comfortable.**
_____	**Kept his/her spot without fidgeting.**
_____	**Acted story out using hands and body.**

Score: _____/8

Comments/suggestions: _____

Kid-Designed Rubric Samples.

within herself. They helped Maya receive professional counseling. The next fall, she returned to school ready to play, ready to participate—smiling.

Perhaps most precious is the undying keepsake that families gain. By project's end, one of the families lost its elder. Through listening to elders, children opened windows into a life unknown and treasured stories that endure.

Lainie Levin has been a storyteller since the ripe old age of ten. Drawing from her Jewish heritage, world cultures, and her own experiences, Lainie crafts stories that "tickle the funny bone and touch the heart." Career highlights include Jackson Storyfest, Fox Valley Storytelling Festival, the Detroit Art Institute, and the Missouri River Storytelling Festival. As a veteran teacher and versatile storyteller, Lainie is no stranger to teaching workshops. She has high expectations for workshops, especially her own. As a result, attendees leave inspired and empowered to act. Topics presented include "Kindred Keepsakes" and "The Busy Teacher's Guide to Storytelling." E-mail: Lainlev@ yahoo.com.

Yvonne Healy is "an Irish pixie of a performer!" Mythology, history, an outrageous family, and a theatrical background converge in her highenergy performances. Healy's audio/video recordings and writings have earned Gold Awards from National Parenting Publications, Children's Music Organization, and America's Story Festival. Educated through Swarthmore College, Tufts University, and continuing professional studies, Healy completes the cycle by teaching in elementary and secondary school residencies nationwide and near her Michigan home. In college classes, professional conferences, keynotes, and workshops, Healy trains others to use her unique methods to foster literacy and explore history. Information is online at www. YHealy.com.

COYOTE AND SKUNK WOMAN: A JOURNEY INTO THE DESERT
By Darlene Neumann

National Standards:

NCSS 4: Students should understand the physical and human characteristics of places; students should understand that people create regions to interpret Earth's complexity; students should understand how culture and experience influence people's perceptions of places and regions.

Objectives:

Gain an understanding of how Native Americans used stories to instruct children; locate and read information on deserts and desert animals to increase their background knowledge; tell a Coyote story.

Resources and Materials:

- "Coyote and Skunk Woman," found in *Navajo Coyote Tales*, is a required resource for this modified unit.
- Books from the media center on deserts and desert animals will be needed for research.
- Internet sites will have information, but reading levels may be high. Sites with pictures and diagrams are especially helpful.

"Coyote and Skunk Woman"
A Navajo story of the trickster Coyote who meets his match in
Skunk Woman

As Coyote was walking in an arroyo, he called for rain to cool him and carry him to many prairie dogs. He asked Skunk Woman to tell the other animals that he was dead. She told Rabbit who told Porcupine who told the prairie dogs. They all went down to the river to see that dead coyote. After Skunk Woman sprayed into their eyes, she and Coyote killed all the other animals. They built a fire, setting the prairie dogs to roast. Coyote suggested they race while they waited. Skunk Woman hid while Coyote ran by. She ate the prairie dogs, stuck their tails upright in the fire, and hid in her hole. When Coyote returned, he decided to eat the prairie dogs before Skunk Woman arrived. He pulled tail after tail out of the fire and went to find Skunk Woman, demanding that she share the prairie dogs. She told him his part was in the fire, but that he could have the bones, as well. Coyote had to be content with the tails and bones.

Instructional Plan:

Our fourth-grade social studies curriculum includes an extensive unit on regions of the United States. Novels set in specific regions are integrated into the unit. As media center director, I was invited to take a reading group for one of two novels: *Lost in the Devil's Desert* (Louis Sachar, Farrar, Straus and Giroux, 1998) or *Holes* (Gloria Skurzynski, Lothrop, Lee & Shepard, 1982). I knew neither would be appropriate for my group of concrete, literal thinkers who were reading at the second-grade level. The challenge would be to find reading material to support the curriculum with differentiated content, while connecting with what the rest of the class was reading.

My nine children brainstormed what they "knew" about the desert. The challenge would be to reexamine their "facts" and to locate stimulating material at their reading level to increase background knowledge. I felt that nothing could be more interesting, entertaining, and instructional than Coyote stories. We discussed how the Navajo people, during long winter nights, used stories to teach clan history and to teach children right from wrong.

I handed out *Navajo Coyote Tales*. "Coyote and Skunk Woman" became their favorite. Although I had not suggested storytelling, the group decided they'd like to tell this story for all the fourth graders.

I asked strategic yet factual questions: "What is an arroyo? Do listeners need to know what an arroyo is?" They decided it was important and should look up "arroyo." Our school library yielded books containing descriptions and photos of arroyos. The group realized that if *they* didn't know what an arroyo was, their audience probably wouldn't either, so they decided to make a poster showing an arroyo. Their finished poster showed exactly what an arroyo is and explained why Coyote needed to be careful in the sudden rainfall.

The students began asking questions about characters. Why was the skunk called a spotted skunk? Didn't all skunks have stripes, like ones that live in our state? Maybe the audience would need another poster to see what the spotted skunk really was. Did the other fourth graders really know what a coyote or a porcupine looked like? Was the rabbit like ones that run in our backyards? Research began in books that were quite readable and then on Web sites written at a much higher level. As curiosity and enthusiasm grew, so did the level of understanding.

Because each student had told a story at our Storytelling Festival earlier in the school year, each of them knew they could tell a story. The hardest parts of telling this Coyote story had already been done because the story had been chosen, read, and reread, and research had strengthened understanding. Students divided the story into segments, focusing on characters. Rereading increased fluency and boosted confidence. After considerable practice sessions, students were ready to tell the story and to share information while using their posters. They had become so excited about their research that some of their favorite facts made their way into the telling of the Coyote story. While local striped skunks just raise their tails, spray, and run, a spotted skunk stands on her front paws and aims her spray directly at her prey's eyes, so that's what Skunk Woman did!

Students invited parents, the principal, special area teachers, special education staff, fourth-grade peers, and second-grade reading buddies. After a confident telling of the Coyote story, colorful posters filled with information about arroyos, the spotted skunk, the jackrabbit, porcupines, and prairie dogs were shared with the audience.

Classroom teachers said that if they hadn't known these children required differentiated curriculum and accommodations, they would never have guessed from their storytelling and their well-researched posters. Parents said that their children could hardly wait to come to reading class. Students said they couldn't believe they had so much fun reading. A mother told me that her daughter had said, "The kids who teased me were wrong: I really can read, and I'm a great storyteller!"

Darlene Neumann is a storyteller and library media specialist. With her clear, pleasing voice and her engaging facial expressions, she paints compelling pictures, inviting children and adults to laugh and cry and revel in the joy of stories. Darlene tells world folktales and shares bittersweet stories about growing up on a Southern Illinois farm. She has told at festivals, international schools, and public libraries, and has conducted storytelling workshops at library conferences, educational conferences, and universities. She coordinates an annual storytelling festival at her school in which each fourth and fifth grader, and some younger students, tells a story. Darlene helps the students choose, learn, and tell their stories. She is also an adjunct professor in storytelling at National-Louis University in Evanston, Illinois. E-mail Darlene at ldneu@tds.net.

LAZY JACK: ELAPSED TIME
By Mike Anderson

National Standards:

NCTM (Measurement) 2: Apply appropriate techniques, tools, and formulas to determine measurements.

Objectives:

Use previously made clocks to practice finding elapsed time; record findings on a data collection sheet and/or create bar graphs to display the collected data.

Materials:

- 11″ × 14″ pieces of poster board for each student
- Brass brads
- Timekeeper's Sheet for each student

The Math Lesson—Elapsed Time Practice:

In this story-based activity, the students will use previously made clocks to practice finding elapsed time. Through cooperative groups, or individually, the students will record their findings on a data collection sheet as well as create bar graphs to display the collected data.

Before beginning the lesson, students make clocks using an 11″ × 14″ piece of poster board. Each student draws/traces two circles onto the poster board, then numbers the clock face (typically, putting on 12, 3, 6, 9 and then adding the other numbers works best). Clock hands are then made and attached to the clock using brass brads.

Then explain that students will be using their clocks to measure elapsed time (the time it takes for something to happen or be accomplished) on a Timekeeper's Sheet (see example below). As the story is being told, the students will individually record the beginning and ending times on the Timekeepers Sheet. Elapsed time is figured when the story is over, using the student-made clocks.

Tell "Lazy Jack," incorporating time elements as demonstrated in the sample below. The complete text of this Jack tale—minus the time elements, of course—can be found in many sources, including *Lazy Jack* by Tony Ross (Dial Books, 1986, c1985).

TIMEKEEPER'S SHEET	Starting time	Ending time	Elapsed Time
1st Event			
2nd Event			
3rd Event			
4th Event			
5th Event			

Timekeeper's Sheet.

Lazy Jack: A Jack Tale, adapted by Mike Anderson

I wouldn't say Jack was lazy, but he sure didn't want to do much besides eat and sleep. One day his mama impressed upon him that he needed to get himself a job and help support the family. The conversation went something like this:

Mama: Jack, you get up and go earn some money otherwise I'm only gonna give you half of what you normally eat!
Jack: OK, Mama.

It was a simple conversation that got the message across in a way Jack could understand. You see, Jack wasn't the most colorful crayon in the box.

That evening Jack went to bed at 10:00 p.m. and got up at 5:45 a.m. Jack sat down to a sumptuous breakfast of fifteen pancakes, six eggs, four glasses of milk, and a bunch of pieces of bacon at 6:15. He didn't finish eating until 7:00 a.m.!

Jumping up from the table, Jack ran to the farmer's house. He got there at 7:45 a.m.

"Mr. Farmer, do you have any work for me to do?"

"Why, yes I do, Jack. I want you to chop these logs into firewood. Can you do that, Jack?"

"Yes, Sir!" replied Jack and he set to work. He chopped that wood from 8:00 a.m. until 12:00 noon.

The farmer was amazed at how much wood Jack had chopped and paid him a dollar!

Jack left work at _____. Jack ran all the way home holding his dollar. Unfortunately Jack's hands were tired from all that chopping and

the dollar slipped from his fingers and vanished before he got home at
_____.

Jack's mama wasn't happy about losing the dollar.

"Jack, when you get money like that you gotta put it in your pocket so you don't lose it!"

"Yes, Mama."

Here is the basic format for the rest of the story (note that the teller should change the elapsed time for each job):

Jack slept from _____ to _____.
Ate breakfast from _____ to _____.
Ran to the farmer's house from ____ to _____.
Worked from _____ to _____
Left work at _____ got home at _____.

The students can use the Timekeeper's Sheet to answer the extended lesson questions. So that the students are not overwhelmed with data, one bit of the story can be used to answer questions, such as the examples below:

1. As the week of Jack's working goes on, his breakfast time gets shorter. Which day did he eat the longest? Which was the shortest? Make a bar graph showing this data.
2. He's tired going home after a long day; how long does it take?
3. How different is this from his time going to work?
4. On which day was he the fastest or the slowest?
5. Does the difference in his travel time change from day to day? Why? Make a bar graph showing this data.
6. Which job took the longest? Which was the shortest? What is the elapsed time difference between the longest job and the shortest job? Make a bar graph showing this data.

For a cooperative group of four, four jobs can be assigned: beginning time setter, ending time setter, the clock master (the one who figures out the elapsed time), and the timekeeper. The jobs rotate after each elapsed time situation in the story.

For the following advanced questions, you'll need to alter the way the story is told:

1. Getting up from the table, Jack runs to the farmer's door. It takes him 12 minutes to get there. What time did he get there?
2. He left the house at 6:30 and got to the farmer's house 15 minutes later. When did he get there?
3. He started chopping wood at 7:05. He quit for lunch at 11:18. He started working again at 12:35 and quit at 4:15. How long did he work that day?

If the students are not good at this skill, the story could be terminally long. An initial lesson may only include writing down the times on the Time-keeper's Sheet and/or making the hands on their clocks match the times. Older students may not need, or you may not want them to use, the class-made clocks. Putting in too many times can easily kill the story. Typically concentrating on just one repeated event is best.

Different groups can be responsible for different events. For example, Groups A and B can be recording breakfast times, Groups C and D can be recording travel times, and Group E and F can be recording work times. This technique can be used with any stories that have repeated events.

Assessments:

Timekeeper's Sheets and bar graphs reflect students' ability to determine elapsed time and record it accurately.

Mike Anderson, from Jacksonville, Illinois, weaves stories, songs, and a wide variety of musical instruments into performances that appeal to all ages. An award-winning teacher of thirty-plus years, Mike wrote and hosted an award-winning TV show. A recipient of multiple Parents' Choice Honors for his storytelling and children's recordings, Anderson has authored several books, including picture books, chapter books, and a book on how to make musical instruments, as well as several magazine articles concerning childhood fears. Mike is a popular presenter at conferences and workshops. He has numerous recordings available featuring storytelling, children's music, and mountain dulcimer. Find him on the Web at www.dulcimerguy.com.

FRACTION FRIENDS
By Gail N. Herman, Ph.D.

National Standards:

NCTM 1: Understand numbers, ways of representing numbers, relationships among numbers, and number systems; develop understanding of fractions as parts of unit wholes, as parts of a collection, as locations on number lines, and as divisions of whole numbers; recognize and generate equivalent forms of commonly used fractions, decimals, and percents.

Objective:

Demonstrate understanding of fractions as parts of unit wholes.

The "ahas!" students have with this storytelling activity are like light bulbs, especially for the children who need more experience with fractions!

Fraction Friends is an active storytelling strategy. It involves kinesthetic learning as well as visual (seeing movement and/or drawing) and verbal modes. Kinesthetic and visual learning have four main benefits over verbal alone: 1) they strengthen memory; 2) they deepen understanding; 3) they promote creative thinking; and 4) they encourage creative communication. When children use this mode of learning, they are feeling the motion and emotion (external and internal) in the environment and in their own bodies. In this lesson, becoming the fractions and seeing the parts move and remain are the keys to understanding.

Here is one of the stories I tell while children mime the characters. Children then create and act out their own stories.

Once upon a time there were six stuffed animals on a store shelf: a parrot, a crab, a frog, a turtle, a teddy bear, and a dinosaur. They were all talking about how they felt. Parrot bragged and spoke in a high, cackling voice, "I'm the best of all six of us. Awk, Awk, I'm the brightest 1/6. My colors cheer people up. I'll get picked before all of you."

The second animal was Crab, and it spoke in a crabby voice, "Nope! I'm the best 1/6 because I'm red and have funny little eyes and big claws. I'm better than real crabs; I'm soft and cuddly and never pinch."

Frog sounded a little sad. "It's not easy being green; green's never seen. I'm just the color of grass. No one will ever pick me." Frog shrugged and gave a heavy sigh.

Turtle was frightened and said, "I'm afraid to get sold. You go first, Crab. I'll just stay here and hide behind Frog so no one will see me."

Fuzzy Bear laughed, "Oh, Turtle, you don't get it at all! It's fun to play out there and get thrown around in the air. I hope I'm picked first." Bear tried to move in front of Frog and Turtle.

The last stuffed animal had a very, very big voice: "Tyrannosaurus. That's me! Call me Tyran for short. I'm the best 'cause I'm a King."

Suddenly, Parrot saw a girl. A hand went up to the shelf and squeezed all the animals. Parrot laughed, "'Bye, 5/6! I'm out of here because I have the brightest colors of all." A flash of color disappeared in a big shopping cart.

All the animals chanted, "'Bye 1/6! Have a good trip!"

"Hmmm," said Crab. "Now there are only five of us left. Only five of six animals left. Oh boy, here comes a grandmother! Maybe I'll be the one to get picked. Yes! She's picking meeeeee."

The rest of the animals said, "So long, 1/6."

Crab looked back at the four animals left and said, "'Bye, 4/6."

Turtle said, "You mean 2/3."

Crab sounded crabby again. "Oh, it's the same thing: 4/6 or 2/3! Whatever!" Crab knew they were six animals, but they were separated into three little groups with two in each group: Parrot and Crab were one group and were picked off the shelf. Then Turtle was hiding behind Frog, and finally Bear and Tyran were sitting together. So there were three little groups with two in each group. Two groups of the three little groups were left on the shelf, 2/3.

Just then, Frog noticed a little boy. "He's looking up and pointing at me. Here comes his mother and she's wearing a green dress! Wow! They like green. 'Bye, 3/6, I mean 1/2. Now half of us are picked."

The three animals on the shelf all said, "'Bye, 1/6."

Now that Frog was gone, Turtle hid behind Bear. Bear said, "Now look who is coming. Someone's wearing a cowboy hat. He probably likes only horses. Oh, wait. He says he wants to hold me."

"'Bye, 1/6," said Tyran to Bear. Turtle added sadly, "We'll miss you, Bear."

Bear wasn't sad at all, "'Bye, 2/6, I mean 1/3. I'm going to the ranch!"

As the lights went out in the store, Turtle and Tyran took deep sighs. "Maybe tomorrow, I'll get picked," said Tyran.

"Hopefully, I won't!" said frightened little Turtle.

And that's the story of Fraction Friends Six. What do you think will happen tomorrow?

Students discuss (some write or draw) their own stories to finish what happened next. The next day, after students share what happened to the other toys, I say, "Now you can create stories about fractions. We will personify parts of a whole. That means we will give human characteristics and feelings to non-living objects that are made of equal parts. We'll act it out!"

I arrange students in groups of three, four, five, six, seven, or more students. Each group decides what they will be. Suggestions: a fleet of cars on a lot, eggs in the refrigerator, a pie, a pack of gum, apples on a tree, etc.

Students discuss the following before performing their stories:

1. Describe how your character feels. Each character should be different. Is your character happy, sad, bragging, frightened, or angry? Speak with a different voice as you introduce yourself and tell how you feel.
2. Give hints about the setting. Example: If it's a refrigerator, you might say, "It's cold in here."
3. Tell who comes to buy or take you. Actually move away from the group. For example, for a pie with four parts, one can say, "Oh, good! Here comes the mother to take meeee. I can't wait. I'm going first. I'm getting out of this freezing cold. Here I goooo! 'Bye, 3/4." The remaining ones answer, "'Bye, 1/4." The second pie piece might say, "Oh, I don't want to leave, I'm scared! 'Bye, 2/4, I mean 1/2. I'll miss you! Sniff. Sniff." The rest of the pie says, "'Bye, 1/4." Of course, if you notice 2/4 are gone, one of you can say, "Wow, half of us are gone already."

4. Decide the ending. Will the story end when all of you are gone? Will one be left? Will everyone be reunited? Also, give the final word. For example, "And that's the story of the Fraction Friends Four!"

This storytelling activity is very successful in helping children conceptualize fractions—especially those kids who didn't get it before! Perhaps because they *became* a fractional part, or perhaps because they could *see* the parts moving away in groups, but whatever the reason, students say it helps them do better on their tests. Aha!

Assessments:

Ask each child to draw or write the group story, providing an opportunity to assess individual grasp of the concept of fractions.

Dr. Gail N. Herman is a professional storyteller, artist in residence, keynoter, and educator. She performs widely across the United States and in other countries. Most recently she collected and disseminated stories on a grant to Estonia, Lithuania, and Latvia. She teaches storytelling for Garrett College in Maryland, Lesley University, the University of Connecticut's Confratute, and the University of Louisiana at Lafayette. She directs a Tall Tale Festival and Tellebration. Gail is published in Better Homes and Gardens, Storytelling Journal, *and* Early Years, *and in the books* Joining In *and* Spinning Tales, Weaving Hope. *Contact Gail at gherman@garrettcollege.edu or at www.gcnet.net/storyteller.*

ZENO'S PARADOX
By Gail N. Herman, Ph.D.

National Standards:

NCTM 5.1: Develop understanding of fractions as parts of unit wholes, as parts of a collection, as locations on number lines, and as divisions of whole numbers; use models, benchmarks, and equivalent forms to judge the size of fractions; recognize and generate equivalent forms of commonly used fractions, decimals, and percents.

Objectives:

Demonstrate understanding of fractions as divisions of whole numbers; use story form to demonstrate understanding of the size of fractions; generate equivalent forms of fractions.

Math is everywhere. Even on the ceiling! When our second and third graders were studying fractions, I decided to spice up the teaching standards with some imagination and motivation. Some students needed more conceptualization and concrete experiences; others needed creative challenges. Naturally, I searched my mind for a story that would get students intrigued about fractions. An author in *The Chronicle of Higher Education* observed that students need more romance in early college math and science courses. By "romance" the author didn't mean budding friendships; she meant activities to help students LOVE the SUBJECTS. It brought to mind a story from a Greek philosopher: Zeno's Paradox—a story about fractions and their infinite progression, when dividing a space in half, and then that half space in half again and again and again. I hoped Zeno didn't turn over in his grave, because I modified the story for my students.

Zeno's Paradox

Once upon a time there was a teeny, tiny fly, Felix, who lived in a humongous mansion. One day, instead of doing math lessons with Uncle Zeno, Felix felt adventurous. He wanted to cross the great wide ceiling. As he prepared for his long, arduous journey, his Uncle Zeno asked, "What are you doing, Felix?"

"Oh, I'm going to walk upside down across the great wide, white ceiling tomorrow morning."

"Why, sonny, you'd best make a plan for resting," said old Zeno, as he warmed up his front legs next to Felix's fire. He had six legs, but it was always those front ones he rubbed together to keep warm. "Nobody's ever crossed that distance without stopping at each of the halfway points. If you don't make the stops, you'll fall off. If you don't make the stops, you'll never get there from here."

"Of course I will!" Felix laughed. He flashed his 142 lenses up at the gleaming white ceiling. But, just to be sure, Felix decided to make a plan for the halfway stops. "I **will** be sure to make the stops, just to be safe," he said. "But I know I can get there from here."

"Well, let's map out all the halfway stops you need to make to be safe. I'm telling you now; no one's ever made it. They all come home just shaking their heads, saying that the ceiling is 'in-fin-ite.' Now what do you suppose that means?"

The question hung in the air. But Felix Fly sat down with Zeno and drew a map of the ceiling on paper. (Storyteller points to the ceiling showing the direction of travel.) Can you figure where his first stop will be? Felix drew a line down the middle of his map. Then he wrote down: "Stop, 1/2 more to go." He drew another line halfway from the middle to the end and wrote: "1/4 more to go." (Storyteller or child points up to the place indicating 1/4 more to travel.) Then Felix Fly pictured setting off again. This time he had to go halfway across the 1/4 of the ceiling that was left. (Teacher draws a map of the ceiling on the board and divides it in half, then divides each half in half, or fourths.) Now let the students figure where the next stop should be (at 1/8). Continue to 1/16.

Finally, Felix Fly had only one inch left to walk. He decided to make another plan of action. He remembered what Uncle Zeno said: "Stop at the halfway mark and you'll be safe." He figured the next stop was a half-inch mark. Then 1/4. Then 1/8. Then 1/16. What was the next? 1/32. Many students will have figured out the pattern. On the board write all the fractions as you or the students say them. How many halfway points do you think Felix could figure? How many more can you figure?

"Will I ever get to the other side with this plan of action?" Felix asked.

Uncle Zeno just smiled. He sure knew how to get his nephew, Felix, to study math, didn't he?

I challenge you to make the longest plan of action you can for Felix. Who can come up with the longest plan? Can you figure out what the next fraction will be? How much further will he need to go during that last inch? Then, for sure, you will know the paradox!

Discuss the idea that in math there is an infinite (never-ending) series of fractional parts. This is what Zeno was trying to teach Felix.

Ask, "What do you notice about the fraction as the distance gets smaller and smaller?" (They will notice that the bottom number gets larger.)

Eager Learners.

Ask them what the bottom number means. (A number of total parts or sections of the ceiling. 1/32 means we divided the ceiling into 32 parts.)

I used this story about the infinite divisibility of space to motivate students to write and think about fractional parts on their own. While standing under the ceiling and pointing up during the initial part of the story demonstration, it intuitively helped my students get the concept of going half the distance left. Remember, each time the fly stopped, he looked ahead and planned to stop halfway. It also challenges them to make the longest plan of action. The students not only had a real concrete visual, the ceiling, but they also enjoyed the lesson because I spoke in strange voices and accents for the characters, especially old Uncle Zeno, and I acted out the fly movements by rubbing my arms together as the old fly's legs would do, rubbing my hands behind my back as wings, or sticking out my elbows.

Although the students' necks were aching from counting squares on the ceiling while they imagined the little fly crossing over the Great White Divide, their pencils were flying as they calculated the stops. Their excitement didn't stop there. Many went home and continued the challenge. The next day lists appeared—stapled, crumpled, taped, and rolled like a scroll. Try it!

Assessments:

Varied lists and forms demonstrate the students' ability to grasp math concepts and generate equivalent fraction forms.

TELL ME WHY: USING POURQUOI TALES IN THE CLASSROOM
By Joan Leotta

National Standards:

CNAEA 1 (Script Writing): Students collaborate to select (and create) interrelated characters, environments, and situations for classroom dramatizations. Students improvise dialogue to tell stories and formalize improvisations by writing or recording the dialogue; NCTE 3: Students apply a wide range of strategies to comprehend, interpret, evaluate, and appreciate texts. Specifically, they work on creating a story that corresponds in form and structure to the model story; NCTE 11: Students participate as knowledgeable, reflective, creative, and critical elements of a variety of literary communities-taking the story that was performed as a model and as a group creating a written story that fits the model; NCTE 4: Students adjust their use of spoken, written, and visual language to communicate effectively. Students learn to use power words (nouns and verbs) to move the action of the story and character change.

Objectives:

Perform an example story; analyze the story using simple examples; review format using outlined folktale; guide the creation of a class story; identify power words; act out story sequence.

Resources:

Web site with some interesting short tales and uses of the tale: http:// teacher.scholastic.com/products/instructor/pourquoitales.htm.

By the time children are in third or fourth grade, they realize the power of using the words "why" and "how," not only to exasperate adults, but also to open new worlds of learning. Since ancient times, these two words have been the engines that power scientific imagination and literary exploration. Folktales can often satisfy the question of why and how something came to be and often present a fanciful way to observe nature and/or an allegorical cautionary tale about human behavior. The accumulated body of these tales has been dubbed "*Pourquoi*" (meaning "why" in French).

Pourquoi tales have broad educational value and are excellent language arts teaching tools. *Pourquoi* structure provides an easily copied pattern that helps children to bridge the gap between listening to oral folklore and writing stories. The tales are great fun for presenters and listeners.

One great advantage of using the *pourquoi* format is that the outcome of the tale is known before the story ends. This lifts creative pressure from young scribes, freeing their creative juices to be applied to imagining how the animal looked in the beginning, and how it changed to look the way it does today.

Third and fourth graders working under guidance can be counted on to invent hilarious situations that bring a character from an imagined starting point to its contemporary existence. Once the writing exercise is complete (written either as a group tale or an individual tale), the floodgates are open for other educational uses of *pourquoi* tales. Complementary art projects provide illustrations for the tales. In social studies exercises, students can search for similar tales in multiple cultures. In science, they can compare the tale's fantastic "facts" with real-life observations and modern scientific knowledge. They can research how the question "why" continues to lead to information and discovery.

Recently, I participated in a workshop with the Washington Opera Society in which fourth graders at a DC elementary school created a *pourquoi* tale that was then used as the libretto for a "homegrown" opera. I performed an example tale and worked with the class to create the group *pourquoi* tale

Bringing the Character and Action to Life.

that became the libretto. The Opera Society provided the musical expertise, as well as the artists for costuming and the sets. A five-step story creation process is one I've used in many classrooms and can be easily replicated.

<u>Step 1: Perform an example story.</u> I generally use a very simple story that relies on action and humor to bring about the change (for instance, "The Tale of the Bear's Tail" or "Fast Talking Turtle"). This is very appealing to third and fourth graders. Several of my favorites focus on (bear or rabbit) tail length. While performing, I deliberately speak more slowly than usual and create each character and incident with plenty of verbal detail and physical action to make it easier for the audience to follow both the story and the form of the story. If the students have read some *pourquoi* tales before the performance, steps 2–5 are much easier.

<u>Step 2: Analyze the story using simple questions</u>. With prepared storyboards or writing on the blackboard, we review the three major parts of the story, starting with the ending (i.e., the animal today). The class provides the details by answering my questions (e.g., How is the tail? Is it long or short?).

Next: The beginning. What was the animal like then? (e.g., long tail)? The action-packed center is last. I begin by asking: What were the three things that happened in the middle of the story to bring our friend from a long tail to a short tail? Then I ask them to order and describe the incidents (other characters, circumstances).

Step 3: Review the format using the tale as outlined. The structured form of the *pourquoi* helps solidify learning to sequence and shapes the beginning, middle, and end of the story. In the beginning, we introduce characters, describe them, and create the setting for the story. In the middle, the action happens. At the end, we have the results of the action and the animal takes on the form we see today.

Step 4: Guiding creation of a class story. I take notes on an easel, record the session on tape, or have another adult transcribe the class comments. You can do all three! Guiding tale construction helps organize the group, gives the class *pourquoi*-form practice, and provides a finished example of their own making for writing their own individual tales. I offer students three choices in each category. Each selection is made by majority vote: first the animal that will change, and then the part of the animal (tail, ears, or size—big/little) that will change. I offer a selection of three to help speed up the process. If the class spontaneously offers a fourth element, I add it to the ballot. These two choices set the beginning and ending of the story. The concept of opposites comes into play. What the animal is like now (long-eared) is the opposite of what the animal was like in the beginning (short-eared). Next, we create the three incidents that cause the change (e.g., big to small). I remind the students that we need three incidents or actions, just as we did in the sample story. The use of three is mythic in folklore, and the limit helps increase the young writers' sense of control over the process. Once the incidents and basic story are outlined, we flesh out the details. Sometimes step four elicits so much comment from the students that step five becomes a fine tuning process.

Step 5: Power words! At this point, I introduce the students to the idea of power words—nouns and verbs. Using examples from the performed tale, I explain that the words must convey how they want the reader/listener to see things. We act out various words, run, skip, or hop, to see how they differ from the oft-chosen "walked." We brainstorm for specific nouns. This time, we work from the beginning to the middle, and then through to the end of the story. In the beginning section, we use our power words to describe the setting and the personality of the main character—especially those traits that will trigger the change. We also introduce sidekicks, friends, and folks of the main creature. I stress showing instead of "telling." Questions guide the creative process throughout. For example, where does the animal live? Is it in the jungle? Is it in the desert? Is it in his or her hometown? What other animals does it interact with? Who are its enemies and friends? How will the animal character be perceived by the other animals? For the action-packed middle, we ask questions such as: What might happen to make the change take place? Will it be a race, a gift, or a question by the main animal character? For the ending, we use many of the same questions asked in the beginning to describe how the animal is now.

Keep the students focused on fun—let them act out the sequences they create. Encourage them to draw the shapes they talk about. All ideas should be recorded and saved. Make sure the students know that even if an idea is not incorporated into this version, the idea can be used in another story, at another time. It's important that students realize that all ideas have value!

Once you have recorded the group story, it can become a class book or the first chapter in a book that includes individual student-written tales. Or the group tale can be made into a play, an opera, or an art project. Once the simple word "why" has set the creative process in motion, the possibilities are endless.

Assessments:

Search for similar tales in multiple cultures; compare "fantastic" facts with real-life observations and modern scientific knowledge; research how the question "why" continues to lead to information and discovery; record the group story for later inclusion in a class book; group tale can be made into a play, an opera, or an art project.

Joan Leotta, a twenty-year veteran story performer, playwright, and author lives in Calabash, North Carolina, after a long career in the Washington, DC, area. She spreads "encouraging words through pen and performance" in schools, libraries, festivals, museums, hospitals, and other venues and is dedicated to using story to heal, encourage, educate, and entertain. Contact her for performing or teaching performance and/or writing at joanleotta@ atmc.net.

THE OVERCOAT
By Robin Bady, Lillian Adorno, and Lisa Radford

National Standards:

NCTE 2: Understanding the human experience; NCTE 5: Communication strategies; NCTE 6: Applying knowledge; NCTE 8: Evaluating data; NCTE 11: Participating in society; NCTE 12: Applying language skills; CNAEA (Visual Arts) 1: Understanding and applying media, techniques and processes; CNAEA (Visual Arts) 3: Choosing and evaluating a range of subject matter, symbols and ideas; NCTM (Problem solving) 2: Solve problems that arise in mathematics and other contexts; NCTM (Problem solving) 3: Apply and adapt a variety of appropriate strategies to solve problems; NCTM (Measurement) 2: Apply appropriate techniques, tools and formulas to determine measurements; NAS 3: Life Science; NS.5–8.6: Personal and social perspectives; NCSS 7: History of science. Life Skills: Self-Regulation, Thinking and Reasoning, Working with Others.

Objectives:

Enhance students' knowledge of ecology and recycling through verbal, visual, and kinesthetic experiences; inspire students to own their personal connection to the problems of pollution; motivate students to make a commitment to conserve natural resources and protect our earth; utilize storytelling as a means of opening up discussion and consolidating students' acquired knowledge.

Materials and Resources:

- Teacher-created storyboards
- Various art supplies such as glue, fabric, sparkles, etc.
- The song "Hob Ikh Mir a Mantl" or "I Had an Old Coat" (available at www. zemerl.com)
- Children's books *Joseph Had a Little Overcoat* by Simms Taback (Viking, 1999) and *Something from Nothing* by Phoebe Gilman (Scholastic, 1992)

Instructional Process:

Storytelling and recycling: A natural connection! What are stories but life reduced, recycled, and renewed? What is garbage but the detritus of our culture? How can we use story to deepen our students' awareness of their ecological power?

On the streets by P.S. 20, an elementary school on New York's Lower East Side, trash is everywhere. The streets are a genuine urban classroom for a recycling program. Although the school population is 52 percent ELL (English Language Learners), with many recent immigrants from China, Bangladesh, India, and Latin American, the children have readily absorbed our modern throwaway culture. During the midwinter academy, Lisa Radford, a cluster instructor who teaches environmental sciences; Lillian Adorno, who teaches fifth grade during the winter and summer academies; and I, the school storyteller, worked together to make the connection tangible in three forty-five-minute workshops. The experience was fun as well as productive. We saw students' perspectives shift as they took ownership of their own ecological habits, learned from each other, and began to think of alternatives.

> "The Overcoat"
> A young tailor makes an overcoat and wears it for years until it is ragged. Unwilling to throw away the memories or the fabric, he takes what is usable and makes a jacket. When the jacket wears out, he makes a scarf, then a tie, and then, when there is almost nothing left, he makes a button. The tailor, now an old man, sews the button on a new overcoat.

Day 1: I told the story "The Overcoat" to the students. The story immediately engaged them, and they began to shout out alternative ways to recycle the fabric. Afterward, we had a lively discussion about recycling: at home, in New York City, in the United States, and in their native countries. That night, their assignment was to make a list of the items in their garbage cans at home.

Day 2: The students were asked to imagine themselves in polluted areas where the air, water, and land were filthy and smelly, and then in a healthy environment with clean air, fresh scents, and beautiful landscapes. We discussed the sensory and visual reactions to each setting.

Reviewing the homework, the students shared their garbage lists as well as their experiences going through the trash. We chose one item from the students' lists and brainstormed ideas of how it could be recycled. Using those ideas, we created a class story of the journey of that piece of debris through various incarnations. (Lillian's class chose a plastic bag; in Lisa's class the students picked a plastic milk jug.)

That night, their homework was to choose one of the items from their list and think of three ways it could be reused.

Day 3: We expanded the warm-up, dividing students into two groups and assigning one group the task of using their bodies to build a tableau (freeze picture) of a polluted landscape. The other group was assigned the task of creating a picture of a clean environment. The students observed each other and reflected on being inside and outside of the tableaux. At this point, the classes diverged.

The students in Lisa's class used storyboards to map out the progression of their recycling tales, drawing pictures and writing notes. Then, each wrote a draft of their story and shared it with another student.

Lillian's class decided to build trash sculptures and brought in empty bottles, old socks, tin foil, plastic bags, and newspapers from home. They built sock puppets, racing cars, flags, boats, and rocket launchers.

Both classes ended with a quiet meditation followed by sharing.

Conclusion:

From the beginning, with their spontaneous interaction with "The Overcoat," the students personalized the concept of recycling. They could identify with the process of the tailor in remaking the coat over and over, and could see other possibilities for reuse. For example, one student used and reused newspaper until it devolved into crayoned confetti pasted on a card for his mother!

There was enthusiastic discussion of garbage as their perspectives shifted from "Gross!" "I won't touch it!" and "That's not mine!" to ownership of their part in the cycle. An interesting dialogue ensued regarding cultural differences. In some of the students' native countries, people threw trash on the streets. One of the students had no list because she had been forbidden to touch the family garbage or share its contents with others.

By the time the workshops were over, the students were sharing their trash for art projects, critically examining the garbage, and working together to create new story ideas as well as recycling ideas to save the Earth's resources.

How could this workshop be expanded? The next lessons would involve sharing, revising, and creating final drafts of their stories, which the students would then publish and/or retell.

Assessments:

Embedded assessment: Through ongoing observation of the depth and quality of the students' homework, group work, and expression through story and visual art, evaluate the evidence of the students' understanding of, and commitment to, the issues of recycling.

Storyteller, director, actor, teaching artist, writer, and musician, Robin Bady has been exploring story forms for over thirty years. She performs throughout the northeast, often working with musicians and visual artists. Her newest project is "Aesop Sez: Fables for Our Times," a collaboration with a cartoonist/animator. She is a teaching artist and staff developer in many diverse schools, and presents storytelling workshops at conferences. She founded Shirazad's Children, a multicultural storytelling ensemble. In former times, she was a member of an ensemble theater company, as well as director of two youth theaters. She lives in Brooklyn, New York, with her husband, Tom, a high school English teacher, and their two cats. E-mail: robbady@aol.com.

Lillian Adorno teaches first grade at P.S. 20. She has the position as grade leader within her school. Together with the other first-grade teachers, she organizes the grade curriculum, assuring that all state standards are being met within the classrooms. She graduated from Marymount Manhattan College with a bachelor of psychology degree. She is currently working on a master of arts degree in early literacy. She is hoping to write and illustrate her first children's story within the next two years. Ms. Adorno lives with her two children, husband, two dogs, and cat. E-mail: lcmystic@aol.com.

Lisa Radford is a Reading Intervention Specialist/Staff Developer, creating and modeling reading lessons in self-contained classrooms and acting as a literacy consultant with regard to children with learning difficulties. Lisa has two master's degrees from New York University, in the psychological foundations of reading and early childhood education. She is a member of Kappa Delta Pi (National Honor Society in Education) and the National Political Science Honor Society. She is a recipient of three NYC Department of Sanitation Golden Apple Awards, as well as a Teachers Network IMPACT II Disseminator

Grant. She is an adjunct professor at Metropolitan College of New York, teaching reading instruction for upper grades and diagnostic and enrichment techniques in reading. E-mail: ps20lisa@yahoo.com.

MERCURY AND THE WOODSMAN
By Linda King Pruitt

National Standards:

NCTE 6: Uses reading skills and strategies to understand a variety of literate texts; NCTE 8: Uses listening and speaking strategies for different purposes.

Objectives:

Students will understand how the five Ws and the five senses can help develop an understanding of character and setting in story.

Materials and Resources:

- Chart of the twelve Olympian gods and the Roman gods
- Storyboard: A series of pictures on separate sheets that show the sequence of the story-The teacher can do this or students can draw the pieces of the storyboard after listening to the story.

Hermes, the son of Zeus, wandered out of his mother's sight within hours of his birth and went searching for adventure. He found the pasture of the gods, where he stole fifty cows from Apollo. Less than one day old, he was already quite shy. He made "shoes" out of bark from an oak tree, making it hard to track him, and then drove the cows backward over places that left no prints.

Hermes was brought before Zeus, but looking innocent, he said, "Me? Why, I'm too young to even know what a cow is!"

Zeus was amused, but made Hermes lead Apollo to the herd where it was discovered two cows were killed. Hermes had divided the meat into twelve portions for the gods. Apollo asked who the twelfth god was, and Hermes answered, "Me!"

Zeus made Hermes his messenger, but he remained a trickster of sorts . . . patron of travelers, thieves, and rogues.

Whenever Zeus visited the earth, Hermes went with him. His acts of kindness did not go unnoticed by the mortals, and soon every traveler who became lost or suffered some hardship called upon Hermes for help.

I had already been using Aesop's fables in classrooms for four years when I added "Mercury and the Woodsman" to my lesson plan. Now, I know that Aesop's fables carry the power and potential to speak to the heart of listeners and open their minds to the message those powerful fables carry, but I was struck by the absolute silence that fell over the classroom as this story of rewards and punishment unfolded. There is nothing like the magic of a golden axe delivered by a Greek god to stir the imagination.

"Mercury and the Woodsman" is a fable that can easily be found in any number of collections of Aesop's fables. My adaptation can be found online at: www.lkpstoryteller.com/mercury.htm. There is also a collection of fables at www.aesopfables.com.

"Mercury and the Woodsman" is about a poor woodsman who loses his axe in a pool of water. As he cries over his loss, the god Mercury appears. Three times, Mercury dives into the pool of water. The first time, he dives in and brings up a golden axe to the woodsman. The honest man tells the god that the axe does not belong to him. Mercury dives in again and brings the woodsman a silver axe. Again, the woodsman tells Mercury that the axe is not his personal axe. The third time, Mercury retrieves the man's old axe. The woodsman is happy and thankful and Mercury is so impressed with his honesty that he gives him all three axes to keep as a reward for his honesty.

Once the woodsman returns home and the villagers hear his story, they hide their axes and call for help from the god Mercury, hoping to retrieve gold and silver axes, but all they get for their dishonesty is a whack on the head and the loss of their axes as well.

More magic takes place as the students begin working their way through the lesson plan.

Instructional Process:

Begin by telling "Mercury and the Woodsman," followed by interactive storyboard sequencing. Volunteers hold pieces of the storyboard while the rest of the class puts the story in the correct order. To reinforce the story sequence, using the storyboard, quickly retell the story as a group.

Because this fable deals with a Roman god, a chart is used to show the twelve Greek Olympian gods and their Roman equivalents. After a quick story on the birth of Hermes, students learn that Hermes/Mercury is a trickster. This will lead to further understanding of his actions in the story. Mercury could easily have given the woodsman his old axe the first time he dived into the pool of water, but he was trying to trick him. The character of Mercury takes on more depth with this information. It is then explained how the five Ws and the five senses can help develop the characters in the story.

These questions are asked of all characters in the story: who they are, what they are doing, where they are, when it is happening, and why they are doing what they are doing. After these questions are answered and students know where the story is happening, the five senses are addressed: what could be seen, smelled, touched, tasted, or heard in the place where the story is happening.

The students now have a richer, fuller picture of the story, an understanding and sense of motivation of the story characters, and they are ready to act out the story.

Divide students into groups and have them take turns acting out the story for the class.

Conclusion:

Two students were very touched by this lesson, and they purchased beautiful books of Aesop's fables and a book on Greek mythology. I cannot think of a better testimony of the power of story. Even shy, quiet students love to participate in fleshing out the story setting because they can see it so clearly. I encourage students and teachers to explore more mythology, fables, and trickster stories from around the world. Simple props can be added, along with sound instruments and imaginations to bring these stories alive in the classroom. More curricular extensions can be found at my Web site: http://lkpstoryteller.com/teacher.htm.

Assessments:

Students contribute to brainstorming character development through the use of the 5 Ws and the five senses and they actively participate in the dramatization of the story.

Linda King Pruitt has been working since 1996 as an artist in residence with the Fullerton School District in Southern California for "All the Arts for All the Kids," teaching creative storytelling to over 2,000 children each year. She has told, taught, and lectured at elementary, middle, and high schools and at colleges, including Cal State L.A., Cal State Fullerton, and USC. Linda has also worked with museums throughout California and has been frequently filmed telling stories for Mission Viejo TV's Storytime Theater. A member of the National Storytelling Network, South Coast Storytellers Guild, and a board member of Los Angeles Story Works, Linda enjoys sharing the oral tradition with young and old.

CHAPTER FIVE

Grades Six, Seven, and Eight

INTRODUCTION
By Jane Stenson

"Huh!"
"A storyteller, wha's that? We hafta listen to a storyteller?"
"Whaddaya mean, I hafta tell a story?"

Many fine adults embrace burgeoning eleven- to fifteen-year-olds because the stakes are so high: caring and knowledgeable adults make a difference. In the middle school child, developmental processes occur that constitute challenges for the age group, as well as for those entrusted with the responsibility for their healthy development and education. This is a time of great excitement and opportunity due to rapid emotional and physical growth, yet it is simultaneously fraught with vulnerability and risk.

These children seek an identity: who they are, where they came from, what the world is like, and where they are going are the thrusts of their daily life, because they will soon be driving cars, earning a living, having their own babies, and voting. They push toward emotional adulthood, and yet they are children. The peer group influences their thinking and their behavior, while parents and teachers speak to them of responsibility to oneself and to society. These years can be a hopeful, idealistic, altruistic time as each middle schooler determines what the world can be. Simultaneously, this adult child may understand and face obstacles that he or she feels will prevent access into the adult world.

Physically, they are all different sizes and shapes and exhibit a natural awkwardness. Just when the peer group dominates their thinking, there is no typical or standard middle school student. Hormones infuse their bodies, causing mood swings and reactive behaviors. The need for active, interactive, and creative expression of the currents of their daily lives is crucial.

Intellectually, they are wonderfully competent, if somewhat tongue-tied. Higher-level thinking in every academic domain causes curiosity and explorations reminiscent of a five-year-old, though the objects of that interest may differ! Interests pursued at this age may become lifelong or be discarded. Simultaneously, many educators feel that the media dominance of TV and video games causes adolescents to think and speak in sound bytes, reducing vocabulary and the ability to converse even (or especially) about strongly held convictions. Teachers know that in middle school what generates the most interest occurs at the intersection of the individual's concern as it relates to a societal or universal concern; negotiating the walk through the forest of life is the middle schooler's dilemma.

Storytelling and adolescents are a natural fit...if only teachers practiced the holistic act of telling stories with these children...if only tellers didn't compromise the intellectual part of their programs. Stories show the individual a path; stories show a variety of options in an accessible way. Content can range from social and cultural issues to nonfiction stories. The conflicts of our time are best understood in a narrative that allows a broad context as well as easier access to remembering! Further, the act of telling encourages discourse, vocabulary, long-range thinking, and an increased opportunity to pursue the implications of decisions and behaviors. Storytelling in the classroom is interactive and active, exactly the way the middle schooler learns best.

DAY OF THE RAPTORS
By Pat Kane

National Standards:

NAS 1: Science as inquiry; NAS 3: Life Science; NCTE 1: Reading for perspective; NCTE 3: Evaluation Strategies; NCTE 4: Communication Skills; NCTE 6: Applying Knowledge; NCTE 8: Developing research skills; NCTE 12: Applying language skills; NCTM (Measurement) 1: Understand measurement; NCTM (Measurement) 2: Apply techniques; NSS 3: Physical Systems; NSS 5: Environmental; NSS 6: Uses of Geography; CNAEA (Theatre) 2: Acting; CNAEA (Theatre) 7: Analyzing; CNEAE (Visual Arts) 3: Subject matter; NETS 1: Basic operations; NETS 3: Technological production tools; NETS 5: Technological research tools.

Objectives:

Analyze a story form and translate to art form; define the flight paths of migrating hawks; identify hawks by field marks and measurements; collect information from library resources and Web sites; social objectives include sharing experiences with classmates; participating in a group; and using academic tools to enjoy the excitement of natural occurrences.

One of the most fascinating phenomena we witness twice each year is the migration of hawks. These masters of the sky are a constant source of wonder and provide a free show if we know how and where to look. Students in grades five through eight who took part in these lessons became more observant of their surroundings, more eager to share experiences with classmates, and more eager to participate in group activities. No wonder! It's holistic education; every academic domain is required in the study of hawk migration.

Resources and Materials:

- Wingspan measurements of hawks, found at www.peregrine-foundation.ca/identification.html
- Maps of hawk migration paths, found at www.hawkcount.org
- Physical map that includes the local region
- Other information on hawks: www.hmana.org
- Roll of plain shelf paper
- Sheet of poster board
- Access to Internet
- Art materials of choice for representations

Instructional Process:

Tell the story:

The Day of the Raptors, or How Hawks Came to Be

In the early times, when the people were just learning to live on the land, there were two brothers, Raptor and Toxor. They were hunters and fishers, with bows and spears swift and sure. They learned swiftness by racing with the deer and the antelope, and patience from watching heron and wolf. The two were inseparable. The brothers were honored among the people, and when they grew to manhood they became the leaders of the tribe.

One day on the way home from the hunt, Toxor asked, "What will you do with your meat? You have already enough for the winter."

"Yes, I know, but there are other hunters who have not been as successful. I will give it to them."

"What! You will just give it? Why not make them give you something in return, or do some labor for you. You are a fool."

"Perhaps," said his brother, "but the strength of the tribe is tested by the weakest member. If my skill keeps all strong, then how am I a fool?"

Toxor had extra meat too, but he traded what he did not need for beads and furs. When there was nothing to trade, he demanded services and kept careful account of what was owed.

After a time, Toxor moved away from the village and took some with him who were attracted by his power. "We will have our own tribe and we will tolerate no weakness. Kill those who have no value to the tribe."

War was waged on Raptor and his tribe families. "Killing serves no good," said Raptor. "Trust in the power of the Great Spirit who honors the gifts you have to live on the land given to us. Run swiftly and hide, but do not kill your brothers."

They did as Raptor bid and one by one they began to change. Raptor himself had a headpiece of white feathers and a cloak of brown. He began to soar high into the sky and called himself Bald Eagle. Great Spirit gave them all feathers to clothe them and a name that suited their skills on the earth. The fisher he called Osprey, and sent him flying over rivers and lakes and oceans. The forest and field hunters he called Red Tail and Vulture and Rough-Legged. Those who were swiftest he called Falcons: Peregrine, and Merlin, and Kestrel.

Soon all of the Raptors were winging their way through the sky. Loud shrieks told the Great Spirit of their delight. To this very day they can be seen in the skies, only today they are also known as hawks. If you watch the sky you will surely see them as they go on their way. And you can hear the cry of Bald Eagle, for he still yearns for the loss of his brother.

<u>Lesson 1: Language</u> Tell the story and lead the class in a discussion about favorite parts and what made them interesting. Have the students separate facts from myth elements of the story. Are there other values portrayed than natural science facts? Assign teams to portray favorite scenes. Supplementary reading: *My Side of the Mountain* by Jean Craighead George (E. P. Dutton, 1988).

<u>Lesson 2: Research through Technology and Library</u> Research the physical characteristics of all raptors. What are their migratory flyways? List the birds of prey that are found in your part of the country. List similarities and differences. List the wingspan of each hawk. (See Web sites under Resources.)

<u>Lesson 3: Math</u> Use the local hawk species and their wingspan for this activity. Using the shelf paper, create a measuring line that extends to seven feet. Mark the line in six-inch increments. On the poster board, create a bar graph with the names of hawks on the vertical and numbers in tens to one hundred on the horizontal. Display the line and graph in the hallway. Students extend arms on the measuring line and compare their arm span to the nearest hawk with the same span. Mark the graph accordingly. This can be monitored by participating classes, but can be open to all in the school. Identification with a hawk adds motivation for further research.

<u>Lesson 4: Geography</u> Display a map of hawk flyways taken from the Web site. On a physical map, locate the flyway that is closest to the local area. How is your region conducive to hawk migration? What natural resources are available to meet their needs?

<u>Lesson 5: Art</u> Students divide the story into sequential scenes. As teams or individuals, portray the scene through some art medium. These can be displayed in the hall or made into a video production to be shared with other classes.

Assessments:

<u>Hard assessment</u>: Class participation in discussions and products of individuals and teams. <u>Soft assessment</u>: Students connect class presentations and activities with real-life observations.

Conclusion:

When this program ran for two weeks, there were less absenteeism and fewer discipline problems, and chatter among the students during free time was mostly about hawks.

Pat Kane was an elementary school teacher for twelve years and served in many positions as a leader in environmental education for thirty years. During her tenure with New Jersey Audubon Society, she co-authored two editions of Bridges to the Natural World: A Natural History Guide for Elementary Teachers. *She incorporated storytelling in the many programs she developed for schools, day camps, and professional development workshops for teachers. Retirement provides more opportunity for advancing the use of storytelling in all areas of the curriculum. Pat continues to offer storytelling and workshops to schools and professional groups. E-mail: prkane@ worldnet.att.net.*

STAR STORIES OF ANCIENT CULTURES
By Larry Neumann

National Standards:

NCSS 1: The student understands how certain cultures became centers of dense population, urbanization, and cultural innovation. Therefore, the student is able to compare the development of religious and ethical belief systems in civilizations and how they legitimized the political and social order [Compare and contrast differing sets of ideas]; describe architectural, artistic, literary, technological, and scientific achievements of these civilizations and relate these achievements to economic and social life [Analyze cause-and-effect relationships]; NCTE 2: Students read a wide range of literature from many periods in many genres to build an understanding of the many dimensions (e.g., philosophical, ethical, aesthetic) of human experience; NCTE 4: Students adjust their use of spoken, written, and visual language (e.g., conventions, style, vocabulary) to communicate effectively with a variety of audiences and for different purposes; NCTE 7: Students conduct research on issues and interests by generating ideas and questions, and by posing problems. They gather, evaluate, and synthesize data from a variety of sources (e.g., print and non-print texts, artifacts, people) to communicate their discoveries in ways that suit their purpose and audience.

Objectives:

Students will learn about the importance of the stars to specific cultures; students will research a selected culture to prepare a PowerPoint presentation on the history, architecture, and star connections of one culture; students will select a star story to learn and tell.

Materials and Resources:

- Access to library references on the chosen cultures.
- Star stories from mythology.
- Outstanding books on archaeoastronomy, defined as the astronomy of ancient cultures, include Aveni's *Stairways to the Stars* and *Echoes of the Ancient Skies*. *Echoes of the Night* is the CD that contains the story of the Great Bear.
- The CD-ROM *StarSites: Ancient Buildings Connecting Earth and Sky* is a terrific source for research on the cultures.
- Access to Hubble or Chandra images of deep space objects is available from NASA online.

Instructional Plan:

Storytelling became the organizing mechanism and anchor for the sixth-grade social studies unit on ancient star sites. The Native American story of the Great Bear introduced the unit, and students found star stories everywhere as they researched ancient cultures. Storytelling was also a way for the students to process their learning, relate to ancient peoples, and develop confidence as experts in that culture.

As the storyteller, I played my Native American flute to call my sixth-grade gifted students together. I told the Abenaki story of the placing of the

Great Bear (Big Dipper) in the sky. In this story, visiting hunters abuse the hospitality of the Abenaki, and set off to chase the bear, which the Abenaki view as a brother. The shaman of the village saves the bear by placing him in the sky as the constellation Ursa Major, the Great Bear. The greedy hunters are set in the sky as well, to forever hunt but never catch their prey. This story, which I accompanied with Native American drum, was an introduction to Star Stories of Ancient Cultures. It also set a tone of respect for ancient cultures for the unit.

Next, students went to the computer lab to explore the ancient cultures of China, the Maya, India, Egypt, and Newgrange through the CD-ROM *Star-Sites*. They listened to an introduction that presented the star connections for the Forbidden City; ancient Mayan temples and ball courts; the Indian observatory of Jantar Mantar; the Egyptian pyramids; and the burial mound of Newgrange. After hearing about all five cultures, students selected a culture to research using electronic resources, print resources from the IMC, and online sources. Their research was shared in the form of PowerPoint presentations for the rest of the class.

The Instructional Media Center director helped students locate collections that contained star stories or myths related to the sky. Some students looked for a story that captured their imagination, while others began searching for a story that would relate to their chosen culture. I worked as storytelling coach and mentor. Students began their work by reading many stories in order to select one that spoke to them. They read and reread their stories, made visual story maps, and practiced telling with partners. Students spent four weeks learning stories, which included the Chinese story of the Milky Way, Native American stories of Coyote and the heavens, Thai star stories, and the Mayan Twins enacting the ball game of the heavenly bodies.

Assessments:

Students also had the option of creating their own myth about the stars. Using the latest images available from NASA, students selected a color print of a deep space object. They brainstormed images that they could see, emotions that the image suggested, and possible settings for their myth. They then wrote the story of how that object appeared in the sky. They found themselves in the same position as the early cultures that looked heavenward and tried to make sense of the patterns in the sky.

The culminating story concert was a huge success, as each student told a story found in a collection or inspired by a deep space image. My student with Asperger's Syndrome relied on his own cryptic story map to organize and help him learn his story. Although this brilliant boy had difficulty relating to his peers, he willingly joined his classmates to tell in the final concert. A shy, reserved girl began to develop confidence and poise as a realization of her own abilities opened before her. From this beginning, she went on to compete in the speech and drama festival, and she secured a part in the next two school musicals. Students finished the unit with a new respect for ancient civilizations and a new wonder at stories hidden within the stars.

Star Stories of Ancient Cultures: Resources

Aveni, Anthony. *Stairways to the Stars: Skywatching in Three Great Ancient Cultures*. New York: John Wiley & Sons, Inc., 1997.

Aveni covers the early cultures in Britain, as well as the Maya and Aztec cultures. Although definitely an adult resource, his clear illustrations and well-focused topics make this book accessible as a resource when students are motivated and interested.

Krupp, E. C. *Echoes of the Ancient Skies: The Astronomy of Lost Civilizations*. New York: Harper & Row, 1983.

Krupp has a chapter on ancient tombs that focuses on Egypt, the Maya, and Newgrange. He specifically discusses the arrangement of the Imperial City and its relationship to the heavens. This is an outstanding adult resource that will have to be supported to use with the middle school students. The book is filled with photos and illustrations to make clear the connections to the stars.

StarSites: Ancient Buildings Connecting Earth and Sky. (CD-ROM) Vancouver, BC: DNA Multimedia Corp., 1996.

This CD-ROM focuses on the ancient cultures of China, the Maya, Egypt, Newgrange, and India. It uses music, interactive maps, and strong visuals to explain how these cultures made use of the stars and heavens in their buildings. It provides a wealth of information in libraries on each culture, as well as a series of information in short, visually engaging topics that even include games and stories. This is a must-have resource for the StarSites unit.

Tsonakwa, Gerard Rancourt. *Echoes of the Night: Native American Legends of the Night Sky*. (Compact disc) Tucson, AZ: Soundings of the Planet, 1992 (1-800-93PEACE).

This CD contains the Abenaki story of the Great Bear. Excellent music and drumming provide a stunning background to stories. Stories tend to be lengthy, so you might want to use excerpts. It would be possible to use the entire recording of the Great Bear story.

Larry Neumann is a teacher of gifted students at Pleasantdale Middle School in Burr Ridge, Illinois. He has worked extensively on stories about the Wright brothers and works with storytelling in middle school classrooms. He has written several musicals, and produces an annual musical at his school. He conducts storytelling workshops, and performs at festivals, schools, and a variety of other venues. E-mail: ldneu@tds.net.

FABULOUS FABLES!
By Elizabeth Rose

National Standards:

NCTE 3: Students apply a wide range of strategies to comprehend, interpret, evaluate, and appreciate texts; NCTE 4: Students adjust their use of spoken, written, and visual language (e.g., conventions, style, vocabulary) to communicate effectively with a variety of audiences and for different purposes; NCTE 5: Students employ a wide range of strategies as they write and use different writing process elements appropriately to communicate with different audiences for a variety of purposes.

Objectives:

Use a variety of strategies to extend reading vocabulary; use content, style, and structure appropriate for specific audiences and purposes; use appropriate verbal and nonverbal techniques for oral presentations.

Materials:

- Copies of the fable "The Dog and the Shadow" or any favorite Aesop fable, a copy for each student in the class
- Copies of Aesop's fables (one different fable per student). Web site: *www.aesopfables.com*
- Paper and pencil
- Graphic organizer of a story map and plot diagram

Instructional Plan:

Ask students if they have ever heard or read a fable. If so, have them share their prior knowledge of this genre. Explain that fables come from the oral tradition of storytelling found in folklore from around the world. A fable is a very short story that is meant to illustrate a point or teach us a lesson. Usually, fables are stories about animals that talk like people and teach us a lesson in life called a moral. Many common sayings come from Aesop's fables, such as "Don't count your chickens before they hatch" and "Honesty is the best policy." Aesop was a legendary Greek fabulist, believed to have been a slave who lived in Samos in the sixth century B.C. and eventually freed by his master. No one is really sure if Aesop really made up these fables; what is certain, however, is that the stories called Aesop's fables are so wonderful that they have been told over and over again for thousands of years.

Read aloud "The Dog and the Shadow" by Aesop as the students follow along. Discuss the events. Call attention to the wording, or the style in which the fable is written. Ask students if it is written in the way that they speak. Ask students to identify any unknown words and to look them up in a dictionary. After discovering the meanings of unknown words, ask them to come up with synonyms for those "vocabulary" words. Have students rephrase each sentence in the story using their own words so that it makes sense to them. By doing this, the students are able to work through the story a bit at a time, re-creating it according to their own prior knowledge.

Review with students the elements of a fable: characters, setting, order of events, and the moral. In most fables the characters are animals. These animals usually represent specific human qualities. The characters are one-sided. They act and talk in a way that shows one quality, such as greed or cleverness. For example, the dog in "The Dog and the Shadow" represents greed. Discuss personification, giving human qualities to nonhuman things. Ask students for examples of personification from cartoons and TV commercials.

Review the concept of a moral. Tell students that fables are meant to teach a lesson or moral. The moral is usually revealed at the end of the fable. Sometimes the moral is delivered as a statement, such as "Be happy with what you have" or "It is easier to think up a plan than to carry it out." Call attention to the moral from the fable "The Dog and the Shadow." Ask students to restate the moral in their own words.

Tell students that fables were and are meant to be heard several times. It is usually easier to appreciate and understand a fable if you hear it more than once. The first time, you enjoy the story. The second time, you can study the characters and find the lesson taught about human nature. Point out to students that storytellers told fables over and over again. As they were retold over the years, they evolved in content, emphasis, and style. To illustrate the process of adaptation by individual storytellers, model for the students a retelling of the fable "The Dog and the Shadow." Change details, but not the main point. Explain that the process of retelling stories results in different versions of the same fable. As a group, compare and contrast the retelling of the fable to the original version that was introduced.

The students will now practice rewriting and retelling their own versions of an Aesop fable. The students will be given a fable to read, restate, and paraphrase in their own words. First, the students will read their fable silently. Then, they will read it out loud to a partner. Next, they should restate the fable and the moral to their partner in their own words. If there are any unknown or unfamiliar words in the text, the students are to look them up in a dictionary. Individually, the students will then work on drawing or writing the events of their fable in the proper sequence on a graphic organizer. The students will also complete a story map and plot diagram to identify the elements of their fable. The students will write a rough draft of the fable in their own words, adding details, dialogue, and better-developed characters to make the story more interesting. The students will peer-edit their rough drafts, checking to see that the story makes sense and that details have been added to the story to

Tellers of Tales.

make it more interesting. They will also check for correct spelling, punctuation, and capitalization. Students will then make a final draft to turn in along with their graphic organizer, story map, and plot diagram.

The students are now ready to become tellers of tales. The students will conclude this lesson by orally presenting their fables to the class. As they deliver their fables, remind them of storytelling techniques that have been introduced in previous lessons. For example, remind them to change their pitch or volume of voice, to make eye contact with their audience, and to use their bodies as they deliver their stories.

Assessments:

Student-generated rubrics, such as the examples provided in Levin and Healey's article, evaluate individual elements of student writing and oral presentation.

Tellers of Tales.

For more than a decade Elizabeth Rose, from Kingston, Tennessee, has been performing traditional Southern folklore, fairy tales, ghost stories, and folktales of many cultures for various audiences throughout the United States. Elizabeth shares stories woven with wit, emotion, and expressive enthusiasm. She has the ability to mesmerize her listeners, transporting them through her image-laden tales of other times and cultures. She has thrilled children and adults alike with her vivacious storytelling in classrooms and at festivals and conferences. Elizabeth has nineteen years teaching experience and she currently teaches eighth-grade reading and American history. She uses the "Power of Storytelling" in her daily curriculum and conducts workshops for other educators on how to effectively use storytelling in the classroom. She is truly captivating in voice and presentation! Elizabeth is also the current director for the National Youth Storytelling Showcase. Please visit her Web site at www.storycast.biz.

SELKIE TALES: EXPRESSING THE STORY
By Lisa Worth Huber

Kiet Miah Falchay, which in Scottish Gaelic means "A Thousand Welcomes."

National Standards:

NCTE 4: Adjust use of spoken language to communicate with different audiences; NCTE 5: Apply knowledge of language structure, conventions to create non-print texts; NCTE 9: Develop understanding of and respect to diversity in language use, patterns, and dialects across cultures; NCTE 12: Students use spoken language for learning, enjoyment, and exchange of information; NCSS 1: Provides interaction with other students who are similar and different; NCSS 2: Creates opportunity to explore cultural traditions.

Objectives:

Discover geographical and historical context for Selkie stories by listening to and then discussing the stories; retell stories to other students; draw and create mandalas based on story sequencing; retell the story as a team, with each student telling a portion of the story.

Resources:

- Doherty, Berlie. *Daughter of the Sea*. New York: Random House, 1997.
- Fry, Rosalie K. *The Secret of Roan Inish*. New York: Hyperion Paperbacks for Children, 1985. (Movie of same name by John Sayles)
- Hunter, Mollie. *A Stranger Came Ashore*. New York: Harper Trophy, 1977.
- Lillington, Kenneth. *Selkie*. London: Faber and Faber, 1985.
- Lockley, Ronald. *Seal Woman*. London: Rex Collins, 1974.
- Williamson, Duncan. *Tales of the Seal People, Scottish Folktales*. New York: Interlink Books, 1992. (Williamson, like some other tellers, refers to Selkies as Silkies.)

Instructional Process:

This program welcomes all students and every learning style. The main objective is to help middle school students fall in love with storytelling as listeners, as tellers, and, later on in the process, as writers. Stories surround us, yet most youth feel disengaged from stories. A high consumption of television viewing by preteens has fostered observers who live outside of the oral tradition. What this strives to accomplish is an awakening of the storyteller in each student. It gives them the tools needed to be active story participants and creators.

In my experience, I have found that this may be the first time students view themselves as intelligent, creative, funny, dramatic, and articulate. After completing this program, many students become consciously engaged in expressing themselves. They've discovered that language is a magical medium through which they can express ideas, images, and feelings that they once kept trapped inside. As an educator, I find it inspiring to watch students take ownership of their creativity in fresh ways, empowered by their storytelling experience.

To teach a love for stories, you must share stories you love. I love Selkie stories. (Selkies are seals that take human form when they are on the land.) Versions of these stories are found throughout the British Isles, but I'm drawn to the place where they originated—the Orkney Islands located at the northwestern tip of Scotland.

Before telling these stories, I place them in their geographical and historical context. Students listen more closely when given clues to a story's mystery. Their excitement is piqued when they discover that the most ancient structures in all of Great Britain are found in Orkney. These structures are older than the pyramids at Giza, the Great Wall of China, and England's Stonehenge. Scholars speculate on who built these structures, but believe it's from their mysterious beginnings that the Selkie stories originated. Following this introduction, students listen with purpose to these ancient seal stories. Purposeful listening is crucial to awakening the storyteller within.

Next, I lay out the plan for the workshop. There will be no script, no written stories to refer to. Instead, I will tell these Selkie stories from beginning to end, just once. The students must listen closely. It will be from this one-time telling that they create their stories. There are numerous Selkie stories. A beautiful rendition is found in Susan Cooper's *The Selkie Girl*. I tell my own version created from many sources, but this isn't necessary. The key is found in just becoming comfortable telling the story. At a minimum, depending on class size, I share two Selkie tales.

After hearing the stories, the students and I discuss them. Key questions include: What happened? What words, expressions, and repetitions did you notice? How did the stories make you feel? Were there characters you particularly identified with, and why?

Next, I divide the class into storytelling teams, one team per story. Each story is divided into parts, one part per student. Then, an outline of the story is created and each part placed on a slip of paper. (These are the only written words allowed.)

I then present the following assignment: students must behave as a team and be supportive of each other. We begin telling the story, one student-teller to the next, like passing a ball. This builds listening skills and community.

Crucial to the success of this program is the requirement that students not memorize what they are going to say. Rather, they must trust themselves to be courageous and create the story fresh each time they tell it. I emphasize that there is no right way to tell a story as long as it comes from the heart. This is a liberating concept, particularly for students who shy away from storytelling and reading. Students with dyslexia and ADD/ADHD are initially quite shy when it comes to exposing themselves through storytelling. It is their transformation that I find most inspiring through this approach—although all students shine.

The second day, after team telling, I segue for visual work. I request that the students draw a story map of what they hear. Often, I present this as a mandala, giving each student a marker and a sheet of white paper with a large circle on it. We talk about mandalas: how they can show one moment of a story, a sequence of a story, even a feeling of a story—whatever they are led to do. Mandalas are great for middle school students who, aware of the traditional story structure of beginning, middle, and end, now need to focus on the story's heart. Sharing these mandalas creates another opportunity for students to listen, speak, and grow community. The following day, after team telling, I ask students to draw a picture of their part of the story. This creates a visual memory cue and helps bring description and nuance to their telling.

Ideally, this program takes five consecutive days. After practicing all week, on Friday, it is time to present before an audience. I frame the event by telling the audience that the students could not memorize the story they are about to tell, and that therefore the listeners will be receiving a story created in the moment.

Every time I present this program, I've noticed that children who rarely speak up, do; students who rarely read ask their parents, often for the first time, to take them to the library to find books on Selkies, seals, or other folktales; students who rarely write begin to write their own versions of their favorite stories. Why? I believe it is because they have discovered how story lives inside each student—not on the page, not on a screen, but in their hearts. They become connected with their own voices. They are validated, listened to, and realize that they have a lot to say and share. In essence, students have learned to embody story.

This curriculum addresses the whole brain and is designed to make storytelling come alive for all types of learners. Because it's multi-sensory, it demonstrates the different abilities each student has, enabling those with different learning styles to witness the different intelligences of their peers, often for the first time.

While I'm partial to Selkie stories, this technique can be applied to all story types. After teachers learned this method, they reported using it with myths, folktales, and legends.

Assessments:

Students draw the part of the story that they learned to tell, creating a visual memory cue and helping bring description and nuance to their telling; sharing mandalas creates another opportunity for students to listen, speak, and grow community.

Lisa Worth Huber is a storyteller, writer, and educator. She holds a master's degree in oral traditions and works with teachers and students developing methods of integrating oral stories into curriculum to enhance reading, narrative and poetic writing, creative inquiry, and social awareness. Currently, she is pursuing a Ph.D. in peace studies and is furthering her research on story narrative. E-mail: lisahuber@earthlink.net.

THOSE CLEVER TRICKSTERS!
By Sherry Norfolk

National Standards:

NCTE 1: Students read a wide range of print and non-print texts to build an understanding of texts, of themselves, and of the cultures of the United States and the world; NCTE 4: Students adjust their use of spoken, written, and visual language (e.g., conventions, style, vocabulary) to communicate effectively with a variety of audiences and for different purposes; NCTE 5: Students employ a wide range of strategies as they write and use different writing process elements appropriately to communicate with different audiences for a variety of purposes; NCTE 6: Students apply knowledge of language structure, language conventions (e.g., spelling and punctuation), media techniques, figurative language, and genre to create, critique, and discuss print and non-print texts; NCTE 12: Students use spoken, written, and visual language to accomplish their own purposes (e.g., for learning, enjoyment, persuasion, and the exchange of information); NCSS I: Culture; NCSS III: People, Places, and Environments.

Objectives:

Research, write, and orally present an original trickster tale, reflecting respect for and some understanding of the culture within which it is set.

Trickster tales speak to kids, especially to kids who are often told that they are too little or too weak to do the things they want to do. These tales proclaim loudly and clearly that brains are better than brawn and that the underdog can come out on top. Since nearly every culture has its trickster stories, they can be drawn upon to help children recognize the similarities and differences in values and beliefs, to identify and build on the patterns in the stories, and to learn from the negative and positive role models exhibited.

Full of laughter, pratfalls, mishaps, and mischief, the trickster tales appeal to listeners of all ages and engage imagination and creativity. They provide a perfect platform for creative writing!

I begin by talking a little about trickster tales and their widespread popularity around the globe, and then launch into some stories: Br'er Rabbit, Anansi, Raven, and Kantchil (and, if the season is right, Coyote) are my favorite tricksters to introduce to this age group. After the first story, we discuss the characteristics of a trickster: What size is he or she? Does he or she use violence? Was the trickster greedy or lazy or helpful? We talk a little about the lessons that might be learned, and then we quickly go on to the next story, followed by a quick compare-and-contrast discussion. How was this trickster the same as or different from the first one? How do these differences reflect the culture from which the story originates? When stories from different cultures or continents are very similar, what might be contributing factors to this phenomenon?

After hearing the stories, kids are ready and eager to make up their own! We start the creative writing by developing a group story. Through our discussion, we've determined that trickster stories follow a similar pattern. We can follow that pattern to create our own story, answering these questions:

1. Where does the story take place?
2. Who is the trickster? *(Students can make up their own character as long as he or she fits the characteristics of a tricksters and is native to the setting.)*
3. What does he or she want? *(Examples: The moon, the gold, the ripest peaches, the king's daughter)*
4. Why can't he or she get it? *(Examples: Someone else has it and won't share; it costs too much and trickster is too lazy to work for the money)*
5. Who has it or can help trickster get it?
6. How does the trickster trick this character so that he can get what he wants?
7. How does the story end? Does the trickster get punished or get away with it?

During this group process, kids offer answers and we evaluate them, question them, include them, or reject them. There are always kids who are disappointed that their ideas weren't accepted, but I remind them that they can use those ideas when they write their own stories, so the idea won't go to waste. On Question 6, we brainstorm as many ideas as possible, evaluate the ideas, and decide by voting on the one we'll use (key steps in problem-solving).

After we've answered the questions, I immediately TELL my version of their new story, adding as much detail as possible. I give characters personalities through postures, voices, and dialogue. I add sound effects, action, motivation, and purpose. The idea is to demonstrate how to turn a series of questions and answers into a story. Don't worry—if you're not comfortable doing this part, you'll have students who are clamoring to give it a try!

Then I ask students to make up their own best answers to the questions. This can be done individually, in pairs, or in groups of three, and I like to allow the kids to make their own decisions about whether to work alone or not. While the most creative ideas usually stem from a group-think process, there are always kids who have already thought up their story and are just dying to get on with it! I wander through the groups, helping un-stick the ones who are stuck, answering questions, and mediating disputes that arise when someone's creative ideas are being defended rather too forcefully. Excitement is in the air!

As soon as they've answered the questions, each student writes his or her own individual version of the story, with lots of dialogue to bring the characters to life. After the rough drafts are complete, we make the voices of the characters—out loud!—and then use evocative verbs and adverbs to describe them so that the reader can "hear" how they sound: gravelly, sweet, powerful, whiny, etc. We add sound effects so that readers can "hear" the dripping of the honey or the splat of the falling hippo (even the most reluctant writers are eager to work on this part!). We act out the characters, and then describe them with vivid adjectives and similes. We move as the characters, and find verbs and adverbs that clearly portray the movement. Finally, students pair up with someone who is not familiar with their story. One partner reads his own story out loud while the other partner acts it out. Whenever the actor is unclear as to what he is supposed to do or who is supposed to be doing it, they both stop and make any necessary corrections, continue until the story is finished, and then switch roles. It's chaotic but productive: problems with logic, continuity, and pronoun usage are usually caught and corrected on the spot!

Now everyone has a trickster tale, and the skills to tell it successfully, having developed character voices, sound effects, and actions during the revision process. After a short rehearsal (I recommend practicing in groups of three), it is time for a Worldwide Trickster Storytelling Festival, featuring original stories and student performers!

Following each story, I ask the audience to tell the storyteller what they *liked* about the story (no suggestions, questions, or criticisms allowed). When the hands go up, the storyteller chooses three or four students to give him that feedback. It's powerful for children to get compliments from their peers—and it's empowering to *give* those compliments, as well!

The success rate for this lesson plan is high because students are approaching writing through all the ways of knowing. They move, they listen, they verbalize, and they visualize. They work in social groups and reflect privately. Even students who can't read or write can successfully create and tell marvelous stories, dictating the story to someone else to write down.

Assessments:

Assess the creative writing against state or local rubrics. I provide a rubric for assessing the storytelling as well. But to me, the best assessment is the huge grin on the face of a student teller who has just told her story and been received with wild applause by her peers. She doesn't need a rubric—she *knows* she's succeeded!

Sherry Norfolk is a full-time freelance teaching and performing artist who leads storytelling and creative writing residencies nationwide. E-mail: shnorfolk@aol.com.

MYTH AND POETRY IN THE MIDDLE SCHOOL CLASSROOM: SPRINGBOARDS FOR TELLING AND WRITING ABOUT LOSS
By Merna Ann Hecht

National Standards:

NCTE 9: Students develop an understanding of and respect for diversity in language use, patterns, and dialects across cultures, ethnic groups, geographic regions, and social roles; NCTE 12: Students use spoken, written, and visual language to accomplish their own purposes.

Objectives:

Engage students in exploring different literary styles through listening, reading, and small and large group discussions; explore and express the themes of loss and love based on the Orpheus myth and selected poetry.

As a storyteller and poet, working with seventh- and eighth-grade students across the curriculum areas of language arts, world history, and creative writing, I often draw upon world myth. A particularly successful springboard for engaging students in creative writing and oral presentation is the Greek myth of "Orpheus and Eurydice." Telling this myth has consistently brought forth solemn and thoughtful responses from the young writers with whom I work. When asked to create original poems related to themes from the Orpheus myth, students have taken the myth to heart and have written with candor, clarity, and depth about loss, betrayal, and love. After I present a myth, I use poetry to deepen the universal themes and to offer students a number of different perspectives and entry points for creating their own poetic and narrative responses.

In the story, Orpheus, the gifted mortal musician, is out walking with his beloved, Eurydice, when a snake suddenly bites her and she dies from its venom. Shattered by the loss, Orpheus is determined, to the horror of his friends, to journey down to the Underworld and implore Hades to allow Eurydice to return to the land of mortals. Orpheus's lyre and mournful songs win him a friendship with Cerebus, the ferocious three-headed dog who guards the gates to Hades and, in any other circumstance, would tear a mortal to pieces. Such is the depth of grief and beauty in Orpheus's music that even hard-hearted Hades is swayed to do what he has never done before and returns a mortal to the land of the living. Hades warns Orpheus that he can only have Eurydice back if he does not look at her until they have returned to the human realm. Close to the end of their long and arduous passage out of the Underworld, Orpheus begins to experience a series of terrible doubts—why is Eurydice so quiet? What if Hades has tricked him? What if she no longer loves him? Panicked, Orpheus looks back and Eurydice screams in lament, "Orpheus! Why?" and she is lost to him for eternity.

Stanley Kunitz, the former poet laureate of the United States, wrote, "... The heart breaks and breaks and lives by breaking. It is necessary to go through dark and deeper dark and not to turn," which manages to condense the themes of the Orpheus myth into one line. I continually look for poems that lend themselves to such breathtaking connections with specific myths in my teller's repertoire. I want the students to make the connections between the language of myth and metaphor and experience how each is a vehicle for expressing deep emotion and exploring one's own inner journey, including issues around loss and betrayal.

Instructional Process:

It will require three to four class periods to implement the sequential steps that result in both written work and oral presentations. Throughout the extended lesson, the objectives are to engage students in exploring different literary styles through listening, reading, and small and large group discussions; to improve their skills in writing personal pieces, chants, and lyric poetry; and to explore and express personally or through persona writing the themes of loss and love in the Orpheus myth and selected poetry.

Before I tell the story I talk with my students about loss and read selected poems from Naomi Shihab Nye's collection *What Have You Lost?* (Greenwillow, 1999). We have a group discussion about loss and list things people lose, including objects; qualities (i.e., courage, trust, innocence); and loss of certain abilities, pets, and loved ones. After the students listen to the Orpheus myth, I read them selections from Kate Hovey's *Ancient Voices* (Simon & Schuster, 2004), a collection of personal pieces written in the voices of Greek gods and goddesses, and "Self-Portrait as Eurydice, poems I, II, and III," from Edward Hirsch's book *Lay Back the Darkness* (Knopf, 2004). I divide the class of thirty students into groups of three and ask that they read the selections I've shared with them out loud in round-robin style. They are asked to choose one of the pieces and practice until they have achieved an expressive and dramatic rendering to present to the class.

Next I give them a handout that says: Loss and betrayal can be difficult topics. Choose a loss you feel safe writing about, or explore feelings of loss and betrayal as they relate to the Orpheus myth. You are asked to choose one of the following four writing prompts. Pay attention to word choice, use of simile and metaphor, use of sensory image, and strong narrative writing that will allow you to write from another point of view in order to create a persona piece.

1. Keeping the Orpheus myth in mind, write a personal poem about loss. Go back and read the poems we have read and discussed from *What Have You Lost?*
2. Write a poem to Orpheus in the voice of Eurydice; the voice of Hades; or the voice of the boatman, Charon. Note that this example by sixth-grade poet Michael Schiralli is an excerpt from the book *Listener in the Snow* (Teachers and Writers Collaborative, 2000): "Good-bye to you / I will be back / I promise I will ... Remember my living soul will always be with you ... I will come back through the light."
3. Create your own version of the Orpheus myth from the narrative perspective of Orpheus, Eurydice, or Hades.
4. Create a chant in which you use repetition to express the mood and feeling of your story or poem. Think about ways this will strengthen your piece for out-loud presentation.

Students presented their finished pieces to the class and discussed them. Each student was asked to evaluate his or her own work with questions about both writing and presentation that referred back to the language arts standards addressed in the lesson. Some of the evaluative questions were: Was the atmosphere and mood you created expressive of what you most wanted to say? How could you have made your piece more expressive, both as a written piece and for your out-loud presentation? Do you think you included enough sensory images and figurative language? Are there places where you might add more? Was your voice as a writer and a speaker reflective of your character's mood, attitude, and situation?

The students were thrilled with the high caliber of their creative work and listened intently to each other. One student wrote of her father's betrayal when he left the family, in a riveting piece called "Father, If I Could Speak to You," with repeating lines in a chant form. Another student wrote a poem entitled "This Is What the Underworld Is," a repetitive line poem offering vivid sensory description of the Underworld. Yet another student wrote a piece titled "Poem to Orpheus"; speaking in the voice of Eurydice, she wrote:

"Sinking in the ground / meters away from the sun / So close but now so far / imagining the sun sweet upon the flowers / All that I hold dear slips away!" (Elizabeth, grade seven, Writers in the Schools, Seattle, 2000). And so it went throughout the student showcase. Deeply moving poems from universal experiences of loss, love, and betrayal were crafted, honed, and shared in a classroom community grown close through the use of story and poetry.

Assessments:

Evaluate writing and presentation that referred back to the language arts standards addressed in the lesson; students evaluate their writing to determine characters' mood, attitude, and situation.

Resources:

I adapt the myth of "Orpheus and Eurydice," combining versions from both:

- Low, Alice. *The Macmillan Book of Greek Gods and Heroes*. New York: Macmillan, 1985.
- Rosenberg, Donna, and Sorelle Baker. *Mythology and You: Classical Mythology and Its Relevance to Today's World*. IL: National Textbook Company, 1992.

Resources for poetry and prose pieces cited and used in the lesson plan:

- Heard, Georgia. *Awakening the Heart: Exploring Poetry in Elementary and Middle School*. Portsmouth, NH: Heinemann, 1999. Lines from the Stanley Kunitz poem "The Testing Tree" are quoted from this book, Chapter 2, "Reading Poetry: Poems Keep Singing to You All Your Life," page 19.
- Hovey, Kate. *Ancient Voices*. New York: Margaret K. McElderry Books/Simon & Schuster, 2004.
- Hecht, Merna, ed. *Asa Mercer Middle School Anthology, Helen Paulus's Class Poetry Anthology*. Seattle: Writers in the Schools, 2002.
- Nye, Naomi Shihab. *What Have You Lost?* New York: Greenwillow Books, 1999.
- Statman, Mark. *Listener in the Snow: The Practice and Teaching of Poetry*. New York: Teachers and Writers Collaborative, 2000. The sample student poem on the writing prompt by Michael Schiralli is from Chapter 5, "Writing About Loss," page 66.

Merna Ann Hecht, poet, storyteller, arts and literacy educator, is a Program Mentor and teaching writer for the Writers in the Schools Program in Seattle. She has been a faculty member at Pacific Oaks College in the Teacher Certification Program where she taught "Language and Literacy" and "Imagination and Cultural Expression in the Classroom." She currently teaches for the Heritage Institute's Educating for Humanity Program, offering courses on bringing social justice teaching to the classroom through storytelling, integrated arts approaches, and writing. Merna received a 1999 National Storytelling Network Community Service Award. Her essays and poetry have appeared in a number of professional journals and small press magazines. E-mail: mernaanna@yahoo.com.

ELVIS MEETS A LITHUANIAN ORANGUTAN IN MAGENTA TIGHTS AT THE DISCO
By Greg Weiss

National Standards:

NCTE 12: Students use spoken, written, and visual language to accomplish their own purposes (e.g., for learning, enjoyment, persuasion, and the exchange of information); CNAEA (Theatre) 1: Creates characters, environments; creates improvisations and scripted scenes based on personal experience and heritage, imagination, literature, and history; CNAEA (Theatre) 2: Interacts as an invented character in improvised and scripted scenes.

Objectives:

Create and present an original story based on a shared set of teacher-generated story prompts.

One of the blessings of teaching a middle school drama exploratory is the satisfaction of teaching "art for art's sake," not being subservient to the core subject areas. Also, with few exceptions, every student in the building is scheduled into drama class for one exploratory rotation each year. This also suggests the greatest challenge. With only six weeks per school year to see each student, time is most precious, especially in a course that focuses on frequent student vocal/physical performance.

Arguably the most universal and fundamental dramatic medium, storytelling provides excellent performance opportunities in the middle school drama curriculum. Seventh-grade students will each engage in four story projects over the course of a two-week unit. The first project is to tell a story from the oral tradition. Then a story is learned/told from a written source. Since one of the main goals of the drama curriculum is to encourage students to trust themselves as the originators of creative endeavor, the next task is an original creation, based on elements of the stories already told. Having told three times in front of their peers, students should have a good working knowledge of story structure and basic telling skills. By now, they should also realize how stories will grow and change with each telling. This brings us to the final project, and the focus of this lesson, a story told from a shared set of prompts.

To begin, the class is polled to come up with an item for each of the following categories: a color, a person, a location/place, a language, an animal, and an object. Prior to soliciting these story prompts, they are encouraged

Vocal/Physical Performance.

to think "out of the box." Next, students are instructed to create a story that will incorporate each of the prompts, each student using the same six prompts. Their goal is to separate each of the six items with as much story as possible. For example, if the items are turquoise, Abraham Lincoln, Texas, Turkish, a wombat, and a balloon, the following would not be a good story: "One day

Presenting the Story.

while walking my pet wombat, named Abraham Lincoln, a crazy man carrying a turquoise balloon approached and asked me how to get to Texas in Turkish." The students are encouraged to space the items apart somewhat evenly in a story, which should last about two minutes. A good story might begin, "The hot Texas sun beat down on the bricks of the school, making the whole building feel like a giant oven. It was hard for the students to concentrate, particularly Johnny, who was terribly bored, especially in history class. He didn't care that Abraham Lincoln was the sixteenth president. His mind drifted into a daydream. He imagined this was what it felt like to be in the Outback of Australia, in the scorching heat of summer. At least that would be something new and different. Johnny could search for marsupials, his favorite kind of animal. Of particular interest would be kangaroos and wombats..."

Students are given one class period to create their stories and to practice telling them to each other. They are encouraged to let characters speak, to create dialogue. At this point, students are not permitted to write their stories on paper. It is reinforced that the story will be different each time it is told. Since they will hear other stories, students are told to respect each others' work, not to "borrow" from each other. After polishing their tales overnight, they will present them for evaluation the next class session.

The evaluation covers the following aspects: successful inclusion of all six prompts, the even spacing of the prompts throughout the story, character, conflict, story structure, sufficient length, and delivery skills. Though everyone is working from the same set of prompts, the results will be as varied and imaginative as the students in the class. This project showcases the uniqueness of each participant in an assignment where it is okay to be weird. It also engages students as audience members. They will listen actively, trying to catch all six prompts, while anticipating the next twist or turn in the story.

Once all stories have been presented, the option still exists to have each student write the story and, perhaps, even draw images to go along with it. Or, if a specific tie-in is desired, the teacher could require that the prompts all fit a particular topic. With possibilities like these, this project can expand into other curricular areas, like language arts, social studies, and art. While this is an ideal project for middle school, it would work well, with little adaptation, in third grade through high school.

Assessments:

At the conclusion of each presentation, feedback is solicited from everyone—students and teachers alike—concerning successful inclusion of all six prompts, the even spacing of the prompts throughout the story, character, conflict, story structure, sufficient length, and delivery skills.

A storyteller and schoolteacher since 1990, Greg Weiss was introduced to storytelling at a seminar taught by Lynn Rubright. Since then, he has attended dozens of workshops and coaching sessions by some of the best storytellers in the business. He has told stories and presented workshops throughout the Midwest and beyond, at major storytelling festivals including St. Louis, Three Rivers (in Pittsburgh), Illinois, and at schools/conferences like Betty Weeks, Northlands, and Northwestern University. Greg serves on the board of the Northlands Storytelling Network. Three-time honoree of Who's Who Among America's Educators, his efforts earned him the Studs Terkel Humanities Service Award from the Illinois Humanities Council. E-mail: gjweiss@ earthlink.net.

THE ART OF EXPRESSIONS AND EMOTIONS IN STORYTELLING
By Diane Williams

National Standards:

NCTE 1: Reading for Perspectives: Students read a wide range of print and non-print texts to build an understanding of texts, of themselves, and of the cultures of the United States and the world; to acquire new information; to respond to the needs and demands of society and the workplace; and for personal fulfillment. Among these texts are fiction and nonfiction, classic, and contemporary works; NCTE 4: Communication Skills: Students adjust their use of spoken, written, and visual language (e.g., conventions, style, vocabulary) to communicate effectively with a variety of audiences and for different purposes; NCTE 6: Applying Language Knowledge: Students apply knowledge of language structure, language conventions (e.g., spelling and punctuation), media techniques, figurative language, and genre to create, critique, and discuss print and non-print texts.

Objectives:

Explore verbal and nonverbal communication skills that will help students to tell stories with emphasis on expressions; practice facial expressions without speaking; practice using words and phrases to express different meanings.

Resources:

- Cole, Joanna. *Best-Loved Folktales of the World*. New York: Doubleday, 1983.
- Goss, Linda, and Marian E. Barnes, ed. *Talk That Talk*. New York: Simon and Schuster, 1989.
- Kimmel, Eric. *The Witch's Face*. New York: Holiday House, 1993.
- Scieszka, Jon. *The True Story of the Three Pigs*. New York: Viking Kestrel, 1989.
- Silverstein, Shel. *The Giving Tree*. New York: Harper & Row, 1964.
- Yolen, Jane. *Favorite Folktales from Around the World*. New York: Pantheon Books, 1986.

Practice:

Verbal, vocal, and visual communication—the three go together. The next time you talk with someone, just try to incorporate one without the other. For example, talk to someone using a plain and simple monotone voice. The listener loses interest in the conversation within the first few minutes.

Let's take this experiment one step further. If you incorporate vocal intonations with expressive pitch, volume, and pauses, the conversation becomes much more interesting. Furthermore, with practice you can master the art of effective communication.

The art of effective communication involves much more than phonation. There is also a universal form of communication called body language, and that's the visual aesthetic needed to effectively relay a message when words are not enough.

Many individuals use their hands, bodies, and facial expressions in a haphazard way. A conscious effort to involve your body by using gestures can enhance communication, and, if coordinated with vocal and verbal command of language, the orator will present a dramatic presentation appropriate for any theatre's stage.

Actors become proficient in the art of effective communication all the time. When auditioning for a role in a play or movie, the director selects the actor who uses pauses, gestures, and phrasing that engage the listener and viewer.

Simple Rules to Follow

- Articulation—Say it with feeling
- Enunciation—Consider how it sounds
- Pronunciation—Say it distinctly
- Verbalization—Focus on the meaning of the words as you project and embody the story—movement and facial expressions should add emphasis to what you say.

Listed below are words or phrases that have been arranged to evoke expressions from the professional as well as the novice storyteller in all of us.

Facial Expressions

Instructions: Use facial expressions to exhibit the emotional traits. Talk about specific visible differences in face and body language.

- Admiration—great job!
- Adoration—love
- Ambiguity (doubtful or uncertain)
- Anger
- Astonishment—shock
- Confidence
- Confusion
- Denial
- Depression
- Expressionless
- Frenzy
- Grief
- Happiness—joy
- Hatred
- Horror
- Hysterical
- Ignoring
- Lecturing
- Melancholy
- Outrage
- Sadness
- Surprise
- Terror

Verbal Expressions

Instructions: Say the word that is written in bold type in the manner specified in the indented column. Example: Say "Well" as if you are disgusted. Now say that same word in an inquiring or questioning manner. Then say it as if you are surprised. Note: To achieve the best results possible, as a precaution students should use only the word to the far left. They should not verbalize any other words for effect.

Start out by practicing words and phrases that students have already been having some fun with. For example: "Duh," "Stop," "Shut up," "Okay," "Hello," "Ya think," "My bad." Then try these:

Well

- Disgust.
- Inquiringly.
- In surprise.

Joyful.

- Let me see (let me think about it)—Pondering something.
- Pleased and ready to move on to the next item.
- Upon seeing a dear friend whom you haven't seen in years.
- What are YOU looking at?!
- What do you think of that?

What

- A question: In what respect? How?
- Do I have toilet paper hanging onto the bottom of my shoe or something?
- Surprise/shock.

Oh

- Okay—that clears things up!
- To express acknowledgement or understanding.
- Whatever!
- You found out something embarrassingly shocking about someone at church.

Confidence.

You'd better not!

- A general warning that something could possibly go wrong.
- An alarming warning of danger.
- Disciplining a child.

Wait

- Angrily.
- (Alarm) A truck just turned the corner in front of someone.
- You're trying to catch up with someone.

Don't do that

- Adamantly!
- Said to a stranger or acquaintance.
- With overwhelming emphasis (a warning).

Darling

- To a dear/loved one.
- Stated as if you are Mr. or Mrs. Hollywood or Queen/King of Elvis Land.

Laughter

- Chuckle.
- Fake.
- Hilarious.
- Snicker.

Whatever

- No matter what you need—you will have it.
- Nonchalantly.
- With attitude! Possibly coming from a teenager.

Assessments:

Students will work in groups and evaluate one another; teachers will observe students and commend best practices; practice skills learned by reading and telling a story with facial and verbal expression; after completing this exercise, teachers can select appropriate stories for the students to retell.

Diane Williams is past board chair for the National Storytelling Network (NSN). She currently serves as the Arts Industry Director for the Mississippi Arts Commission and as the president of the Central Mississippi Storyweavers Guide. Diane lives in Madison, Mississippi. E-mail: dwteller@aol.com.

AMERICAN CHOICES, AMERICAN VOICES: TELLING THE STORY
By Kevin Cordi

National Standards:

NCTE 1: Students read a wide range of print and non-print texts to build an understanding of texts, of themselves, and of the cultures of the United States and the world; NCTE 3: Students apply a wide range of strategies to comprehend, interpret, evaluate, and appreciate texts; NCTE 4: Students adjust their use of spoken, written, and visual language (e.g., conventions, style, vocabulary) to communicate effectively with a variety of audiences and for different purposes; NCTE 7: Students conduct research on issues and interests by generating ideas and questions, and by posing problems. They gather, evaluate, and synthesize data from a variety of sources; NCSS IV: Individual Development and Identity: Examination of various forms of human behavior enhances understanding of the relationships among social norms and emerging personal identities, the social processes that influence identity formation, and the ethical principles underlying individual action.

Objectives:

Information literacy—extended research of an American historical figure or event; use results to write and present a narrative about that person or event and bring history to life.

Students often don't engage in history because they feel it does not connect with them; however, this assignment allows students to step into a historical time and/or a historical person's shoes. It allows him or her to imagine what Albert Einstein might have felt as he decided on his theory of relativity. It puts the student in Maria Mitchell's place as she struggled to be recognized as the first woman astronomer, or in Kathy Wright's earthbound shoes, wishing she could fly with her brothers Wilbur and Orville. In this lesson, students explore the people who made the choices that changed history and allowed their voices to be heard. This is why I designed "American Choices, American Voices: A Look into History."

To begin, ask the class how a person their age, living during or experiencing the following events, might have felt: the landing on the moon; the assassination of JFK; the wonder of the first flight; invention of the telephone; being the first woman to go to college; being the first African American kid to go to a desegregated school; staging the first sit-in; signing the Declaration of Independence; being captured and placed in a Civil War prison; building the first automobile; being a Rough Rider; spending a night in a Birmingham jail.

We discuss how being a teenager might change the viewer's perception of an event, and then I ask students to brainstorm a list of people in American history, directing them to list as many as they can who have played a significant role in history. We don't worry if individuals are considered major or minor characters; we simply list them. You might also brainstorm time periods or events that have occurred in American history. No matter how small or large, simply list them.

Decide on two or three events or people who would be interesting to investigate. Talk about how looking at these people through the eyes of a middle school–aged student might change the way they see it. How much knowledge would be important? What would be their interest concerning the subjects?

Collectively share what students know about the events and people they chose. What else will they need and want to know? Send them to the media center to discover as much as they can about the person or time. They should make sure to collect many vantage points and even find the trivial information because that can help make a good story; for example, what did the historical person's parents think of him or her? What pets did he or she have as a child?

Student Assignment:

Select facts and incidents that best represent the event or person. Identify transitional times and turning points to recount, e.g., What event led to the first space walk? What were the high points of Thomas Edison's years? Begin to organize and select the information that tells the event or person's story.

If you are studying an *event* of the past, decide how you will take the listeners in your class back to the time period you want them to visit with you. Are you returning with the help of a time-traveling device? Are you already in the past? Were you dreaming in class and woke and found yourself at the New York World's Fair?

Choose your perspective: inside or outside? Are you telling the story as a person from the outside (present time) looking in? Are you a young Abraham Lincoln or Harriet Beecher Stowe telling the story from the inside?

Choose to be a historical person *at your own age* or view an event from the vantage point of a young person during the historical time. Gather resources from books, magazines, and Web sites that portray many perspectives of the event or person.

The Storytelling Structure:

Lance Hensen, a Cheyenne storyteller and writer once said to me, "Stories are gifts; we take them and receive them." With this thought in mind, a story should have:

An "Unwrapping" Beginning: Just as a special gift has wrapping paper that is unwrapped to reveal the gift, so does a story. Think of a beginning besides "This person's name is . . ." that unwraps a certain part of this person or event's "life" and reveals that there is more to be heard.

The Gift: This is the actual fabric of the story. Instead of telling all you can, entice us with the most interesting or controversial facts about your person or event. Often mysteries about the event or person can hold our attention as listeners. Make sure that you have at least ten true statements (historical facts); however, in telling the story you may add historical fiction, such as Ben Franklin taking a walk downtown to see his sister, as long as it does not change the significance of who he is.

A "Wrapping" Conclusion: Much as a precious gift is rewrapped and put away to savor at another time, a story must follow suit. Find a way to end, perhaps with a question.

Ways to Spice the Storytelling:

To make the storytelling a special event for the students, try some of these ideas:

1. Dress the part: allow students to dress as the characters or in the time period. I highly recommend that you encourage them to represent their characters with clothing or props to help place themselves in the time period or as the person.
2. Add an emcee: ask the emcee to pose as a radio broadcaster or TV newscaster, or simply as someone who entices us to listen to find out more about the person. The proper "set-up" can help the teller and the story.
3. Invite special guests: important, knowledgeable guests such as history teachers or a local historian can help add an extra dimension to the work. Make sure students are forewarned about these visitors!
4. Q&A: after each presentation, encourage audience members to ask relevant questions about the event or character. The storyteller should stay "in character" as he or she answers these questions. You might ask the audience to portray reporters, researchers, etc.
5. Create a CD or tape recording of the stories. Students can record either before or during the performance.
6. Ask students to create a PowerPoint presentation after the story is completed.
7. Create an interactive Web site.

Reflection:

My class at first did not really know the people and events that shaped America; however, as one student said it, "I have walked their history and now I understand the road." Some of my students set out to study someone like Harriet Tubman, but found the first woman astronomer along the way. Some told the story of the Revolutionary Mollie Pitcher, who provided water to the soldiers on the battlefield. Others explored the local connection to the Dust Bowl, and still others told stories of Orphan Train riders. Once the students were vested, they researched their stories and the history connected to them. We recorded our work in a professional studio, which is available at www.youthstorytelling.com.

History came alive because the students made the choice to bring the story to life. You can do this in your classroom, and you, too, will find that American history has wonderful, engaging, and inviting stories to tell.

Assessments:

The Q&A session described above is a powerful way to learn the depth of each student's research and understanding of the person or event portrayed.

Kevin Cordi is an award-winning teacher of fourteen years and is "the first full-time high school storytelling teacher in the country." He is finishing a

Ph.D. at Ohio State University, studying narrative storytelling and process drama and teaching. He is the co-author, with Judy Sima, of Raising Voices: Youth Storytelling Groups and Troupes. *He was awarded the "Golden Bell Award" by the California Board of Education, marking his program one of the top fifty exemplary educational programs in the state. You can reach him at www.youthstorytelling.com.*

THROUGH THE EYES OF YORK
By Bobby Norfolk

National Standards:

NCSS II: Time, Continuity, and Change; NCSS IV: People, Places, and Environment; NCTE 1: Students read a wide range of print and non-print texts to build an understanding of texts, of themselves, and of the cultures of the United States; NCTE 4: Students adjust their use of spoken, written, and visual language (e.g., conventions, style, vocabulary) to communicate effectively with a variety of audiences and for different purposes; NCTE 6: Students apply knowledge of language structure, language conventions (e.g., spelling and punctuation), media techniques, figurative language, and genre to create, critique, and discuss print and non-print texts; NCTE 7: Students conduct research on issues and interests by generating ideas and questions, and by posing problems. They gather, evaluate, and synthesize data from a variety of sources; NCTE 12: Students use spoken, written, and visual language to accomplish their own purposes.

Objectives:

Develop and perform first-person narratives based on the lives of members of the Corps of Discovery; through the resulting performances, students will not only educate their own class members about a variety of explorers and the expedition, but will be fully prepared to teach students in lower grades as well.

Assembly programs in schools are tricky these days—the content must adhere to rigorous academic standards, must by accessible for a fairly wide range of listeners and learners, and must be entertaining and engaging enough to keep them all listening. Maybe that's why my one-man show, which brings the Lewis and Clark Expedition to life "through the eyes of York," the only African American in the Corps of Discovery, is so popular with elementary, middle, and high schools. This program was developed after years of careful research into the expedition itself and York in particular, and in it, I use a lot of humor, action,

The Explorers See the First Prairie Dogs.

and graphic detail to engage young listeners who often have never even heard of the Louisiana Purchase, much less the expedition to explore it.

Programming of this type is often used to introduce a theme or unit of study, to interest the students in the content, pique their curiosity, and make them eager to learn more—and it works! One teacher reported that her fourth graders refused to return to their classroom after the performance—they demanded to go to the library and get more information about York and the other explorers! This kind of enthusiasm is also demonstrated during the question-and-answer session after the program, during which kids ask a zillion questions: How many people died on the expedition? How many horses did they take on the LoLo Trail in the Bitterroot Mountain Range? How many horses survived? How many people actually went to the Pacific Ocean? Teachers are always amazed at their kids' questions, and are eager to capitalize on their enthusiasm in the classroom.

One way to capitalize on that enthusiasm is described in the lesson plan below, which my wife, Sherry, conducts to build on the learning that began during the assembly program.

The Lesson:

Get ready by discussing the York performance and how it was developed. Stress that it took research, research, research! Ask students what made it grab and hold their attention: voices, sound effects, actions?

The Rocky Mountains!

Develop first-person narratives about the explorers by first modeling a short (two- to three-minute) first-person narrative performance—Seaman the Dog is highly recommended. Make it fun, use a "doggy" voice, and scratch your fleas and mosquito bites every once in a while!

Send groups to discovery centers about the Corps of Discovery. NOTE: provide a variety of materials for this purpose. The following Web sites are recommended for concise, specific information:

1. www.nps.gov/jeff/LewisClark2/Activities&Kids/CorpsProfiles.htm
    Excellent, short profiles with links to more detailed information. Site developed by the Museum of Westward Expansion, St. Louis, Missouri.
2. www.pbs.org/lewisandclark/inside/idx_corp.html
    Researched and written by Irving W. Anderson, past president of the Lewis and Clark Trail Heritage Foundation.
3. www.lewisandclark200.gov/edu/corps/cfm
    Developed by the Department of the Interior, this site provides specific biographical information on members of the Corps.

Guide students in writing the narrative by providing focus. Ask kids to take notes about what they find interesting—no dates of birth, death, etc.—just events. After they have developed their notes, ask them to think of one or two words that describe this person's personality (brave, foolhardy, resourceful, etc.). Then ask them to write down the events that support that opinion. In other words, they should SHOW, not TELL. In fact, the personality words they choose should not even have to appear in their text, because the events they choose to share should illustrate them clearly to the listeners.

Ask kids to pair off, read their narratives to their partners, and see if the partner can guess what the words they chose were. If not, partners should help the writer to research events that will do the job, or discuss what traits were actually illustrated by the anecdotes in the narrative.

The research is complete, and now the students will learn to bring the explorers to life. Practice performance techniques such as vocal expression, body language, and gesture. First, ask kids to think about the voice their character would have—loud, soft, high, low, slow, fast, mean, etc.—and demonstrate it by introducing their character to the group in the character's voice.

Next ask kids to think about the way their character would hold him- or herself—tall and straight, hunched over, with a limp, etc. What did that person carry (everyone carried something all the time!)? How would they carry it? Now ask kids to walk around the room in character, carrying their loads: climb mountains, slog across the prairies, slosh through streams.

Rehearsal in small groups will provide an opportunity for students to become comfortable with their characterization and the content of their narrative. Groups of three are optimal. Each student becomes the character and tells/reads his or her narrative using the voice and posture and acting out the anecdotes whenever possible.

Following rehearsal, your class is ready to present their own Performances of the Corps of Discovery!

This lesson plan for the "living museum" has been used in fourth-grade to eighth-grade classrooms, and the results are always exciting! The kids are eager to learn as much as possible about their explorers, and will read and read and read until they feel confident. They develop postures, voices, and characteristics that bring their explorers to life in humorous, sympathetic, and imaginative ways. Their listeners remain engaged, ask intelligent questions, and learn even more!

The technique can easily be modified to follow any first-person performance. Musicians, authors, artists, historical figures, scientists, and mathematicians can all be explored using this method, making learning reciprocal, multifaceted, and fun! It's a win-win situation when storytelling comes to school!

Assessments:

Follow each oral presentation with a question-and-answer session, during which audience members can explore additional facets of the explorer's experiences. This provides further opportunity to assess the depth of understanding of the individual explorer and his or her role in the expedition itself. Or, the class may decide to have an afternoon of the living museum, inviting other classes and parents who can walk around and interview the historical figures!

Bobby Norfolk is well known for his high-energy performances and lively animation. His stories promote character education, cultural diversity, and self-esteem, and are geared for audiences of all ages. From park ranger to TV host, recording artist to author, Bobby has traveled an interesting life path that is revealed by his creative stories and crowd-pleasing concerts, enriched with language, movement, and clever sound effects. He has been awarded three Emmys and several Gold Parents Choice awards for his work. Web site: www.bobbynorfolk.com.

TELLING THE STORY OF OUR SCHOOL
By Nancy Fraleigh

National Standards:

NCTE 3: Evaluation Strategies: Students apply a wide range of strategies to comprehend, interpret, evaluate, and appreciate texts. They draw on their prior experience, their interactions with other readers and writers, their knowledge of word meaning and of other texts, their word identification strategies, and their understanding of textual features (e.g., sound-letter correspondence, sentence structure, context, graphics); NCTE 4: Communication Skills: Students adjust their use of spoken, written, and visual language (e.g., conventions, style, vocabulary) to communicate effectively with a variety of audiences and for different purposes.

Objectives:

Collect alumni stories on tape; create character dimension from detail and explanation given by alumni; practice interviewing skills and techniques on evoking information; catalog the collection of stories for storing and preserving archives; compare and contrast taped accounts from a variety of time periods.

Materials:

- Contact information for alumni
- List of agreed-upon questions
- Tape recorders
- Cassette tapes
- Tape storage boxes and labels

"This is a dead document," I proclaimed as I threw the book onto the floor. The document in question was a book compiled to commemorate the 100th birthday of our school. A lot of work had gone into it, and it was a wonderful gesture. There were pictures, jokes, advertisements, news clippings about administrators, but most of all, lists and lists of past graduates.

"Who were these kids? What did they do at lunch? What were their shows like? Their concerts? Their baseball games? Their spelling bees? What did they want to be when they grew up? Until we know these things, this is not a record honoring a group of young people who went to this school. This is just a pile of paper." I think I was getting their attention. "So what can we do about it? Do these kids deserve a REAL record of their time here?"

A spirited discussion ensued, and they decided that yes, every generation deserves to be known, to be understood. What then?

"We could interview them, take notes, and type them up."

"We could get the graduates to write their stories for us." The ideas were starting to flow.

"We could make a display like they do in museums."

"Oh! I know!! Have you ever heard of an *archive?*" Nobody was familiar with the word, so I told them. "It's a place where you keep public records and documents. What if we had people come in and tell their stories while we taped them? Then we could figure out a way to catalog the tapes and make an archive out of them."

"Then we could listen to them anytime we want."

"And we could add to them whenever we wanted to. Like, every year we could tape a few more graduates. This could get really big."

"But what would we do with it?" asked one skeptic. "I mean, why would we WANT to store a bunch of old tapes?"

"It's the story of our school, dummy. We could look back and see how they did things a hundred years ago, and how different it was from the way we do things now. We could see how much we have changed . . . how far we have come." I was glad she said that, so that I didn't have to. It is great when the students become the teachers.

"OK, so if you all think that this is a good idea, how shall we begin?"

How Shall We Begin? As students move through the grades, we want them to work toward "fleshing out" and expanding the characters in their writing. When we point out how one-dimensional the lists and lists of student names are, we emphasize the need for detail, explanation, and "story." We, indeed, DO NOT have a living piece of writing without that. By bringing the school document to life, we provide students with a prime example of what EVERY document should be.

Grade Level and Subject Matter Whether they are just finishing elementary school, or are ready to leave middle school and progress to high school, they are grasping the concept of moving from one level of education to another. There are graduations and good-byes involved, and there are ideas to preserve.

Instructional Process:

Decide Whom to Interview: We decided to interview the five inductees to our district's Hall of Fame that year. We also decided to interview ten graduates of our school that year. We used them to practice our interviewing skills, before the alumni came in.

Decide What to Ask: Small groups met to compile a list of twenty questions that they would want to ask. We then shared lists and compiled one master list. They were also advised to compose generic questions that could be asked of ANY graduate, so that comparing the different generations would be easier.

Practice: Student groups were assigned to interview this year's graduates, in order to perfect their techniques. Invariably, students allowed their subjects to give brief answers, rather than expanding into a story. If the first tape is not satisfactory, students should have an opportunity to hear a well-done example, and then retape their subjects.

Isolate Vocabulary: Students should go through their tapes and identify words that might not be understood by another generation (such as slang). They will then write up a list of vocabulary and definitions, to be stored with the tape.

Tape the Alumni: When students are ready, alumni may be brought in to be taped. Students should be reminded that they must "draw out" their subjects in order to get their "stories." Each alumnus may be given to a small group to work with. Besides taping them, students must also be alert to vocabulary that they may need to define (by asking their subjects BEFORE they leave).

Plan Who Will Be Taped Next Year: Keep a growing archive that can be used in many, many ways.

Label and Store the Tapes.

Assessments:

Students can write a story from the viewpoint of one of the taped subjects. Write a "Back to the Future"-type story, using the taped subjects as characters. Compare and contrast two or more of the taped subjects from different decades.

Nancy Fraleigh is a high school–level storytelling teacher at Hanford High in California. She and her students delight elementary school audiences every Wednesday afternoon in what they call "Afternoon Delights." Also an experienced history teacher, her love of story and history has led her to create this alumni archive project. Her students love preserving the stories of the past. She is also currently compiling a book of stories surrounding the development of girls' and women's ice hockey in California. Anyplace that people will tell, you'll find Nancy with her tape recorder. E-mail: hcky2118@aol.com.

THE DEVIL'S HIGHWAY: AN EXPLORATION OF MATH AND SOCIAL STUDIES
By Althea Jerome

National Standards:

NCTM 6: Instructional programs should enable all students to solve problems that arise in mathematics and in other contexts; NCSS 5: Social studies programs should include experiences that provide for the study of interactions among individuals, groups, and institutions; NSS.1 (U. S. History): Living and working together in families and communities now and long ago. Understand the history of the local community and how communities in North America varied long ago; NSS.2 (U. S. History): The history of students' own state or region. Students understand the people, events, problems, and ideas that were significant in creating the history of the state.

Objectives:

Analyze elements of a story about the Natchez Trace to increase understanding of life in that region of America during the early 1800s; create math problems to solve using content from *The Devil's Highway* and background information about the Natchez Trace.

Materials and Resources:

- *The Devil's Highway*, by Stan Applegate. Atlanta, GA: Peachtree Junior Publications, 1998. ISBN 1-56145-184-3.
- Overview of Natchez Trace: http://www.scenictrace.com
- A park map of the Natchez Trace Parkway: http://www.nps.gov/natt/pphtml/maps.html
- A CD player and recording to play while the story is read aloud. Example: *Trail of Tears, A World Symphony*; Lee Johnson. Intersound Records #3722, 1998.
- Paper, pencil, calculator, ruler to create graphs, etc.

Introduction:

How would you like to go on a long journey—a journey in time and history? Come with me to a place once populated by wild animals, Native

Americans, European settlers, post riders, boatmen, citizens, soldiers ... and outlaws! Today, the Natchez Trace is a National Parkway, a road that stretches from Natchez, Mississippi, to Nashville, Tennessee. It is both a park and a roadway that is only one mile wide at its widest point and nearly 450 miles long.

Our journey will take us back to a time when the western border of the United States was the Mississippi River. The Louisiana Territory was purchased by the United States at about the same time. In the early 1800s, rivers and streams were the equivalent of today's interstate highways. There were no trains or cars then, and there were no motors to power riverboats. The young United States of America depended upon farmers in the areas of Kentucky, Tennessee, and Mississippi to provide valuable products and food to support a growing nation. For about twenty years, boatmen floated down the Mississippi River on keelboats to sell their products to merchants in Natchez, Mississippi. Then they returned to their homes on foot via the Natchez Trace, a prehistoric trail. When their products were sold and their boats were broken apart and sold for lumber, these boatmen walked northeast toward Nashville on the Natchez Trace with pockets full of money.

The book *The Devil's Highway* tells what might have happened to Zeb and Hanna, ages fourteen and ten, as they traveled on the Natchez Trace in the early 1800s. Their story is rich with excitement, emotion, and intrigue. Zeb and Hanna provide a youthful perspective from which to view an era of America's history. Their story also offers an opportunity to examine questions about economic development and the law of supply and demand in a historical context. Further, a study of the Natchez Trace creates a historic and social tapestry through which students can utilize and develop mathematics problem-solving skills.

Process:

1. The teacher will provide an overview of life in the early 1800s near the Mississippi River and along the Natchez Trace as an introduction to the story of Zeb and Hanna from *The Devil's Highway*.
2. The teacher will introduce the creative visualization activity: students will listen to an excerpt from *The Devil's Highway* with their eyes closed and with background music playing. After hearing the story, individual students will be asked to name images they "saw" or recalled from the story.
3. Students will listen to the story a second time. This time they will be permitted to move as though they are actors in the story. They will keep their feet in one place while moving their arms and bodies in a standing position, demonstrating hiding, throwing, running, walking, swimming, riding, singing, etc.
4. The teacher will communicate facts about what life might have been like for the boatmen, robbers, innkeepers, Native Americans, and soldiers who traveled across or lived on the land.
5. The teacher will divide the class into small groups that will create math problems for their classmates to solve. The groups will be assigned a role from the

characters listed in #4. Student problems should contain aspects of content related to the study of the Natchez Trace.

6. The teacher will monitor group activity and then select the three best problems from each group. Students will solve the problem created by their classmates and then discuss the processes they used and the challenges they encountered while creating the problems or solving them.

Conclusions:

"Unless students can solve problems, the facts, concepts, and procedures they know are of little use. The goal of school mathematics should be for all students to become increasingly able and willing to engage with and solve problems." *The Principles and Standards for Teaching Mathematics,* page 182.

Capturing students' interest is the first step in creating an effective lesson. By building a math lesson around an exciting passage of a story from America's history, students are invited into the learning setting in an imaginative way. Further, they are given the opportunity to develop their own understanding of history through the group activity of creating math problems for their classmates to solve. Active engagement with the content of the lesson and peer reflection and assessment encourages student engagement and willingness to continue to solve problems.

Assessments:

Evaluate the student-created problem, giving consideration to both the math and social studies content; student groups will grade their classmates' work on the problems their group created. Reflect and discuss what students learned about the history of the Natchez Trace and how problem solving was an important requirement for people who traveled there; compare and contrast with present-day lifestyles.

In the past five years, Althea Jerome has visited nearly 100 schools as a teaching artist offering professional development, standards-based instruction, classroom modeling and coaching, arts instruction, and strategic planning that emphasizes arts education. She is a musician and educator with almost thirty years' experience working with pre-kindergarten through graduate-level university students. In addition to work in schools, she has held leadership positions in the Mississippi Music Educators Association (MMEA) and the Mississippi Alliance for Arts Education (MAAE). From 2002 to 2005, she served as a member of the Network Leadership Committee of the Kennedy Center Alliance for Arts Education Network. In June 2005, she received the Arts Service Award from the Mississippi Alliance for Arts Education. E-mail: ajerome@ comcast.net.

KOFI'S HAT: WHAT WE BELIEVE AND WHY
By Caren Neile, Ph.D.

National Standards:

NCSS IV: Individual Development and Identity: Examination of various forms of human behavior enhances understanding of the relationships among social norms and emerging personal identities, the social processes that influence identity formation, and the ethical principles underlying individual action; NCSS V: Interactions between individuals, groups, and institutions.

Objectives:

Prioritize and clarify values; discuss and role play conflict resolution procedures; examine and role play tolerance-building activities; examine the disconnect between values and behavior.

Resources and Materials:

- 8–10 small pieces of paper and pen or pencil for each student
- Whiteboard and marker or a substitute

How do you engage students who, almost by definition, are disengaged? That was my challenge when I entered a GED-preparation class in Miami's Overtown community to present a series of storytelling-based lessons centering on the archetype of the Hero's Journey. This group was ages sixteen to twenty-one, although the lesson under more regular circumstances is appropriate for grades seven through twelve.

> The story used was "Kofi's Hat," a cautionary West African tale of two brothers and two sisters who get along perfectly. The couples marry and happily settle on adjacent yam farms. When they decide to pool their resources and work together, they win the village's annual yam contest, much to the dismay of the perennial winner, Kofi.
>
> Kofi then creates a hat that is different on the right than on the left, walks down the road between the two farms, and causes dissension between the couples as to what the hat actually looked like. They stop speaking to each other and never work together again.

How these young adults took pleasure in listening to this story and determining what they would do in the situation! It obviously struck a chord with them.

Process:

1. We "warmed up our instruments" by each stating our names loudly and clearly and saying in a word or two what mattered to us most in life.
2. I then gave each student eight slips of paper with the following words on them: CAREER, EDUCATION, FAMILY, FRIENDS, GOD, HEALTH, MONEY, USA. I asked them to put the slips in order of their importance in their lives. Then I asked them to call out their lists and wrote down the words in order, so that I could compare and contrast lists for the group.
3. We talked about what a values system is, how it is developed, and how our values may or may not determine our behavior.
4. I then told "Kofi's Hat." Twice in the middle of the telling, I stopped and asked them how they would handle the situation. (Once it was how to win the yam contest from Kofi; the next time it was how to win back the yam contest from the two couples.) After they called out their responses, I asked them to give more responses based on the priorities in their list of values. This made for some very interesting answers—as well as plenty of discrepancies between values and answers, which led to more than one "aha" moment for the students!
5. I told a short personal story about a time that I was betrayed—and how I handled the situation. We discussed the story. Surprisingly, my story of betrayal led to a lively, mirthful discussion of whether or not to forgive and forget, of how to make decisions the next time we are found in a similar situation of stereotypes and prejudices. Perhaps because the group is comprised primarily of African American juvenile offenders, comments and questions were directed to me about typical white and black behavior. Life stories that relate to folktales often promote strong responses about people and values.
6. Because our overall program curriculum is based on the Hero's Journey, we then related the lesson to one of the characteristics of a hero—a strong, consistent values system that influences behavior. We also discussed what the lesson tells us about being the hero of our own lives, that is, we can make wise choices once we know what our values are.
7. We wrapped up by relating the storytelling to their own lives: how storytelling helps exercise the imagination so that they can imagine alternatives in their own lives, just as they were able to brainstorm so many alternatives to the story.
8. We ended as we usually do, with a "cool-down" exercise, a generic, fictional group story, each person contributing a line.

Assessments:

A short essay that describes what the student got out of the lesson, and includes his or her own related story.

An additional step in the process, depending on the group and the amount of time available, is to discuss the possibility of positive and negative values systems. In this class, the values expressed were all socially acceptable, but that might not always be the case.

Other variations to the method include (a) asking the students to write their own values on the cards, or agree on a set of eight or ten, rather than providing them, and (b) asking students to retell the story through Kofi's perspective.

I can honestly say without reservation that this was the best educational experience I have had in thirty years of teaching. The students were mesmerized by the story and activities, with more and more of them eager to jump in and contribute as the lesson progressed.

Who would have believed that a West African folktale could touch, and teach, streetwise urban teens? Only a storyteller!

"Kofi's Hat" was told by Susan O'Halloran, La'Ron Williams, and Antonio Sacre in the video *Tribes & Bridges at the Steppenwolf Theatre* and was printed in O'Halloran's diversity curriculum "Kaleidoscope: Valuing Differences and Creating Inclusion." www.susanohalloran.com.

Caren S. Neile, MFA, Ph.D., is founding director of the South Florida Storytelling Project at Florida Atlantic University. Dr. Neile serves on the national board of the Healing Story Alliance and is founding managing editor of Storytelling, Self, Society: An Interdisciplinary Journal of Storytelling Studies. *She has performed and presented workshops and lectures throughout the United States, in Canada, and in the Caribbean. Her publications include* Hidden *(co-author, University of Wisconsin Press, 2002) and chapters in* Entremundos: New Perspectives on the Life and Work of Gloria Anzaldua *(Palgrave Macmillan, 2005), and* The Storytelling Genius of Elie Wiesel *(McFarland, forthcoming). She is a 2005 recipient of a National Storytelling Network Oracle award for Regional Service and Leadership. She can be reached at carenina@bellsouth.net.*

WE ALL CAN GET WHAT WE WANT
By Susan O'Halloran

National Standards:

NCSS I: Culture; NCSS III: People, Places, and Environments; NCSS IV: Individual Development and Identity.

Objectives:

Learning the four steps of successful win-win negotiations: reassure yourself and each other that "each of us can get what we want;" (your gain is not my loss;) state your desires and look for the wants below your wants ("What will you get by having ...?"); listen to and try on the other person's perspective until each person feels completely understood; find common ground: what ideas can fulfill both of our deepest desires? (Win-win, not win-lose or compromise.)

This is a teaching story, and in that regard it differs from every other contribution to this book. The story sets out to explain social studies curriculum in character development within the narrative structure. It is a storytelling style that can be emulated and accessed in Susan O'Halloran's "Kaleidoscope" curriculum, accessible from her Web site: www.susanohalloran. com. It is an artistic contribution that teaches.

Once upon a time there lived a royal family who fought all the time. In fact, the royal family had a long history of arguing. They squabbled over how many stallions should pull their carriages, how many soldiers should make up their army, even what kinds of flowers should grow in the palace gardens. However, there was one thing everyone in this family could agree on: the ancient solution to resolving all conflict was stupid.

Years before, a magician had given the king and queen a map and a key. He told them they would find a box that contained "the secret to all conflicts." The king and queen searched and searched and finally found the spot marked with an "X" on the map. They dug and uncovered a simple, plain wooden box; the key fit perfectly. Inside the box was a small paper scroll with only a few words inked in black calligraphy. It read, "We All Can Get What We Want."

"That's ridiculous!" the king and queen squealed simultaneously. For the next many years, it was the only thing on which this royal family could agree. The king and queen put the box and the note inside a glass case and hung it on a wall in the family's living chambers. Whenever someone wanted to let off some steam, one of them would point to the glass case and read the scroll out loud: "We all can get what we want."

"That's absurd!" said the king. "There's never enough to go around. Some lose and some win. That's what battles are all about."

"I agree," said the queen. "For example, if I want the higher-backed throne and you do too, then it would be impossible for both of us to get what we want."

"What?" said the king. "You want *my* chair?"

And so it went. Every time they or their children would agree that the so-called secret had been a terrible hoax, one or the other of them would give an example to prove their point and, within moments, they'd all be arguing. But one of their children, the youngest daughter, grew tired of the bickering. The same fights went on year after year, and the hurt feelings piled higher and higher till the very air in the castle was thick with rage.

When it came time for her to marry, the daughter picked a neighboring prince whom she thought would be different. However, when the prince came to the palace to ask for the daughter's hand, within minutes, he was arguing too. The king and queen had started another round of scoffing at "We all can get what we want" when the prince joined in.

"I agree. What if I wanted the land that borders both our king-doms to the north," the prince said theoretically to the king, "and you wanted that exact same land? Then it would be impossible for both of us to get what we want."

"What? You're going to take the land to the north of us?" the king shouted. "I won't stand for it!"

The screaming got louder and louder until the young princess could stand it no longer. "Stop it!" she yelled. "Can we have no peace? Surely there's some other way to settle things than arguing all the time. Father, did the magician say nothing more except to find the box? Do you think he left something out?"

"Perhaps," said the king, and he calmed down for a moment. "Actually, the magician said that there were two parts to 'the secret to all conflict.' But your mother and I were so appalled by the illogic of what we had read on the first scroll that we never looked further."

"Where is the second part of the secret?" the princess asked.

The queen pointed to the scroll on the wall. The princess took the scroll off the wall and turned it over. On the back was another map showing a second place to dig.

"You can come with me or you can stay," the princess said to the prince. "But I will only marry the man who wants the second part of the secret as badly as I do."

The prince already loved the princess very much, and so he lost no time in deciding to join her. They left as the king and queen and all the girl's brothers and sisters argued about whether or not they should go too.

They didn't. The prince and princess traveled alone across fields, through forests, around ponds, and over rugged hills. They passed shepherds tending flocks, peasants goading oxen across streams, and merchants carrying their wares to the nearest towns. And when, days later, they finally reached the place marked "X" on the second map, right next to a lake and a waterfall at the edge of a forest, the prince and princess began to dig. Out came a box much the same as the one that had held the first scroll. This box was not locked, and when they opened it, another scroll was inside.

"You read it," the prince said to the princess.

The princess lifted the scroll from the box and held it in her hand. "Whatever this says," she said to the prince, "I want us, for the time being, to pretend it is true, whether it makes sense to us or not."

The princess unrolled the scroll and read, "Find the wants below the wants and reassure each other throughout."

It was a good thing that the princess herself had suggested they pretend to believe the scroll, for if not, she would have been the first to snap, "This is ridiculous!"

"Okay," said the prince, "let's try it. Let's take one of our first arguments—where we will live. Since neither of us is the firstborn, we do not inherit our parents' kingdoms, but they will make us a present of whatever piece of land we choose. And I love the flatland my parents rule by the ocean."

"And I," said the princess, "wish to live in my father's castle in the mountains. That seems like opposites, but . . ."

"But," the prince continued, "for the moment we'll pretend we both can get what we want."

Then, remembering the backside of the newest scroll, the princess added with great reassurance in her voice, "And I want both of us to get what we want and I won't give up until we find a resolution. So what is the want below the want? What do you get from living by the ocean?"

The prince smiled. "The sun and the sound of water." And then, remembering to reassure her, he said, "I'm sure we can figure this out. I want to live with you in a place where we can both be happy. So tell me, what do you get by being in the mountains?"

"The crisp air, the breeze, the smell of pine trees, and walks in the woods," said the princess.

They looked at each other and laughed, for their needs, they saw, were not so incompatible; the very spot where they sat was perfect—a lake next to a forest with sun and the sound of water, pine trees, and a cool, light breeze. In fact, it's the very land on which they built their house and spent their remaining contented days together.

Oh, and about the family. I can't tell you that they completely stopped arguing, but when they sat and listened to the prince and princess resolve their conflicts, they realized this was great sport too. Could they find the common ground below seeming opposites? What ingenious solution would encompass *both* their needs? The prince and princess's constant declaration, "We can work this out!" became almost as much fun for the family to say as "That's ridiculous!"

Unfortunately, the story about how absurd it was to believe that "We all can get what we want" started earlier. The belief that it's impossible to settle conflicts without fighting has had more time to travel across many more lands. So maybe you'll tell this story instead and help to spread the word: most of the time, whatever the conflict, it's possible for all of us to get what we want.

Assessments:

Enjoy and discuss the story. What does it teach? Is it a true story? Or is it a true story even though the facts of the story are not true?

Susan O'Halloran is a writer, story artist, television personality, and keynote speaker whose work explores the complex issues of social justice. She is the author of four books and the producer of video and films, including Tribes & Bridges at the Steppenwolf Theatre *and* More Alike Than Not: Stories of Three Americans—Catholic, Jewish, and Muslim. *The* Chicago Reader *says O'Halloran "has mastered the Irish art of telling stories that are funny and heart-wrenching at the same time." Susan was a National Storytelling Network keynote speaker in 2003 and a featured teller at the National Storytelling Festival in Jonesborough in 1996 and 2004. She lives in Evanston, Illinois, and can be reached at www.susanohalloran.com.*

SUGGESTED RESOURCES

Compiled by Judy Sima

Judy Sima *is an award-winning storyteller, author, and educator. Her performances and workshops have been featured at conferences, festivals, schools, and libraries throughout Michigan and across the country. As a teacher-librarian for more than thirty-five years, she has introduced many young people to the art of storytelling through her middle school storytelling troupe. Judy's book,* Raising Voices: Creating Youth Storytelling Groups and Troupes *(Libraries Unlimited, 2003, co-authored with Kevin Cordi), has received numerous awards and accolades, including Storytelling World Honor Award, VOYA Five Foot Bookshelf, and the Anne Izard Storytellers Choice Award. Judy has been telling stories professionally since 1987. She is a frequent presenter at the National Storytelling Conference, Northlands Storytelling Network, American Association of School Librarians, Michigan Reading Association, and the Michigan Association for Media in Education. Her many articles have been featured in* Storytelling Magazine, Library Talk, Book Links, Oasis Magazine, Tales as Tools, Beginner's Guide to Storytelling, Telling Stories to Children, *and others. Judy is the recipient of the Michigan Association in Media's Ruby Brown Award for Individual Excellence and the National Storytelling Network North Central Region Service and Leadership Award. Visit her Web site at www.JudySima.com.*

STUDENT RESOURCES—SINGLE TITLES

Applegate, Stan. *The Devil's Highway*. Atlanta: Peachtree Junior Publications, 1998.
Bang, Molly. *Wiley and the Hairy Man*. New York: Macmillan, 1976.
Berry, Jack. "The Elephant, the Tortoise, and the Hare," *West African Folktales*. Evanston, IL: Northwestern University Press, 1991.

Bruchac, Joseph. *The First Strawberries: A Cherokee Indian Tale*. New York: Dial, 1993.

_____. "The Girl Who Was Not Satisfied with Simple Things," *Iroquois Stories: Heroes and Heroines Monsters and Magic*. Trumansburg, NY: The Crossing Press, 1985.

Burritt, Amy. *My American Adventure: Big Things Happen When You Reach Really High*. Grand Rapids, MI: Zondervan Publishing House, 1998.

Climo, Shirley. *The Irish Cinderlad*. New York: Harper Trophy, 2000.

Coleman, Evelyn. *White Socks Only*. Morton Grove, IL: Albert Whitman, 1996.

Cooper, Susan. *The Selkie Girl*. New York: M. K. McElderry Books, 1986.

Courlander, Harold, and George Herzog. "The Cow-Tail Switch," *The Cow-Tail Switch and Other West African Stories*. Illustrated by Madye Lee Chastain. New York: Henry Holt and Company, Inc., 1947.

DeAngeli, Marguerite. *Big Book of Nursery and Mother Goose Rhymes*. Garden City, NY: Doubleday, 1954.

Demi. *The Empty Pot*. New York: Henry Holt, 1990.

Doherty, Berlie. *Daughter of the Sea*. New York: Random House, 1997.

Dubois, Paul. *Abiyoyo Returns*. Simon & Schuster Books for Young Readers, 2006.

Evans, Freddi Williams. *The Battle of New Orleans: The Drummer's Story*. Gretna, LA: Pelican Publishing, 2005.

_____. *A Bus of Our Own*. Morton Grove, IL: Albert Whitman & Company, 2001.

Flack, Marjorie. *Ask Mr. Bear*. New York: Macmillan, 1968.

Fox, Mem. *Wilfred Gordon McDonald Partridge*. Brooklyn, NY: Kane/Miller, 1984.

Gag, Wanda. *Gone is Gone: Or the Story of a Man Who Wanted to Do Housework*. New York: Coward, 1935.

Galdone, Paul. *The Greedy Old Fat Man*. New York: Clarion, 1983.

_____. *Henny Penny*. New York: Seabury Press, 1968.

George, Jean Craighead. *My Side of the Mountain*. New York: Dutton, 1988.

Gilman, Phoebe. *Something from Nothing*. New York: Scholastic, 1992.

Hardendorff, Jeanne. *Slip! Slop! Gobble!* Philadelphia: Lippincott, 1970.

Harper, Wilhelmina. *The Gunniwolf*. New York: Dutton, 1967.

Hewitt, Kathryn. *The Three Sillies*. New York: Harcourt Brace Jovanovich, 1986.

Hitte, Kathryn. *Boy, Was I Mad!* Illustrated by Mercer Mayer. New York: Parents Magazine Press, 1969.

Hong, Lily Toy. *How Ox Star Fell from Heaven*. Morton Grove, IL: Albert Whitman, 1991.

_____. *Two of Everything*. Morton Grove, IL: Albert Whitman, 1993.

Hoose, Phillip. *It's Our World Too! Stories of Young People Who Are Making a Difference*. Boston: Little, Brown and Company, 1993.

Isele, Elizabeth. *The Frog Princess*. New York: Crowell, 1984.

Kent, Jack. *The Fat Cat: A Danish Folktale*. New York: Scholastic, 1971.

Kimmel, Eric. A. *Garlic and Onions*. New York: Holiday House, 1996.

_____. *The Greatest of All*. New York: Holiday House, 1991.

_____. *Sword of the Samurai*. New York: Harcourt, Brace, 1999.

_____. *Three Sacks of Truth*. New York: Holiday House, 1993.

_____. *The Witch's Face*. New York: Holiday House, 1993.

Lillington, Kenneth. *Selkie*. London: Faber and Faber, 1985.

Lockley, Ronald. *Seal Woman*. London: Rex Collins, 1974.

Louie, Ai-Ling. *Yeh-Shen*. New York: Philomel, 1982.

MacDonald, Margaret Read. *Fat Cat: A Danish Folktale*. Little Rock, AR: August House Little Folk, 2001.

_____. *Pickin' Peas*. New York: Harper Collins, 1998.

_____. "What a Wonderful Life," *Shake-It-Up Tales*! Little Rock, AR: August House, 2000.

Martin, Bill. *Knots on the Counting Rope*. New York: Henry Holt, 1987.

Martin, Rafe. *The Rough-Faced Girl*. New York: Putnam, 1992.

Mayo, Margaret. *Tortoise's Flying Lesson*. New York: Harcourt Brace, 1995.

_____. *When the World Was Young: Creation and Pourquoi Tales:* New York: Simon & Schuster, 1996.

McCaughrean, Geraldine. "The Bat and the Basket," *Starry Tales*. New York: Margaret K. McElderry, 2001.

McDermott, Gerald. *Anansi the Spider: A Tale from the Ashanti*. New York: Holt, Rinehart, and Winston, 1972.

McGovern, Ann. *Too Much Noise*. New York: Houghton Mifflin, 1967.

Miller, Theresa. *Joining In: An Anthology of Audience Participation Stories & How to Tell Them*. Cambridge, MA: Yellow Moon Press. 1988.

Ness, Caroline. "How Big Was Mango?" *The Ocean of Story: Fairy Tales from India*. New York: Lothrop, Lee & Shepard, 1996.

Nye, Naomi Shihb. *Sitti's Secrets*. New York: Simon & Schuster, 1994.

Pierr, Morgan. *The Turnip*. New York: Philomel Books, 1990.

Poe, Edgar Allan. "The Raven" and "The Cask of Amontillado," *The Complete Tales and Poems of Edgar Allan Poe*. New York: Random House, 1938.

Polacco, Patricia. *Aunt Chip and the Great Triple Creek Dam Affair*. New York: Philomel, 1996.

_____. *Babushka's Doll*. New York: Simon & Schuster Books for Young Readers, 1990.

_____. *Babushka Baba Yaga*. New York: Philomel: 1993.

_____. *The Bee Tree*. New York: Philomel, 1993.

_____. *Mrs. Katz and Tush*. New York: Bantam, 1992.

_____. *The Keeping Quilt*. New York: Simon & Schuster Books for Young Readers, 1998.

_____. *My Ol' Man*. New York: Philomel, 1995.

_____. *Rechenka's Eggs*. New York: Penguin Putnam Books for Young Readers, 1996, c1988.

_____. *Thunder Cake*. New York, Philomel, 1990.

Poole, Amy Lowry. *How the Rooster Got His Crown*. New York: Holiday House, 1999.

Ross, Tony. *Lazy Jack*. New York: Dial Books, 1985.

Rubright, Lynn. *Mama's Window*. New York: Lee & Low Books, 2005.

Sanderson, Ruth. *Cinderella*. Boston: Little, Brown and Company, 2002.

Seeger, Pete. *Abiyoyo*. New York: Simon & Schuster Books for Young Readers, 1963.

_____. *Abiyoyo Returns*. New York: Simon & Schuster Books for Young Readers, 2001.

Serwer, Blanche. *Let's Steal the Moon*. Boston: Little, Brown and Company, 1970.

Sherlock, Philip M. "Ticky-Picky Boom-Boom," *Anansi the Spider Man*. New York: Crowell, 1954.

Sierra, Judy. *Wiley and the Hairy Man*. New York: Lodestar Books/Dutton, 1996.

Simms, Laura. *The Squeaky Door*. New York: Crown, 1990.

Stevens, Janet. *The Tortoise and the Hare*. New York: Holiday House, 1984.

Taback, Simms. *Joseph Had a Little Overcoat*. New York: Viking, 1999.

Taylor, Mildred. *Roll of Thunder, Hear My Cry*. New York: Dial Press, 1976.

Tolstoy, Alexi. *The Great, Big, Enormous Turnip*. New York: Watts, 1968.

Tompert, Ann. *Grandfather Tang's Story*. New York: Crown Publishers, 1990.

Uchida, Yoshiko. *The Wise Old Woman*. New York: McElderry Books, 1994.

Want, Rosalind. *The Fourth Question*. New York: Holiday House, 1991.

White, Mark. *The Tortoise and the Hare: A Retelling of Aesop's Fable*. Minneapolis: Picture Window Books, 2004.

Yagawa, Sumiko. *The Crane Wife*. New York: Morrow, 1981.

Zemach, Margot. *It Could Always Be Worse*. New York: Farrar, Straus & Giroux, 1976.

_____. *The Three Wishes*. New York: Farrar, Straus & Giroux, 1986.

STUDENT RESOURCES—COLLECTIONS

Arkhurst, Joyce. *More Adventures of Spider*. New York: Scholastic Book Services, 1964.

Berry, Jack, coll. and trans. *West African Folktales*. Edited by Richard Spears. Evanston, IL: Northwestern University Press, 1991.

Bonnet, Leslie. *Chinese Folk and Fairy Tales*. New York: Putnam, 1958.

Botkin, Benjamin. *Treasury of American Folklore*. New York: Crown, 1944.

Bruchac, Joseph. *Iroquois Stories: Heroes and Heroines Monsters and Magic*. Trumansburg, NY: The Crossing Press, 1985.

Chase, Richard. *Grandfather Tales*. New York: Houghton Mifflin, 1948.

_____. *The Jack Tales*. New York: Houghton Mifflin, 1943.

Chinen, Allan. *In the Ever After: Fairy Tales and the Second Half of Life*. Wilmette, IL: Chiron Publications, 1989.

Cole, Joanna. *Best-Loved Folktales of the World*. New York: Doubleday, 1983.

Courlander, Harold, and George Herzog. *The Cow-Tail Switch and Other West African Stories*. New York: Henry Holt and Company, Inc., 1947.

_____. *The Hat-Shaking Dance and Other Tales from the Gold Coast*. New York: Harcourt, Brace, 1957.

Credle, Ellis. *Tall Tales from the High Hills*. New York: Elsevier-Nelson, 1957.

Davis, Donald. *Jack Always Seeks His Fortune: Authentic Appalachian Jack Tales*. Little Rock, AR: August House, 1992.

DeSpain, Pleasant. *Tales of Wisdom and Justice*. Little Rock, AR: August House, 2001.

_____. *Thirty-Three Multicultural Tales to Tell*. Little Rock, AR: August House, 1993.

_____. *Twenty-Two Splendid Tales to Tell From Around the World, Vol. 1 & 2*. Little Rock, AR: August House, 1994.

_____. *Sweet Land of Story: Thirty-Six American Tales to Tell*. Little Rock, AR: August House, 2000.

Fry, Rosalie K. *The Secret of Roan Inish*. New York: Hyperion Paperbacks for Children, 1985.

Goss, Linda, and Marian E. Barnes, ed. *Talk That Talk*. New York: Simon and Schuster, 1989.

Greenaway, Kate. *A Apple Pie and Traditional Nursery Rhymes*. New York: Knopf, 2002.

Grimm, Jacob, and Wilhelm Grimm. *The Complete Grimm's*. New York: Pantheon, 1972.

Haviland, Virginia. *Favorite Fairy Tales Told in England*. Boston: Little, Brown and Company, 1959. Also: *Favorite Fairy Tales Told in Czechoslovakia, Denmark, France, Germany, Greece, India, Italy, Japan, Norway, Poland, Russia, Scotland, Spain, Sweden*.

Hearn, Lafcadio. *Cleanings in Buddha-Fields*. New York: Houghton Mifflin, 1897.

Holt, David, and Bill Mooney. *Ready-To-Tell Tales: Sure-fire stories from America's Favorite Storytellers*. Little Rock, AR: August House, 1994.

Hovey, Kate. *Ancient Voices*. New York: Simon & Schuster, 2004.

Hunter, Mollie. *A Stranger Came Ashore*. New York: Harper Trophy, 1977.

Jacobs, Joseph. *English Folk and Fairy Tales*. New York: Putnam (n.d.).

Jerrold, Walter. *The Big Book of Nursery Rhymes*. New York: Portland House, 1987.

Low, Alice. *The Macmillan Book of Greek Gods and Heroes*. New York: Macmillan, 1985.

MacDonald, Margaret Read. *Look Back and See: Twenty Lively Tales for Gentle Tellers*. Bronx, NY: H. W. Wilson, 1991.

_____. *Shake-It-Up Tales*. Little Rock, AR: August House, 2000.

_____. *Twenty Tellable Tales: Audience Participation Folktales for Beginners*. Bronx, NY: H. W. Wilson, 1986.

Many Voices: True Tales from America's Past. Jonesborough, TN: National Storytelling Press, 1995.

McCaughrean, Geraldine. *Starry Tales*. New York: Margaret K. McElderry, 2001.

Montgomery, Noah. *Twenty-Five Fables*. London, New York: Abelard-Schuman, 1961.

Morgan, William, coll. *Navajo Coyote Tales*. Sante Fe: Ancient City Press, 1988.

Ness, Caroline. *The Ocean of Story: Fairy Tales from India*. New York: Lee & Shepherd, 1995.

Nye, Naomi Shihab. *What Have You Lost?* New York: Greenwillow Books, 1999.

Orgel, Doris. *The Lion and the Mouse and Other Aesop Fables*. New York: DK Publishers, 2001.

Osborne, Mary Pope. *Favorite Greek Myths*. New York: Scholastic, 1989.

Ozaki, Yei. *The Japanese Fairy Book*. Rutland, NY: C. E. Tuttle, 1970.

Pinkney, Jerry. *Aesop Fables*. New York: Seastar Books, 2000.

Poe, Edgar Allan. *The Complete Tales and Poems of Edgar Allan Poe*. New York: Random House, 1938.

Pugh, Ellen. *Tales from the Welsh Hills*. New York: Dodd Mead, 1968.

Raines, Shirley. *Tell It Again!* Beltsville, MD: Gryphon House, 1999.

Rosenberg, Donna, and Sorelle Baker. *Mythology and You: Classical Mythology and Its Relevance to Today's World*. Skokie, IL: National Textbook Company, 1992.

Sanfield, Steve. *The Feather Merchants and Other Tales of the Fools of Chelm*. New York: Orchard, 1991.

Schwartz, Howard. *The Diamond Tree*. New York: HarperCollins, 1991.

Scieszka, Jon. *The True Story of the Three Pigs*. New York: Viking Kestrel, 1989.

Seeger, Pete. *Pete Seeger's Storytelling Book*. New York: Harcourt, 2000.

Seeger, Ruth Crawford. *American Folksongs for Children*. New York: Doubleday, 1948.

Seki, Keigo. *Folktales of Japan*. Chicago: University of Chicago Press, 1963.

Sherlock, Philip M. *Anansi the Spider Man*. New York: Crowell, 1954.

Sherman, Josepha. *Trickster Tales: Forty Folk Stories from Around the World*. Little Rock: August House, 1996.

Silverstein, Shel. *The Giving Tree*. New York: Harper & Row, 1964.

Singer, Isaac Bashevis. *Zlateh the Goat*. New York: Harper & Row, 1966.

Tashjian, Virginia. *Juba This and Juba That*. Boston: Little, Brown and Company, 1995.

_____. *Once There Was and Was Not*. Boston: Little, Brown and Company, 1966.

Uchida, Yoshiko. *The Sea of Gold and Other Tales from Japan*. New York: Scribner, 1965.

Williamson, Duncan. *Tales of the Seal People, Scottish Folktales*. New York: Interlink Books, 1992.

Wyndham, Lee. *Tales the People Told in Russia*. New York: J. Messner, 1970.

Yolen, Jane. *Favorite Folktales from Around the World*. New York: Pantheon Books, 1986.

_____. *Gray Heroes: Elder Tales from Around the World*. New York: Penguin, 1999.

STUDENT RESOURCES—MULTIMEDIA

Burch, Milbre. *If the Shoe Fits: Cinderella Tales from Around the World*. [Compact disc] Order: www.kindcrone.com.

Butt, Janice. *Livin' Above Her Raisin.'* [Compact disc] Order: teachtale@mindspring.com.

Ferlatte, Dianne. *Sapelo: Time is Winding Up*. [Compact disc] Order: www.dianeferlatte.com/order.html.

Gillard, Marni. *Without a Splash: Diving into Childhood Memories*. [Compact disc] Order: www.marnigillard.com.

Healy, Yvonne. "The Healy Cross," *Stories from the Heart of the World*. [Compact disc] Order: www.cdbaby.com/cd/yvonnehealy or Stories@Yhealy.com.

Levin, Lainie. "The Great Banana Flight of 1978," *Signature Stories*. Order: lainlev@yahoo.com.

Lieberman, Syd. *Intrepid Birdmen*. [Compact disc] Order: www.storytelling.org/Lieverman/#anchor904458.

Seeger, Pete. *Abiyoyo and Other Story Songs for Children*. [Sound recording] Washington, DC: Smithsonian/Folkways, 1989.

StarSites: Ancient Buildings Connecting Earth and Sky. [CD-ROM] Vancouver, BC: DNA Multimedia Corp., 1996.

StoryWatchers Club. *Adventures in Storytelling*. [DVD series] Indianapolis: Sax Media Group, 2006.

Tsonakwa, Gerald Rancourt. *Echoes of the Night: Native American Legends of the Night Sky*. [Compact disc] Tucson, AZ: Soundings of the Planet, 1992. 1.800.93PEACE.

TEACHER RESOURCES—CLASSROOM APPLICATIONS
AND PRACTICES

Adler, Nancy. *Telling Tales at School: A Handbook for Teaching Storytelling in Workshops and in the Classroom.* 3rd ed. Self-published. Phone: 801-224-6861.

Appel, Libby. *Mask Characterization: An Acting Process.* Carbondale and Edwardsville: Southern Illinois University Press, 1982.

Ashton, Will, and Diana Denton. *Spirituality, Ethnography and Teaching.* New York: Peter Lang, 2007.

Aveni, Anthony. *Stairways to the Stars: Skywatching in Three Great Ancient Cultures.* New York: John Wiley & Sons, 1997.

Barton, Bob, and David Booth. *Stories in the Classroom: Storytelling, Reading Aloud, and Roleplaying with Children.* Portsmouth, NH: Heinemann, 1990.

Beck, Isabel L., et al. *Questioning the Author: An Approach for Enhancing Student Engagement with Text.* Newark, DE: International Reading Association, 1997.

Bolak, Karen, Donna Bialach, and Maureen Dunphy. "Standards-Based, Thematic Units Integrate the Arts and Energize Students and Teachers." *Middle School Journal.* Westerville, OH: National Middle School Association, May 2005, Volume 36, 9–19.

Booth, David, and Bob Barton. *StoryWorks: How Teachers Can Use Shared Stories in the New Curriculum.* Markham, ON: Pembroke Publishers, 2000.

Bradbury, Ray. *Zen and the Art of Writing and the Joy of Writing: Two Essays.* Santa Barbara, CA: Capra Press, 1973.

Brinkley, Douglas. *The Magic Bus: An American Odyssey.* New York: Harcourt Brace and Company, 1993.

Brody, Ed, and others. *Spinning Tales, Weaving Hope: Stories of Peace, Justice, & the Environment.* Philadelphia: New Society Publishers. 1992.

Bruun, Erik, and Robin Getzen. *Home of the Brave: America's Tradition of Freedom, Liberty, and Tolerance.* New York: Barnes and Noble Books, 2001.

Burnaford, Gail, ed. *Renaissance in the Classroom Arts Integration and Meaningful Learning.* Mahway, NJ: Lawrence Erlbaum Associates, 2001.

Changer, Jerilynn, and Annette Harrison. *Storytelling Activities Kit: Ready-to-Use Techniques, Lessons & Listening Cassettes for Early Childhood.* West Nyack, NY: The Center for Applied Research in Education, 1992.

Collins, Rives, and Pamela J. Cooper. *The Power of Story: Teaching Through Storytelling.* 2nd ed. Scottsdale, AZ: Gorsuch Scarisbrick, 1997.

Cooper, Patsy. *When Stories Come to School: Telling, Writing, and Performing Stories in the Early Childhood Classroom.* New York: Teachers & Writers Collaborative, 1993.

Davis, Donald. *Writing as a Second Language: From Experience to Story to Prose.* Little Rock, AK: August House, 2000.

Egan, Kieran. "Narrative in Teaching, Learning, and Research." *Critical Issues in Curriculum.* New York: Teacher's College Press, 1995.

_____. *Teaching as Story Telling: An Alternative Approach to Teaching and Curriculum in the Elementary School.* Chicago: University of Chicago Press, 1986.

Einstein, Albert, "Letter to Jacques Hadamard," *The Creative Process.* Edited by Brewster Ghiselin. New York: A Mentor Book, 1957. 43–44.

Suggested Resources

Ellis, Brian "Fox." *Learning from the Land: Teaching Ecology through Stories and Activities*. Englewood, CO: Teacher Idea Press, 1997.

Erickson, H. Lynn. *Stirring the Head, Heart and Soul: Redefining Curriculum and Instruction*. Thousand Oaks, CA: Corwin Press, 1995.

Feagans, Laura. "The Development and Importance of Narratives for School Adaptation." *The Language of Children Reared in Poverty*. New York: Academic Press, 1982. 95–116.

Gillard, Marni. *Storyteller, Storyteacher: Discovering the Power of Storytelling for Teaching and Living*. York, ME: Stenhouse, 1996.

Hamilton, Martha, and Mitch Weiss. *Children Tell Stories: Teaching and Using Storytelling in the Classroom*. 2nd ed. Katohah, NY: Richard C. Owens, 2005.

_____. *Stories in my Pocket: Stories Kids Can Tell*. Golden, CO: Fulcrum, 1996.

Harvey, Stephanie, and Anne Goudvis. *Strategies that Work: Teaching Comprehension to Enhance Understanding*. York, ME: Stenhouse Publisher, 2000.

Haven, Kendall. *Super Simple Storytelling: A Can-Do Guide for Every Classroom, Every Day*. Westport, CT: Libraries Unlimited, 2000.

Heard, Georgia. *Awakening the Heart: Exploring Poetry in Elementary and Middle School*. Portsmouth, NH: Heinemann, 1999.

Horowitz, Rosemary. *Elie Wiesel as Storyteller of His People*. Jefferson, NC: McFarland, 2007.

Hrebic, Herb, and Bob Cahill. *Stack the Deck: Check the Deck*. Chicago: The Stack the Deck Writing, Inc., 1994.

Kane, Patricia F., Dale A. Rosselet, and Karl Anderson. *Bridges to the Natural World: A Natural History Guide for Teachers of Grades Pre-K through 6*. Bernardsville, NJ: New Jersey Audubon Society, 2003.

King, Nancy. *Dancing with Wonder: Self-Discovery through Stories*. Belgium, WI: Champion Press, 2005.

_____. *Playing Their Part: Language and Learning*. Portsmouth, NH: Heinemann, 1996.

_____. *Storymaking and Drama: An Approach to Teaching Language and Literature in Secondary and Post Secondary Levels*. Portsmouth, NH: Heinemann, 1994.

Kinghorn, Harriet R., and Mary Helen Pelton. *Every Child a Storyteller: A Handbook of Ideas*. Englewood, CO: Teacher Idea Press, 1991.

Krause, Anne Marie. *Folktale Themes and Activities for Children: Pourquoi Tales*. Englewood, CO: Teacher Idea Press, 1999.

Krupp, E. C. *Echoes of the Ancient Skies: The Astronomy of Lost Civilizations*. New York: Harper & Row, 1983.

Langer, Ellen J. *The Power of Mindful Learning*. Reading, MA: Addison-Wesley, 1997.

MacDonald, Margaret Read. *The Storyteller's Start-Up Book: Finding, Learning, Performing and Using Folktales*. Little Rock, AR: August House, 1993.

National Storytelling Press. *Beginner's Guide to Storytelling*. Jonesborough, TN: National Storytelling Press, 2003.

_____. *Tales as Tools: The Power of Story in the Classroom*. Jonesborough, TN: National Storytelling Press, 1994.

_____. *Telling Stories to Children: A National Storytelling Guide*. Jonesborough, TN: National Storytelling Press, 2005.

Niemi, Loren, and Elizabeth Ellis. *Inviting the Wolf In: Thinking about Difficult Stories*. Little Rock, AR: August House, 2001.

Norfolk, Bobby, and Sherry Norfolk. *The Moral of the Story: Folktales for Character Development*. 2nd ed. Little Rock, AR: August House, 2006.

Pierce, Mark, and Karen Jennings. *Storytelling Tips & Tales*. Tucson, AZ: Good Year Books, 1998.

Rubright, Lynn. *Beyond the Beanstalk: Interdisciplinary Learning through Storytelling*. Portsmouth, NH: Heinemann, 1996.

Sawyer, Ruth. *The Way of the Storyteller*. New York: Viking, 1962.

Schank, Roger. *Tell Me a Story: Narrative and Intelligence*. Evanston, IL: Northwestern University Press, 1990.

Schwartz, Marni, Ann M. Trousdale, and Sue A. Woestehoff, eds. *Give a Listen: Stories of Storytelling in Schools*. Urbana, IL: National Council of Teachers of English, 1994.

Short, Kathy G. *Literature as a Way of Knowing: Strategies for Teaching and Learning*. York, ME: Stenhouse Publishers, 1997.

Sima, Judy, and Kevin Cordi. *Raising Voices: Creating Youth Storytelling Groups and Troupes*. Westport, CT: Libraries Unlimited, 2000.

Statman, Mark. *Listener in the Snow: The Practice and Teaching of Poetry*. New York: Teachers and Writers Collaborative, 2000.

Stevenson, Lauren M., and Richard J. Deasy. *Third Space: When Learning Matters*. Washington, DC: Arts Education Partnership, 2005.

Stolley, Richard, ed. *Life: Century of Change, America in Pictures 1900–2000*. Boston: Bullfinch Press Book, 2000.

Swope, Sam. *I am a Pencil: A Teacher, His Kids, and Their World of Stories*. New York: Henry Holt, 2004.

Tally, Steve. *Almost America: From the Colonists to Clinton*. New York: Harper Collins Books, 2000.

Tobin, James. *Great Projects: The Epic Story of the Building of America, from the Taming of the Mississippi to the Invention of the Internet*. New York: The Free Press, 2001.

Van der Post, Laurens. 1961. *Patterns of Renewal*. Wallingford, PA: Pendle Hill Publications #121, 1961.

Wagler, Mark, Ruth Olsen, and Ann Pryor. *Kids' Field Guide to Local Culture*. Madison, WI: Madison Children's Museum, 2004.

Wells, Gordon. *The Meaning Makers: Children Learning Language and Using Language to Learn*. Portsmouth, NH: Heinemann, 1985.

Williams, Michael, ed. *The Storyteller's Companion to the Bible*. Nashville, TN: Abingdon Press. 1991.

Yolen, Jane. *Touch Magic: Fantasy, Faerie & Folklore*. Little Rock, AR: August House, 2000.

Zipes, Jack. *Creative Storytelling: Building Community, Changing Lives*. New York: Routledge, 1995.

TEACHER RESOURCES—THEORY AND RESEARCH

Applebee, Arthur. *The Child's Concept of Story: Ages Two to Seventeen*. Chicago: University of Chicago Press, 1978.

Suggested Resources

Armstrong, Thomas. *Multiple Intelligences in the Classroom.* 2nd Ed. Alexandria, VA: Association for Supervision & Curriculum Development, 2000.

Brand, Susan Trostle. *Storytelling in Emergent Literacy: Fostering Multiple Intelligences.* Albany, NY: Delmar Publishers, 2001.

Caine, Renate Nummela, and Geoffrey Caine. *Making Connections: Teaching and the Human Brain.* Reading, MA: Addison-Wesley, 1994. 100–101.

Coleman, Daniel. *Emotional Intelligence.* New York: Bantam Books, 1995.

Engel, Susan. *The Stories Children Tell: Making Sense of the Narratives of Childhood.* New York: W. H. Freeman, 1995.

Einstein, Albert. "Letter to Jacques Hadamard," *The Creative Process.* Edited by Brewster Ghiselin. New York: A Mentor Book, 1957. 43–44.

Gardner, Howard. *Frames of Mind: The Theory of Multiple Intelligences.* New York: Basic Books, 1993.

_____. *Multiple Intelligences: The Theory in Practice.* New York: Basic Books, 1993.

Hannaford, Carla. *Smart Moves: Why Learning is Not All in Your Head.* Arlington, VA: Great Ocean Publishers, 1995.

Jensen, Eric. *Arts with the Brain in Mind.* Alexandria, VA: Association for Supervision & Curriculum Development, 2001.

_____. *Brain-Based Learning.* San Diego, CA: The Brain Store, 2000.

_____. *Education with the Brain in Mind.* Alexandria, VA: Association for Supervision & Curriculum Development, 2000.

Schiller, Pam. *Start Smart: Building Brain Power in the Early Years.* Beltsville, MD: Gryphon House, 1999.

Sousa, David. *How the Brain Learns.* 2nd ed. Thousand Oaks, CA: Corwin Press, 2000.

Williams, Linda Verlee. *Teaching for the Two-Sided Mind: A Guide to Right Brain/ Left Brain Education.* New York: Simon & Schuster, 1983.

Wolfe, Patricia. *Brain Matters: Translating Research into Classroom Practice.* Alexandria, VA: Association for Supervision and Curriculum Development, 2000.

WEB SITES

Aesop's Fables. http://www.aesopfables.com

Anderson, Mike. www.dulcimerguy.com

Bristow, Thom. www.thomtells.com

Brown, David K. *Children's Literature Web Guide.* http://www.ucalgary.ca/ ~dKbrown

Burch, Milbre. www.kindcrone.com

Canadian Peregrine Foundation. http://www.peregrine-foundation.ca/

Chace, Karen. *Researching Stories on the Internet: A Webliography of Storytelling Resources.* [CD-Rom] http://www.StoryBug.net

Claflin, Willy. www.willyclaflin.com

Cordi, Kevin. http://www.youthstorytelling.com/meetkevin.htm/

Ellis, Brian "Fox." www.foxtalesint.com

Ellis, Elizabeth. www.elizabethellis.com

Fairy Tales and Fables. http://www.fairy-tales.org.uk/

Folklore and Mythology. http://www.pitt.edu/~dash/folktexts.html

Ford, Lyn. http://www.storyteller.net/tellers/lford

Forest, Heather. *Story Arts.* http://www.storyarts.org/

Gillard, Marni. www.marnigillard.com

Hawk Migration Association of North American. http://www.hmana.org/

Healy, Yvonne. www.YHealy.com

Herman, Gail. www.gcnet.net/storyteller

Hmong Cultural Tour. http://csumc.wisc.edu/cmct/HmongTour/howwedidit/index.htm

Kids' Guide to Local Culture. http://csumc.wisc.edu/cmct/HmongTour/howwedidit/ LOCAL_KIDS_GUIDE_WEB.pdf

Kids' Storytelling Club. http://www.storycraft.org

Kinsella, Marilyn. *Teacher/Teller Pages.* http://marilynkinsella.org/teachetellerr.htm

Lloyd, Angela. www.angelalloyd.com

Louis and Clark 200. http://www.lewisandclark200.gov/edu/index.cfm

MI Story: Calendar of Michigan Storytelling. http://www.MichiganStorytelling.com

Museum of Westward Expansion. *The Louis and Clark Journey of Discovery.* http://www.nps.gov/jeff/LewisClark2/HomePage/HomePage.htm

National Storytelling Network. http://www.storynet.org. Phone: 800-525-4514 or 423-913-8201.

National Youth Storytelling Showcase. http://www.storycast.biz/index.php/ z-natyouth/

Norfolk, Bobby. www.bobbynorfolk.com

Norfolk, Sherry. www.sherrynorfolk.com

O'Halloran, Susan. www.susanohalloran.com

Park Street Cultural Tour. http://csumc.wisc.edu/cmct/ParkStreetCT/index.htm

Pruitt, Linda King. http://www.lkpstoryteller.com

Rose, Elizabeth. www.storycast.biz

Rubright, Lynn. www.lynnrubright.com

Scholastic. "Teaching With Pourquoi Stories." http://teacher.scholastic.com/products/ instructor/pourquoitales.htm

Sima, Judy. www.JudySima.com.

Stenson, Jane. www.storytelling.org/Stenson

Storytell. http://www.twu.edu/COPE/slis/storytell.htm

Williams, Diane. http://www.dwteller.com/

Youth, Educators, and Storytellers Alliance. www.yesalliance.com

Youth Storytelling. www.youthstorytelling.com

Zemerl. Interactive Database of Jewish Song. http://www.zemerl.com

Index

Index

Index

About the Authors

From the International Storytelling Center in Jonesborough, Tennessee, to the Hong Kong International School in Hong Kong, China (and hundreds of places in between!), **SHERRY NORFOLK**'s passion for storytelling incites the imagination of young and old audiences alike. In addition to an electric stage presence, developed through professional storytelling since 1981, she embodies the term "teaching artist"—that is, an artist who can not only talk the talk but walk the walk.

As a teaching artist, she leads residencies and workshops internationally, introducing children and adults to storymaking and storytelling. She is on the roster of seven state arts councils, a testimony to her value as a teaching artist. Her dedication to and deep interest in children and literacy have been recognized with national awards from the American Library Association, the Association for Library Service for Children, the National Association of Counties, and the Florida Library Association. Sherry is the co-author, with her husband, Bobby, of *The Moral of the Story: Folktales for Character Development* (August House, 1999); they are currently working on a series of Anansi stories for the new August House Story Cove label. Visit her Web site at www.sherrynorfolk.com. E-mail Sherry at shnorfolk@aol.com.

JANE STENSON is an award-winning teacher and a storyteller. A classroom teacher for over forty years, she currently teaches kindergarten at the Baker Demonstration School in Evanston, Illinois; the school is affiliated with National-Louis University, where Jane is an adjunct professor. Her main teaching interests are the relationship between storytelling and literacy, storytelling and nonfiction (science and history narratives), creating classroom activities that develop that relationship, and encouraging teacher research projects that document the significant role storytelling can provide in today's classrooms. She has presented her work at several national conferences for storytellers and educators. Further, Jane produces the university's annual Betty Weeks Storytelling Conference for Educators and Evening Concerts. As a storyteller, Jane has infused the Baker Demonstration School with storytelling. Middle school students are rewarded with storytellers' nonfiction narratives. Second through fifth graders are entertained and educated with folktales and personal stories. Pre-kindergarten through first graders enjoy participation stories and folktales from their teachers and professional storytellers. In the school, storytelling encourages student writing and speaking and listening. Jane and John, her husband of thirty-nine years, live in Evanston, Illinois, and have three sons and two grandchildren. She enjoys gardening and has recently learned to play the guitar. E-mail Jane at jane@janestenson.com.

DIANE WILLIAMS is past board chair for the National Storytelling Network (NSN). She is a recipient of the Regional Leadership and Service Award, and is a scholarship and research grant recipient from the organization. She was a 1999 finalist in the National Storytelling Contest. Twice nominated for the Mississippi Governor's Award for Excellence in the Arts, she has performed storytelling and conducted educational arts workshops in every nook and cranny in her home state. She conducted four separate storytelling tours in Germany for the Department of Defense Dependent Schools and boasts of storytelling inside of an inactive volcano on Oahu in Hawaii. Diane currently serves as the Arts Industry Director for the Mississippi Arts Commission and was formerly on their touring arts roster and arts education demonstration roster. She currently serves on the advisory board for the Mississippi Alliance for Arts Educators. She is the founder of the Central Mississippi Storyweavers Guild and recently co-established a Mississippi chapter of Spellbinders, Inc., an organization that trains elder volunteers for intergenerational storytelling. She enjoys supporting other artists and their work. Born in New Jersey, she currently resides on a farm in Madison, Mississippi, with her husband, Ray, and their cows. Diane has two adult sons. Visit her Web site at www.dwteller. com. E-mail Diane at dwteller@aol.com.